Bloomer and Before

Edward Giles

Steve Bloomer, at the peak of his record-scoring career.

BLOOMER
AND BEFORE

EDWARD GILES

The **Hallamshire** Press 2002

To Jim Smith,
the manager who guided Derby County into
the Premiership in his first season with the club.

© 2002 Edward Giles

Published by the Hallamshire Press
The Hallamshire Press is an imprint of
Hallamshire Publications Limited

Typeset by Hallamshire Publications Limited
Portmadog, Gwynedd

Printed by Cromwell Press Ltd, Trowbridge, Wiltshire

British Library Cataloguing in Publication Data:
  A catalogue record for this book is available from the British Library.

ISBN 1 874718 64 4

Contents

By the same author:

Derby County Days
from Carter and Doherty to Storer and Ryan, 1944–1956

Journeys with Jobey

**Steve Richards at the monument erected in Derby's Lock-up Yard in
memory of his grandfather, Steve Bloomer,
Derby County's record goalscorer.**
(Derby Evening Telegraph)

Foreword

By Steve Richards

grandson of Derby County's record goalscorer Steve Bloomer, and a journalist who was sports writer with the Daily Herald *and the* Sun *in the 1960s before going to the United States, where he worked alongside the greatest of all goalscorers, Pele, when the Brazilian was under contract to Pepsi-Cola to promote junior football on five continents. Also, together they produced a world-distributed ghosted daily column from four World Cup Finals in West Germany, Argentina, Spain and Mexico. Steve Richards is now living in retirement in Surrey.*

IT IS FAIR TO ASSUME that Steve Bloomer would have tipped his black bowler hat to the experienced football author Eddie Giles for this tribute to his art of goalscoring roughly a century on.

He would also acknowledge the contributions of his contemporaries in a media age when headlines were less striking but stars still over-received the star treatment.

Fortunately, Giles's gargantuan study offers shared recognition of Bloomer team-mates like the Goodall brothers, Ben Warren, Jimmy Methven, and later Derby County figureheads such as Harry Storer and George Jobey.

This comprehensive book also platforms the controversial Bert Mozley view that the Bloomer Memorial we had erected in 1996 was no more than an unwelcome intruder in what he inaccurately termed Derby's 'Fish Market'.

In fact, the Monument stands in the city's historic 'Lock-up Yard', where there was a florist, a picture-frame shop, a pub, an Italian restaurant and then four mini-fish stalls, all bordering the arched public walk-through to the main Market Hall.

Steve himself would have preferred this intimacy shared with Rams fans and others on their shopping sprees. The Bert I knew (he is now Canada-based) was a rare attacking right-back in the mould of Ramsey, Armfield and Cohen, and whose commendable forward approach naturally left gaps behind.

One gaping gap in this Mozley 'attack' is that I, for one, never heard him propose pre-'96 having a grandiose statue or any suchlike memorial at either the Baseball Ground or Pride Park, both of which have honoured their great one with only the same moveable wall plaque.

Now there's a hint, Bert!

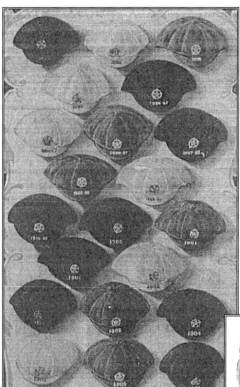

Some of Bloomer's caps...

...and his medals: Shield 1887, 1890, 1891, 1892; v. Scottish League 1897, 1899, 1900, 1901, 1904, 1905; v. Irish League 1896, 1898, 1899, 1900, 1901, 1902, 1903; FA Cup 1898, 1899; Robey Charity 1905, 1906; Bass Vase 1905; Burton Charity Cup 1892.

Preface

THIS is my third book about Derby County. The first one, entitled *Derby County Days*, concentrated upon the years from 1944 to 1956 when I was on the editorial staff of the *Derby Evening Telegraph*, and during which the Rams experienced one of the most eventful periods in their long history by winning the FA Cup for the first (and still only) time, but seven seasons later found themselves in the Northern Section of the Football League's Third Division through two relegations.

The second book, *Journeys With Jobey*, looked back to the decade and a half leading up to the Second World War—the seasons from 1925–26 of George Jobey's managership. These began on another high note with the promotion back to the First Division that had been so narrowly missed in the previous two campaigns, but ended on another low one, in 1941 while the club's closedown because of the war was still in force, when a joint FA–League Commission found that illegal payments had been made throughout those years to entice some of the game's top players to the Baseball Ground. Derby County were fined £500, several directors suspended, and a ban imposed on George Jobey that, though lifted in the meantime, kept him out of football until he made a brief, unhappy return with Mansfield Town in the Third Division early in the 1950s.

This third book, as the title *Bloomer and Before* indicates, goes still further back into Derby County's colourful history—right back, in fact, to their controversial formation as an offshoot of the Derbyshire County Cricket Club in 1884, and then forward again to the beginning of the Jobey era. It starts by recalling how the Rams (as they were quickly nicknamed after the county's military mascot) had to overcome both resentment by local rivals, who regarded them as unwanted interlopers luring away their best players, and some early heavy setbacks on the field before establishing themselves among the foremost clubs in the country and becoming one of the dozen founder members of the Football League in 1888.

Memorable League matches with which Derby County's eventful story is liberally laced include their two record victories, a game that contradicted mathematics by consisting of three halves, and the 'test' they dramatically recovered to win to preserve the First Division status they eventually surrendered 12 years later, in 1907. The period under review extends to the switchback existence that followed, with a couple of Second Division championships offset by two more relegations, culminating in the bleakest season in the club's history up to that time.

The reminiscences of the Rams' record in the FA Cup during those days are no less incident-packed. From the deflation of a seven-goal trouncing when they first played in the competition, and their heaviest-ever 11–2 defeat in the opening round on Merseyside, they recovered to register one of the most consistent sequences of progress by seven times reaching the semi-finals, and three times the final, in nine seasons—but all without carrying off the trophy even once. And in the third of those finals they were Bury'd by what still stands as the biggest margin of the lot in conceding six goals without reply. In those circumstances, it was scarcely surprising that the tale of the Gypsy's Curse, which decreed they would win neither the Cup nor the League, gained so much credence.

Also brought back to mind are such milestones in the County's career as the severing of their link with Derbyshire cricket, their move to the Baseball Ground, and their formation into a limited company.

Of the numerous outstanding individuals who come into the telling, the central character is Steve Bloomer, the legendary forward who was the most prolific scorer of his day, for both club and country, and who, as an automatic choice for soccer's Hall of Fame, still holds a high place among the greatest goal grabbers the game has known. A complex personality, described by one of his contemporaries as 'a tyrant', but also 'quite a peaceable person', he very reluctantly departed to Middlesbrough after dominating the Derby scene for 14 seasons, but readily returned to a hero's welcome and, reinstated as captain in the twilight of his playing career, fittingly inspired the promotion back to the First Division from which the Rams had so swiftly fallen in his absence.

The man who, as manager, brought Bloomer back to Derby also features prominently in these chapters. He was Jimmy Methven, a canny Scot (is there any other kind?) who was with the Rams, except for a short break when the club closed down during the First World War, from 1891 to 1922—for the first 15 of those years as their regular choice at right-back before embarking upon almost as many seasons of managership. Bloomer himself was not far short of that exceptionally long period of service in adding spells behind the Baseball Ground scenes, first as a coach and later as a general assistant, after one of his overseas coaching engagements had caused him to be interned in Germany during the war.

The ending of both those admirable connections with the County was influenced by impaired health. Failing eyesight contributed to Methven's eventual exit; Bloomer succumbed to respiratory difficulties that a specially organised cruise to Australasia could not dispel.

Other gifted footballers in this parade of personalities from Derby County's early years include the inimitable, but so dissimilar, Goodall brothers—the scholarly 'quiet and gentle' John; the robust, controversial Archie, the soccer Strong Man who was the captain the club suspended just before a Cup Final. The differences between them extended even to the countries for which they played. John Goodall, who gave the term 'hat-trick' a new meaning as Bloomer's mentor, reached the Rams direct from being in Preston's double-winning Old Invincibles team of the first Football League season. With Bloomer, he is one of the eight former Derby County players, listed in the appendix, among the 100 Football League Legends. He is also in another select band who played cricket for Derbyshire as well as football for Derby County.

Four of those leading exponents of both games represented England in Test cricket. One of them, Frank Sugg, was at the centre of cricket revolt that is also recalled. Another, William Storer, was a member of a famous family which later produced, in his nephew Harry, the cricketer-footballer who, like Jimmy Methven, gave Derby County sterling service as both player and manager.

Tragedy sadly comes into the account with the fatal injury that William Cropper, a promising Derbyshire all-rounder, suffered on the football field. And in the terrible, untimely end of Ben Warren, who for several years was generally considered to be the best wing-half in the English game. Warren, an indefatigable captain and, ironically, a real stickler for fitness, emulated John Goodall's guidance of Steve Bloomer by taking under his wing his Newhall neighbour Jack Atkin, a full-back who was only too willing to follow his advice and excellent example in rigorous training, and who developed into a model of consistency and loyalty in making Derby County his only League club over some 15 years.

Jack Robinson, at the head of the Rams' impressive parade of Derbyshire-born goalkeepers and for several seasons the best in England, is another outstanding performer to be put strongly in the spotlight—though it is also recorded that, like one of the others, Jack Fryer, the manner of his departure left a lot to be desired. In Robinson's case, too, there was later an allegation of attempted player poaching which raised Derby hackles.

In these pages you can also read of the goalkeeper who packed brown paper under his jersey to protect him from the Derby ground's bitter winds; the manager who deserted the Rams for a club in turmoil; the County winger who scored five goals in the club's record victory; an epic ride on horseback from Derby to Kilmarnock—and back; the Scot who scored four goals on his international debut but was never capped again; the scandal of the absconding secretary; a match played in fancy dress; a gold medal awarded

**Jimmy Methven, pictured in November 1952, the month before
his 84th birthday, while he was living with his daughter
Constance and son James in the Derby suburb of Littleover.**
(Derby Evening Telegraph)

for Walking the Hoop; an oversight that started a momentous career; the six-goal hero who escaped celebrating fans disguised in a frock coat and bowler hat; the player known as the 'Squire of Spondon'; the priest who was sent to bring back two players who had been lured away; the Derby trio dubbed the 'Busy Bees'; the coach who called the police to escort one of his players from the ground; a disaster at Ibrox; the 'Siamese Twin' who made his fortune in Canada; the 'pocket Hercules' who broke scoring records; the forward banned for 30 years; the £2,500 transfer that caused an uproar; a protest at the selection of a 16-year-old; the Cup Final dream that came true; moves from Derby that took one player to a Cup winner's medal, another to England caps…

And that is just a selection.

In compiling this book, I have relied mainly on information I have gathered and filed over a good many years, but to fill in some of the gaps I have been indebted to the publications by Breedon Books, in their excellent *Complete Record* series, concerning Derby County and Sheffield Wednesday, by my old friends Gerald Mortimer and Keith Farnsworth, respectively, and Middlesbrough, by Harry Glasper.

For the clarification of other points I have been most grateful to have the assistance of Ken Smales, a former secretary of Nottingham Forest FC, Michael Forman, a life vice-president of the Forest club, Wade Martin, the Stoke City historian, David Barber, of the Football Association's library, Jack Rollin, Executive Editor of Rothman's Football Yearbook, Anton Rippon, R. Taylor, secretary of Alfreton Town FC, Keith Howard, Sheffield Wednesday's official statistician, Gordon Sharrock, of the *Bolton Evening News*, Terry Frost, the official Bradford City statistician, Mervyn Baker, of Bristol, and the secretaries of the Barnsley, Bristol City and Leicester City football clubs.

Sincere thanks, too, to another old friend, Steve Richards, grandson of Steve Bloomer, who has very kindly consented to provide a foreword and gone to the trouble of checking through the manuscript besides loaning me some photographs from his private collection. He and I go back a very long way to the 1940s, when we were both starting out along the journalistic trail in Derby.

Additional photographs and other items, from the collection of my late step father, George Richards, have been kindly loaned to me by Mrs Delia Richards, the widow of my half-brother Michael. My thanks, too, for other pictures, to the *Derby Telegraph*, my old friend Malcolm Brodie, who until his retirement was Sports Editor of the *Belfast Telegraph* for many years, Mrs Betty Potts, daughter of Fred Flanders, Derby County's youngest player when he made his debut, Joe Stack, of the Derby photographic firm W.W. Winter, and Raymonds Press Agency. I have been unable to trace the source of some photographs, and hope that owners will not take exception to their being used.

Once again, I am also greatly obliged to Pauline Climpson, Managing Director of The Hallamshire Press, Jenny Sayles and other members of her staff, for their friendly help and advice in getting all this into print. Their ready co-operation and expertise in publishing are much appreciated.

Last, but certainly not least, the usual appreciation is due to my tolerant wife Joan, for putting up with the hours I have spent tapping away at the keyboard when I am sure she could have suggested what she would see as better ways of filling in my spare time around the house or in the garden. She, at least, will be relieved to know that I have now exhausted the records of the Rams that I kept with all the eager enthusiasm of youth. Against that, though, I still have many of football in general—and of cricket too…

CHAPTER 1

A Resented Arrival

An offshoot of Derbyshire cricket – W.D. Clark, the 'missing' manager – Record reverse among early heavy defeats – Seven FA Cup semi-finals in nine years and the biggest beating in a final – The Gypsy's Curse – Fixture boycott as Derby Midland head strong local criticism before amalgamation – Historic triumph for Derby Junction – Blackburn land Cup treble in replay at Derby

W E BEGIN WITH AN OVERLOOKED MAN. Harry Newbould is generally said to have been the first manager appointed by Derby County, in 1900, yet the prospectus issued in August, 1896, when the club became a limited company, names one W.D. Clark as the manager among the list of officials.

Even with the inclusion of Clark, who originally joined the club as assistant secretary, there were only five Derby County managers from the time of the club's formation in 1884 until George Jobey's lengthiest reign was at first interrupted by the outbreak of war in 1939, after the first three matches of his 15th season, and then unhappily ended in 1941 by his suspension following a joint FA-League inquiry into the payment of illegal bonuses and inducements. Since then there have been treble that number. There were five managers in fewer than eight years between the departure of Dave Mackay towards the end of 1976 and the arrival of Arthur Cox early in the 1984 close season for a stay that stretched into a tenth year. Since then, another spell of stability under Jim Smith has been abruptly ended by the rapid changes made during the 2001–02 season.

Formed as an offshoot of Derbyshire CCC with the main object of bolstering the county cricket club's ailing finances, and also to give their players the chance of some organised football in the winter months, Derby County experienced fluctuating fortunes in going through their first dozen years without a manager. They lost their first match by five goals, and their first FA Cup-tie by seven, both without scoring themselves. They also suffered their heaviest-ever defeat in another early venture in the national knock-out competition, falling in the first round by an 11–2 margin away to Everton.

In the Football League, too, they had a mainly struggling existence until, in its sixth season, they suddenly shot up to a final third place behind Aston Villa and Sunderland, giants of the game who were then in the midst of each claiming three titles in the course of six successive years—with three more to come between them in the next five. Life among that elite looked like being brief indeed for Derby when they promptly clung

W.D. Clark, who was appointed manager, though a very different role from today's, when Derby County became a limited company in 1896.

Harry Newbould, who managed Derby County and Manchester City before becoming secretary of the Players' Union.

to First Division status with a desperately narrow victory in one of the 'test' matches that then decided promotion and relegation, but back they bounced to go close to the League and Cup double only a few months before it was decided to incorporate the club under the Companies Acts.

The 1895–96 season ended with the Rams runners-up to Villa, four points behind, and denied a place in the Cup Final against the Wednesday by a late goal for Wolverhampton Wanderers in a semi-final at Perry Barr, Birmingham. That was the first of seven semi-finals in which Derby took part in nine consecutive years, the first four of them in succession. On three of those seven occasions they won through to the final, only to lose each time and with increasing severity—ultimately by what is still the biggest FA Cup Final defeat of them all. It was a sorry tale of hopes dashed at the brink that gave rise to the Gypsy's Curse, a belief of the superstitious which lingered for more than half a century until the Cup was at long last collected in the first final after the 1939–45 War.

The Curse, decreeing that Derby would win neither the Cup nor the League (for which, at the highest level, they had to wait another 26 years after that still solitary Cup triumph), was supposedly laid by a disgruntled gypsy who had been ousted from what became the County's Baseball Ground home. Those who believe in such things might just as well have pinned the blame on somebody connected with one of the rival clubs that Derby County's arrival on the footballing scene pushed into the background—and eventual oblivion. For, with just one exception, the newcomers were seen as arrogant, unwanted interlopers, regarded by some with considerable alarm and by others with acute resentment.

The players in this 1895–96 Derby County group are—Back row: Methven and Leiper. Middle row: Cox, Goodall (A.), Robinson, Kinsey, Staley. Front row: Goodall (J.), Paul, Miller, Stevenson, McQueen. On ground: Bloomer and McMillan.

That sole exception related to the team on whose right wing Harry Newbould exploited his prowess as a sprinter in his younger days. A contemporary account tells us that 'of the Derby clubs, none showed the same magnanimous and generous feeling towards the County as St. Luke's'. Much of the animosity among the rest arose from the defection of a number of their best players, then all amateurs, to the ambitious new organisation. Indeed, the ill-feeling in that respect erupted so vehemently, with some remarks being expressed in what one report described as 'not over-polite language', that William Morley, the cricket club committee member whose namesake son spurred him to advocate the soccer venture, was provoked into offering a strong public answer to the critics. In refuting charges of robbing neighbouring sides of their talent, Morley pointed out that those who had changed allegiance had done so voluntarily, and 'no monetary inducement was held out to them'.

Another bone of contention stemmed from the original adoption of the name Derbyshire County by the cricketers' soccer cousins. That wider range of title raised not a few jealous hackles, especially among the august members of the Derbyshire Football Association who maintained that only they could field a county team. Consequently, there was soon a diplomatic truncation to the long-familiar town (now city) prefix, but without any diminution of the determination to remain as representative of the whole of Derbyshire as the players of the summer game.

Nowhere was the anti-Derby County faction more fervent than in the ranks of Derby Midland, the railway works club that had been ruling the soccer roost in the borough, if not the county. Having already caught national attention by reaching the third round of the FA Cup, in which they had lost only narrowly to Wednesbury, Midland had recently taken part in the first Derbyshire Cup Final. There, however, they had been beaten by Staveley, who were to repeat that success the next season and continue to be regular finalists during the early years of a competition in which the only other winners of the trophy were Heeley (1886) and Derby Junction (1888).

Staveley further emphasised their strength around that time by progressing to the FA Cup's fourth round before going out to Blackburn Rovers, who were heading for the first of three consecutive victories in the final, but before the end of the next decade Derby County had left the North Derbyshire club and all their other neighbours behind to such an extent that they were carrying off both the Derbyshire Cup and the Derbyshire League championship with their reserve team.

The County's name caught on at once with the public, and, although the new club naturally had their setbacks, they gained in prestige through having the wholehearted backing of the cricket club's influential personalities. Even so, the intensity of the criticism with which they had to contend early in their existence can be accurately gauged from these comments by one of the Derby Midland club's committeemen:

> There is no wonder that many who worked hard for years in the interests of local football should feel sore when they remember that a new club, claiming to represent the county, stepped in and tried to reap all the advantages by players ready-trained for them at the expense of other clubs. It is not likely to be forgotten, either, that this self-dubbed County club pettishly deserted the [Derbyshire Football] Association—which is the true representative of Derbyshire county football—because they could not have everything their own way.

That last reference, not fairly expressed as it transpired, was to an unfortunate squabble with another local side, Long Eaton Rangers, that resulted in Derby County's disqualification from the Derbyshire Cup competition in their first season. This developed from a misunderstanding over the date of their third-round tie, with the DFA hearing deciding in favour of Rangers despite the fact that the Long Eaton club's secretary admitted to 'inadvertently' proposing, by letter, a date that was a week before the one on which his team turned up to find no opponents awaiting them.

The hearing was told that both clubs had suggested in correspondence that the match should be played on January 10th, 1885, but that the letters had crossed in the post. Because of this, and the fact that their wishes appeared to be mutual, the Long Eaton officials had not considered it necessary to confirm that date. When, however, the Rangers' letter was produced at the DFA meeting, it was seen that they had, in fact, proposed January 3rd for the game. This difference had led Derby County to assume, in the absence of any reply to their own letter, that no date had been decided, and they therefore contended that, in accordance with the Association's own laws, the match ought to be staged on the last available date, January 17th—the Saturday after the one Long Eaton thought they had arranged.

Derby County were so incensed when the DFA decision went against them that Samuel Richardson, their secretary, withdrew the club's players from the Derbyshire team in which they had been chosen for a match with the Hallamshire Association. He did so with the full approval of the men concerned, one of whom, skipper Frank Sugg, issued the following statement:

H.A. Morley, G.H. Bakewell and myself have decided, for the future, to play for our own team in preference to the Association, as we consider the Association, as at present constituted, is a complete farce. And so long as the business is carried on in such an unusual and partial way, they will find it a difficult task to get a team in the field at all.

Sugg, who, as a prominent cricketer, was at the centre of another controversy that is recalled in the next chapter, was stung into his strong comments by criticism of the County in letters published in the local newspapers. Among the fiercest of those critics was someone who dubbed himself 'A Lover of Justice'. He wrote:

Anyone who is in full possession of the facts upon which the dispute hinged will undoubtedly come to the conclusion that the Association arrived at a thoroughly impartial decision. The disqualification of the County is wholly attributable to the defiant attitude they assumed, and if the way in which one of their luminaries arrogantly attempted to intimidate the Association has recoiled upon their own heads, they must submissively bear the burden. If the County executive think of 'smashing' the Association by their withdrawal, and the retirements from the offices of the Association of some of their influential abettors, they are greatly deluded.

In light of Long Eaton's admitted oversight, it could be reasonably argued that a fairer, unbiased, opinion was offered by the *Derby Daily Telegraph* when it stated:

As far as we are able to judge, the correspondence does not conclusively prove that the County entered into an arrangement and then wilfully broke it. All sorts of accusations have been made, not only as to the motives actuating the members of the Association who were present and voted, but also with regard to their attitude towards the County club generally. That there is some feeling against the County on the part of some other clubs will not, we think, be denied. Such a thing, however, ought not to exist. All clubs, we suppose, exist for the promotion of football, and the County have certainly introduced matches of a higher class than we had been frequently accustomed to in Derby. In the circumstances, it was highly desirable that a representative of the Press should have been invited to the meeting of the Association to give an unvarnished account of what took place. Which side is right and which is wrong is a point that will never be satisfactorily settled, but the dispute has had unhappy results, leading to the resignation of the Hon W.M. Jervis from the presidency [of the DFA] and the virtual secession of the County club from the Association.

The Hon. William Monk Jervis, brother of the third Viscount St. Vincent and uncle of Lord Harris, an England cricket captain who held major posts with the MCC and was the dominant figure in Kent cricket for almost 60 years, was president of Derbyshire County Cricket Club, which he helped to establish, from 1871 to 1887. He was a useful cricketer in his younger days, but he was past his best by the time of the Derbyshire club's formation, and in his only appearance for the county, against Lancashire at Derby in 1873, he was dismissed for nought and six. London-born, he was a member of MCC from 1860 until his death at Quarndon Hall, near Derby, in 1909 at the age of 82.

Derby County's participation in the Derbyshire Cup had aroused an adverse reaction even before the mix-up over the Long Eaton date. The question had been raised as to 'whether it is in accordance with the rules governing Association football for a county team to compete for their own cup'. Those who put forward that argument emphasised that a county club could draw their players from the other teams in the district, whereas local clubs could not do so without laying themselves open to a charge of professionalism. Consequently, they maintained, the Rams possessed an unfair advantage.

Holders of a contrary view pointed out that two similar cases had previously occurred in the FA and Scottish Cup competitions, and in neither of them had the claim to take the match by default been allowed.

Quite apart from all the to-do over the Derbyshire Cup expulsion, Derby County's relationship with Derby Midland became so prickly that they refused to make any fixtures with the railwaymen despite the disapproval of some of their supporters who appealed instead for a quick healing of the breach. Paradoxically, Long Eaton Rangers were the Rams' only local opponents during the 1885–86 season which followed their dispute with that club. The County gained a comfortable away victory in that encounter, and just over a year later they gave stronger evidence of their growing stature by also winning their first meeting with Staveley, to whom they were drawn away in the FA Cup.

Defeat for Derby loomed as Staveley held onto a lead they gained shortly before half-time, but the tie was transformed by two goals in the last ten minutes from Isaac Monks, leader of the attack who made his only League appearances for the County at centre-half in their first three games of the following inaugural season.

Derby County scored six goals in both the next two rounds, against Ecclesfield and Owlerton, but they were then derailed at Crewe as the Derby challenge in the competition was robustly carried forward by the Junction club, previously known as Junction Street Sunday School, who were then posing the biggest threat to the County's supremacy in the immediate Derby area. After disposing of Chirk by an only goal while the Rams were failing by the same margin in Cheshire, the Junction pulled off an historic triumph by beating Blackburn Rovers, so recently holders for three successive years, by 2–1 at the Arboretum ground. That took them to a semi-final at Stoke against West Bromwich Albion, another of the clubs about to join Derby County as founder members of the Football League, and they were by no means disgraced in losing by 3–0 to the players who went on to beat Preston 2–1 in the final.

The Junction, however, had reached the summit of their achievement, and the fact that they, too, were being left behind by Derby County was underlined in the 1888–89 season when the Rams not only were elected to the League but also defeated the Junction, against whom they had gone unbeaten through four previous meetings, in the Cup's first round. A year later, Derby Midland themselves had a final fling of FA Cup glory by scoring three goals without reply from Nottingham Forest on the day, in another first-round match, when Derby County suffered that alarming relapse of crashing to their record 11–2 defeat, after leading 2–1, when they met Everton on 'a sea of mud' at Anfield.[1]

John Goodall, of whom more later, scored both Derby goals in that debacle. Three Everton players did the hat-trick—Alec Brady (who will also crop up again, in another controversial Cup context), Fred Geary and Alfred Milward. Geary, who came from Nottingham, notched another hat-trick when he made his debut for England in Belfast the following year, and the month after that match he and Milward were among the four players Everton supplied for the game against Scotland at Blackburn in which Goodall scored England's opening goal in their 2–1 win.

Derby Midland's Cup run in 1890 was halted at Bootle in the next round, and very soon afterwards they also came to the end of their road as an independent club in the most unexpected manner. The introduction of professionalism had presented them with what eventually became insurmountable problems, and when they ended the 1890–91 season more than £100 in debt the railway company's directors ordered them either to revert to amateurism or wind up their affairs. They found that first choice unacceptable, encountering almost unanimous opposition, so when, to widespread surprise considering the bad blood between them, Derby County offered an amalgamation, the Midland committee had little hesitation in falling in with the suggestion. As one local newspaper observed, 'extremes do sometimes meet'.

The boycott on fixtures between the clubs had been lifted to the point where they had met ten times, with four wins apiece and goals figures of 17–13 in the County's favour. The merger became official in June, 1891, and the joint management was vested in a committee of 16 elected by guarantors of not less than £5 each to the club funds who were already being invited by the Rams from among their supporters. Three of the 16, Walter Butt, Fred Knowles and R.G. Ward, were nominated from the Midland's ranks. More than £600 was quickly subscribed, and, with further investments being made, the rejuvenated Derby County were able to put a decent amount in reserve and therefore progress on a sounder footing.

They also benefited from the arrangement whereby they acquired the pick of the Midland's players. Previously, for their first season they had snapped up two of the best of them, wingers George Bakewell (their second signing after William Morley's other son, Haydn) and Charlie Ward. Now they welcomed in such sterling recruits as full-back Jonathan ('Jonty') Staley, half-back Ernest Hickinbottom, who had also played for neighbouring Darley Abbey, and a couple of forceful forwards, winger Sam Mills and William Storer, the Derbyshire and England wicket keeper–batsman who was also a bowler good enough to take more than 200 first-class wickets. Storer, who filled all five of the then standard forward positions in fewer than 30 first-team games for the Rams, was the brother of the Woolwich Arsenal and Liverpool goalkeeper whose son was to render Derby County exceptional service as both player and manager.

It was not all one-way traffic in the arrangement between Derby County and the Midland. In return, the railway club took on a number of the Rams' reserve players, though there was one drawback for them when they had to withdraw from the Midland

---

1. Everton, who, like Derby County, were formed from a cricket club (St. Domingo's Church), played their home games at Stanley Park and Priory Road before moving in 1884 to the site in Anfield Road which was to become the home of their Liverpool rivals. A big increase in rent led to Everton's leaving Anfield for Goodison Park, on the opposite side of Stanley Park, where they first played in September, 1892.

Counties League because a club's second team, which is what the Midland then amounted to, were not welcomed into membership.

Of the Midland men who switched to Derby County, Staley put in the longest spell of playing service in staying for just over ten years before completing his career in Derbyshire with Ripley Athletic. For much of his time with the Rams he was forced into a reserve role after losing his place through injury during his second season, but his patience was rewarded when the player who had replaced him, Joe Leiper, had to drop out for the same reason after the first home match of 1898–99. Staley stayed in for the rest of that season, gaining a Cup runners-up medal against Sheffield United, and he went on to reach almost 150 League and Cup appearances.

Leiper, whose nickname 'Fossil' belied the alert, adventurous approach he brought to the English game from his home club, Partick Thistle, ended just short of 180, including three Cup semi-finals and the 1898 losing final against Nottingham Forest. Having gone close to a First Division championship medal in the Derby team that finished second to Villa in 1896, he picked up one in the Second Division with Grimsby Town in 1901 before rejoining Partick by way of Chesterfield.

Ernie Hickinbottom, who was born at Darley Abbey, played once for Derby County in their initial League season, and on rejoining them from Midland he took his total of games just past the half-century. It was back at the Baseball Ground that he died while watching the Rams' last match before the outbreak of the Second World War in September, 1939.

Haydn Morley,[2] like William Storer, was among the Derby County players who played cricket for Derbyshire, and it was fitting that he should be the first player to be signed by the Rams because he was influential with his brother in persuading their father to press for the formation of the football club. After the entry into the Football League, however, he played only four more times for the first team, late in the League's inaugural season, before leaving for the Wednesday, whom he captained, as an amateur full-back, in the 1890 FA Cup Final against Blackburn Rovers.

That match at Kennington Oval resulted in a demoralising defeat for his new club, by a 6–1 margin that was to stand as a record for the final until his old club crashed 6–0 to Bury at the Crystal Palace in 1903, but for Morley it ended on a literally high note as he was carried from the field on the shoulders of fans paying tribute to his plucky display against overwhelming odds.

Blackburn Rovers were then kings of the Cup, for that was the fourth time they had won it, following the hat-trick of wins they completed in a replay at Derby—and a year later they carried it off yet again. They were finalists six times in 10 years, losing 1–0 on the first occasion, in 1882, to Old Etonians, who were beaten by Blackburn Olympic, 2–1 after extra time, in the next season's final. Then came the three successive victories in the final by Rovers, giving Blackburn a team in the final for five consecutive years. Rovers almost reached the last stage three other times before the turn of the century,

---

2. Morley played just one match in Derbyshire's first team against Notts, who won by 10 wickets, at Nottingham on May 7th–9th, 1891. He opened the innings with L.G. Wright, scoring 12 and eight. Derbyshire totalled 213 and 182, Notts 364–8 dec and 32 for no wicket.

'Jonty' Staley, one of the Rams' recruits
from Derby Midland.

Joe Leiper, who played in three Cup
semi-finals and one final.

going out in the semi-finals to Wolves in 1889 (after a replay) and 1893, and to Notts County in 1894.

Three of Blackburn's six goals against the Wednesday in 1890 were scored by England winger William Townley, whose hat-trick in a final has been emulated by only Jimmy Logan (for Notts County in 1894) and Stan Mortensen (for Blackpool in 1953) both against Bolton Wanderers. When Rovers' other England winger, Joe Lofthouse on the opposite right flank, scored their sixth goal with only a few minutes left for play sections of the 20,000 crowd caused the game to be held up by stampeding towards the pavilion, where preparations were being made for the presentation of the trophy and medals. The delay lasted for about four minutes before police and soldiers helped the referee, Major Marindin, to restore order, and in the short time remaining Blackburn might have scored a seventh time but for Morley's intervention.

After finishing with football, Morley formed a bowls club and ran a brass band as a hobby. In club cricket, he was a successful batsman with Belper Meadows, whom he captained during the early 1890s in succession to F.R. Spofforth, the 'Demon' fast bowler of Australian Test fame who also played for Derbyshire. So active did Morley remain that he continued his work as a solicitor until he was in his nineties—and even then it took the amputation of a leg, resulting from a scratch on a foot that became infected, to enforce his retirement. He died at Hathersage the following year, in May, 1953, at the ripe old age of 92.

One of the biggest disappointments of his long life apart from that heavy beating by Blackburn was also connected with the Cup. He was unable to obtain the ticket for which he applied in writing when Derby County reached an all-ticket semi-final at Sheffield Wednesday's ground after the 1939–45 War.

CHAPTER 2

Contrasting Starts at Bolton

*Future Derby favourite on mark against them in their
losing debut – Spilsbury the Rams' first scorer – Thorny
subject of professionalism – Sugg sparks protest – Four Test
cricketers among Derbyshire players with Derby County –
A soccer fatality – Unlucky Higgins – Bakewell opens
League account – Ever-presents in the Plackett family*

BOLTON was the setting for the first match in which Derby County took part, and for the first one they played in the Football League—with very differing outcomes. On September 13th, 1884, they were beaten 5–0 when they made their entrance away to Great Lever, a district of the Lancashire town long since absorbed into that area of concentrated population known as Greater Manchester. On September 8th, 1888, they began League life by beating Bolton Wanderers 6–3 at Pike's Lane after conceding two goals in the opening five minutes and going three down shortly afterwards.

This was Derby County's all-amateur line-up on the day of their debut, with the clubs from which they were recruited in brackets: L.F. Gillett (Derby School); H.L. Evans (Derby School), Frank Harvey (Derby St. Luke's); Albert Williamson (Sawley), Haydn Morley (Derby Midland), Harry Wharmby (St. Luke's); George Bakewell (Derby Midland), W. Shipley (St. Luke's), B.W. Spilsbury (Corinthians), A. ('Jammer') Smith (Long Eaton), Charlie Ward (Derby Midland).

Two weeks after that deflating start, the first home match was played against Blackburn Olympic, who earlier that year had failed to retain the FA Cup in losing to Queen's Park in a semi-final at Nottingham—and had then seen the trophy stay in Blackburn with their Rovers rivals, who won it for the first of three successive years by beating the Scottish amateurs at Kennington Oval.

For Olympic's visit, Derby County fielded: Gillett; Evans, Morley; Exham, Thorpe, Hickinbottom; Bakewell, Spilsbury, Chevallier, Smith, Ward. The distinction of being their first-ever scorer fell to Old Reptonian Benjamin Ward Spilsbury, who was at Cambridge University when he turned out three times for England over the next two years. Against Olympic, he snatched an early lead with a superb effort, only for another defeat to be suffered despite further goals by Chevallier and Ward. Near the end, Derby were denied a 4–4 draw when the visitors' crossbar was struck by Chevallier, a schoolmaster colleague of Irishman George Exham at Repton who had been twice a winner and twice a loser in FA Cup finals with Old Etonians—on the last occasion as a runner-up against the Olympic after extra time.

Ben Spilsbury, who was born only a few miles outside Derby, at Findern, and had left his teens, on the first day of March, 1884, just a matter of weeks before teaming up with the County, made a scoring entry into international football against Ireland in Manchester the following February. A year later, he bagged four of England's six goals in another defeat of the Irish, in Belfast, and on the last day of the same month, March, 1886, he was awarded his third cap in a 1–1 draw with Scotland in Glasgow. The England scorer in that game was Tinsley Lindley, who also played alongside Spilsbury for the famous Corinthians amateur side as well as Cambridge University, and whose imposing collection of other clubs included the Casuals, Notts County, Crusaders, Swifts, Preston North End and Nottingham Forest.

Spilsbury, who captained the Cambridge football team in his final year, also won a Blue at athletics. At Repton, where cricket was another of his sporting strong suits, he won the long jump for four consecutive years, breaking the school's record. After gaining his degree, he continued his soccer career with Derby County, excelling with hat-tricks against Ecclesfield and Owlerton in successive rounds of the FA Cup in 1887, but he played only once for the club in the Football League, scoring in a 4–2 defeat away to Aston Villa, and he made his farewell appearance in the narrow first-round Cup victory over Derby Junction early in 1889. Alexander ('Sandy') Higgins, Derby's leading scorer for their first two League seasons, got the only goal in that game.

Soon afterwards, Spilsbury emigrated to Canada, where he worked as a land agent, and he died there, at Vancouver, in August, 1938, shortly after his 74th birthday. Lindley, a scorer in each of his first nine matches for England (and in two of the four others), was called to the bar after leaving Cambridge, and later became a county court judge. His achievements as the Nottingham Special Constabulary's chief officer earned him an OBE in 1918. He, too, died at 74, in 1940.

In Derby County's opening match with Great Lever, Spilsbury and his new team-mates were outsmarted by a cultured forward, making his first foray into English football, who was to become one of the finest the Rams have ever possessed: John Goodall. He did the hat-trick (some sources credit him with as many as all five of the home side's goals), a feat he repeated when he definitely did all Great Lever's scoring, again without reply, in that season's return game at Derby.

Those heavy defeats helped to regurgitate the thorny subject of professionalism, which had first been raised officially four years earlier by C.W. Alcock, secretary of the Football Association. Bowing to what he saw as the inevitable, he suggested that professionalism should be legalised, but delegates at the FA's next annual meeting thought otherwise. Consequently, a rule was introduced forbidding any payments other than expenses and the equivalent of wages lost by taking time off from work to play football. This, however, served only to drive professionalism underground. Those clubs which had openly imported talent at a price resorted to so-called 'shamateurism' —and Great Lever, ostensibly an amateur Bolton club, were among them.

The split between the amateur-minded South and the growing influence of the professional-minded North was widened when Preston North End, whose manager, Major Will Sudell, made little attempt to disguise the fact that his men received payment, were disqualified from the 1883–84 FA Cup competition following a protest by their fourth-round opponents, Upton Park. The major was not short of allies, and matters were brought to a head when Burnley also incurred the FA's disfavour for tempting a Scottish player from Accrington. The Burnley officials promptly rounded up other clubs to attend a meeting which was held in Manchester shortly after Derby County's visit to Great Lever, and as a result of this an FA sub-committee reported that it was 'expedient to legalise the paid player under stringent conditions.'

In due course their report was adopted, and in July, 1885, at a special general meeting at Anderton's Hotel in London's Fleet Street, the proposal was carried by 35 votes to five—but with the proviso that 'professionals must qualify for the Cup and Association matches by birth, or by residence for more than two years within six miles of their club'.

In view of those developments, it is interesting to recall that a few days after Derby County had got off to their losing start at Great Lever in 1884, the *Telegraph* evening newspaper in Derby published a letter from an aggrieved fan who, writing under the *nom de plume* 'Amateur', stated:

> The Preston North End and Accrington football teams have been the principal sufferers from the ill-timed and inadvisable attack on professionalism. I say ill-timed and inadvisable because it is a well-known fact that almost every team of importance—especially in Lancashire—have to resort to employing strangers to keep up their strength. The local point is in connection with the match between Great Lever and Derby County, in which the latter suffered a crushing defeat. And is it to be wondered at in view of the fact that nearly every player in the Great Lever side hailed from different clubs of good repute? If, by employing players, clubs can give the public a better exhibition of the game, I say it would be better to acknowledge professionalism at once, for it must inevitably come to it sooner or later. Every club will then have the chance of engaging good players, and football will become not only a Saturday-afternoon game but will also be played on other days of the week.

Prophetic words! But 'Amateur' would surely be speechless, if not scriptless, if he were around today to see to what obscene financial excesses professionalism has taken soccer—and sport in general for that matter. As for his reference to Great Lever, the truth of his words can be appreciated from this list of the players, with their other clubs, who trounced Derby County back in September, 1884: Trainer (Wrexham); Holden (Darwen), Lucas (Kilmarnock); Whittle, Rostron (Darwen), Gallagher (Johnstone Rovers); Walkenshaw (Kilmarnock), Livesey, Goodall, J. (Kilmarnock), Waugh (Glasgow Northern), Hay (Kilmarnock). Quite a representative side, to say the least!

Wrexham-born James Trainer, known as the 'Prince of Goalkeepers', went on to win all but one of his 20 Welsh caps while with Preston North End, where he became a clubmate of John Goodall in moving from Bolton Wanderers in 1887. He reigned supreme for more than a decade at Deepdale, but missed picking up a Cup-winner's medal against Wolves in 1889 because he was then still a couple of months short of the two-year residential qualification.

Derby County lost not only their first two fixtures, against Great Lever and Blackburn Olympic, but also the next two, against Notts County (1–3) and Stoke (0–2), before ironically gaining their first victory at the expense of the one club that did not openly object to their formation. In the Derbyshire Cup competition they defeated St. Luke's 3–1 with goals from Bakewell, Spilsbury and 'Jammer' Smith, and they made further progress in that competition by beating Wirksworth 4–2 before their disqualification because of the dispute with Long Eaton Rangers.

Game in Fancy Dress

A game in fancy dress was played at the County Ground in Derby on January 31st, 1894, between a Derby County team and a side comprising members of the Grand Theatre's *Babes in the Wood* pantomime, to raise funds for the players' stall at the bazaar which was held at the Drill Hall the following March to save the Rams from financial disaster. The match raised about £50, and the bazaar realised more than £1,000.

The Derby County team included Jimmy Methven (dressed as a negro), Johnny Goodall (Bold Bad Baron), Johnny McMillan (Old Mother Shipton), Jack Robinson (Fat Bobby), Joe Leiper (Old Sarah), Archie Goodall (Crash 'em), and Ernest Hickinbottom (Yeoman of the Guard). Steve Bloomer, due to appear as a convict, dropped out through illness.

By then, only a week after accounting for St. Luke's, their interest in the FA Cup had also ended with that 7–0 thrashing in the first round. Without Chevallier and Spilsbury, and with the Derbyshire cricketer Frank Sugg little more than a passenger on the wing after unwisely agreeing to play despite not feeling well, they folded up in the second half against Walsall Town after holding those visitors to a one-goal lead up to the interval. The suffering goalkeeper—as when Derby had let in five goals in their debut game at Great Lever—was L.F. Gillett, who three years earlier had kept a clean sheet in helping Old Carthusians to beat Old Etonians in the FA Cup Final at Kennington Oval.

Frank Sugg, who was joined in the Derby team against Walsall by another Derbyshire and England batsman, William Chatterton, had spent the past cricket season with his home county (he was born at Ilkeston) after starting out with Yorkshire the previous year, but he put in only two more with Derbyshire before being tempted away to Lancashire. That led to sections of the Derby crowd barracking to such an extent in showing their displeasure over the manner of Sugg's departure when the Red Rose county were the visitors in 1888 that Albert ('Monkey') Hornby, the Lancashire captain, led his men off the field and caused a hold-up of about a quarter of an hour. It was with considerable difficulty that he was persuaded to finish the game, which his side won by four wickets.

Until then, Lancashire had been Derbyshire's most regular opponents—the only county, in fact, who had been prepared to arrange home and away matches with them during the first three seasons of their existence. But relations between them were so soured by the Sugg affair that almost five years went by before they were in opposition again, although that regrettable situation was not helped by Derbyshire's temporary loss of first-class status from 1887 to 1894. In any case, Lancashire's domination of Derbyshire was so emphatic on the cricket field in those days that the double victory they gained over them in the season before the falling-out was their 11th in the 18 years they had been meeting—six of them in succession. And Derbyshire had beaten them only four times out of 35 since winning their opening game by the deceptive margin of an innings and 11 runs in 1871.

Frank Sugg, whose brother Walter also played cricket for Derbyshire (from 1884 to 1902), was in the England teams that defeated Australia at the Oval and in Manchester, for a 2–1 series win, on either side of his controversial reappearance at Derby in Lancashire's ranks. He was twice runner-up, and once third, in the Derbyshire batting averages, albeit with modest figures at a time of comparatively low scoring generally, but it was during his 13 seasons with Lancashire, for whom he qualified by residence, that he enjoyed his greatest successes. In completing more than 10,000 runs for his adopted county, he scored 15 centuries and exceeded 150 in an innings on six occasions.

A strapping six-footer, he was a man of many sports. In addition to cricket, in which he also held the record for throwing the ball, and soccer, at which he played for Burnley, the Wednesday and Bolton Wanderers besides Derby County, he excelled at long-distance swimming, reached the final of the Liverpool amateur billiards championship, and won prizes for rifle shooting, bowls, putting the shot and weight lifting. Quite a fellow. By a sad coincidence, he and Walter died within a few days of each other, in May, 1933.

Like Frank Sugg, William Chatterton was renowned more for his cricket than his football. Unlike Sugg, he stayed on long enough with Derby County to make five appearances in their first League season, scoring his only goal at that level from inside-right in a home defeat by Everton. Again like Sugg, he became one of four Test cricketers (the others were William Storer and Arnold Warren) to have played for the Rams, winning his one cap, as Derbyshire's first England player, against South Africa at Cape Town during the 1891–92 tour on which he was the MCC's heaviest scorer. He captained Derbyshire for three of his 21 seasons with the county which ended in 1902.

William Cropper, a promising Derbyshire cricketer who suffered a fatal injury while playing football, and (right) L.G. Wright, the leading Derbyshire batsman of his day who also played for the Rams.

Chatterton, who both began and ended his life in Cheshire—he was in only his 50th year when he died of consumption at Flowery Field, Hyde, in 1913—was Derbyshire's leading run-getter, with just over 11,600 runs, until overtaken by L.G. Wright, another prominent cricketer to play briefly for Derby County in League football. Levi George Wright, better known by just the initials of his forenames, also scored one League goal in a home defeat (by Preston's Invincibles), and he occupied three positions in his four appearances—centre-half, full-back and centre-forward. He played soccer for his home club, Oxford City, before moving to Derby in 1881 to take up the post of assistant master at St. Anne's School, and he joined Derby Midland, from where he was among the Rams' recruits, after soon switching to work as a clerk for the railway company.

As an opening batsman, he recovered from an uncertain start with Derbyshire to exceed 15,000 runs and make 20 first-class centuries before retiring at the end of the 1909 season. He was then 47, and *Wisden* observed that he was 'probably a better player at the age of 40 than at any other period of his career.' The esteemed cricket annual also described L.G. as 'one of the finest batsmen who has ever appeared for Derbyshire' when he died at Derby on January 11th, 1953, only four days before his 91st birthday.

Another Derbyshire cricketer of Derby County's early days was William Cropper, an accomplished all-rounder whose promising double career was tragically cut short only a couple of weeks after his 26th birthday by a fatal injury suffered on the football field. By then, early in 1889, he had left the Rams and was playing for Staveley against Grimsby Town at Clee Park. Ironically, it was with the intention of reducing the risk of his being injured, because he was due to play in a representative match against Glasgow on the following Saturday, that he was moved from the centre of the attack to the right wing, a position in which he was not accustomed to playing.

In going up for a high ball, he was accidentally caught in the stomach by the knee of Grimsby defender Dan Doyle. Although he had to be carried off the pitch, the seriousness of his injury was not readily realised. Overnight, however, his condition deteriorated despite medical attention, and he died the next day from a ruptured bowel. Blameless as Doyle was, feeling against him in particular, and Grimsby in general, was so strong in the Sheffield area that the Wednesday club prudently decided to cancel both their fixtures with the Town that season.

Although naturally very distressed by the tragedy, Doyle felt able to resume his place in Grimsby's team in time for the following month's second-round FA Cup-tie in which they controversially lost to a Preston side heading for the first League and Cup double. Doyle went on to enjoy the most successful phase of his career while with Glasgow Celtic, making eight appearances for Scotland from 1892 to 1898.

Of the Derby County players who were called upon during the club's first four seasons but did not turn out for them again when they entered the Football League at the end of that period, one of the most consistently reliable performers was Sam Lawrence, a defender from the Burton district. Having impressed when, at the age of 18, he faced the County with the Strollers in a Birmingham League Cup-tie, he accepted an invitation to assist Derby's new club the next Saturday and stayed on after helping them to a comfortable win. Frequently he was the full-back partner for Arthur Latham, formerly of St. Luke's and Derby Midland, who followed some five years as a Derby player with nearly 30 more as the County's trainer before leaving for his Norwich reunion in that latter role with Frank Buckley, the former Rams and England half-back who had then newly been appointed manager of the East Anglian club.

Sam Lawrence was in his mid-eighties, still living in the Burton area at Shobnall, when he looked back on his spell with Derby County by recalling:

> I played as an amateur. I received about five shillings [25p in modern money] in expenses for each match—nothing more. At work they got rather annoyed with me because I had to have quite a lot of time off. One match with Derby I particularly remember was played at Kennington Oval, in 1886 I think, when we beat the famous Corinthians side, containing nine amateur internationals, by 3–2. We caught a special train to London at 8 am, and the fare was then four shillings. On Derby station I met Ben Spilsbury, one of my team-mates, who was also a Corinthian. Our goalkeeper was Harry Bestwick, from Long Eaton Rangers, who, like me and Spilsbury, played in all the four FA Cup-ties Derby played in the last season before the League was formed. We had a couple of big wins, in both of which Spilsbury did the hat-trick, before losing by an only goal at Crewe.

Bestwick, in common with Spilsbury, played only once for Derby County in the sterner professional sphere of League football. For most of the first season at that competitive level, the club's goalkeeper was Joe Marshall, a signing from Staveley who then moved to Derby Junction. Marshall stood between the sticks at Bolton when the League got under way in 1888 in a team that included only two members of the side fielded at Great Lever in 1884—George Bakewell and Albert Williamson, who between them made more than 100 appearances over the League's first three seasons before being transferred together to Notts County in 1891.

These were the men who battled so hard to give the Rams their winning start as one of the League's dozen founder members: Marshall; Latham, Ferguson; Williamson, Monks, Roulstone; Bakewell, Cooper (L), Higgins, Plackett (H), Plackett (L).

Latham's full-back partner, Archie Ferguson, an import from Hearts, also played for Preston before emigrating to the United States. Walter Roulstone, a powerful wing-half who followed Williamson from nearby Sawley Rangers, became the first to complete a century of first-team appearances for Derby County in being a regular choice for five seasons before a knee injury forced him out. He was later with Heanor Town and his home club, Castle Donington Town.

Of Bakewell's colleagues in the forward line, Lewis Cooper was beginning his second spell with Derby, having first left them for Grimsby Town, and 'Sandy' Higgins went on also to take part in the first League match played by Nottingham Forest. Having been the Rams' main marksman in each of their first two League seasons, with 11 (plus one in the Cup) and 14 goals respectively, Higgins was Forest's top scorer for two seasons in the Football Alliance, with 22 and 26, before getting both their goals in a 2–2 away draw with Everton when they started out in the First Division in 1892.

Early the previous year, though not fully recovered from injury and not feeling too well, he scored five of Forest's 14 goals when they gained the record FA Cup away win against Clapton at Upton Park. In the Alliance, he scored four against Darwen, Crewe and Lincoln, and hat-tricks against Burton Swifts and Grimsby Town, but found goals harder to come by on reappearing in the Football League with Forest. In 47 games he totalled just 18 before retiring at the end of the 1893–94 season.

Higgins, whose outstanding scoring achievements while with Derby County were both at the expense of Aston Villa in 1889 home games—four goals in a 5–2 win during March, and all five, without response, in late December—must rank as one of the unluckiest footballers at international level. As a Kilmarnock player, he obtained half of Scotland's eight goals against Ireland at Hampden Park in 1885, yet he never represented his country again. His son, another Alex, was more fortunate. During a lengthy stay with Newcastle United, after starting out, like his father, with Kilmarnock, the younger 'Sandy' Higgins was capped four times, won a League championship medal, and played in two FA Cup finals—once as a winner (against Barnsley in 1910, after a replay).

The younger Higgins also played for Forest after briefly rejoining Kilmarnock following the First World War. At the beginning of the 1920–21 season he emulated his father by making a scoring League debut for them—also in a 2–2 draw, at home to Stoke City in the Second Division. A year later, Forest won promotion as champions, but without Higgins. By then he had moved to Norwich City, from where he returned to live on Tyneside and wound up his playing career with several local teams.

The first scorer for Derby County in the Football League was George Bakewell, whose excellent service over the previous four seasons since his move from the Midland also made him an automatic successor to the club's captaincy for that historic encounter with Bolton Wanderers. Bakewell, who was to resume with the Rams as a member of

George Bakewell, Derby County's second signing and their first scorer in the Football League.

Arthur Latham, trainer who made a one-match comeback in a goalkeeping emergency.
(Derby Evening Telegraph)

their committee after his short stay with Notts County, shared Derby's scoring at Pike's Lane with Lew Cooper and Lol Plackett. Each of them contributed two goals as the visitors, who were ahead by the interval after their early shocks, staged a revival that surpassed even the one the Wanderers had made against them in a friendly game at the same ground the previous season. On that former occasion it had been Derby who had gone into an early two-goal lead, only to be held to a 5–5 draw in a pulsating finish during which Bolton had scored twice within a few minutes.

The Plackett brothers, Henry and Lawrence, who formed the Rams' left wing on the first day of League football were members of a well-known Breaston family that could field complete cricket and soccer teams. Both joined Derby County from a Long Eaton club—Lol from the Alexandra in 1886, Henry from the Midland two years later—and both left for Nottingham Forest in 1889. Lol, mainly an inside-forward, alone played in all 22 of Derby's games in their first League season, though Higgins and Roulstone both missed only one match and Latham just two.

More than 30 seasons on, another descendant of the Plackett brood, Sawley-born Sydney, a wing-half, alone played in each of the County's 42 League fixtures when they regained a place in the First Division as runners-up to Sheffield Wednesday in 1925–26.[1]

---

1. Strictly speaking, this Sheffield club was then officially still known as 'The Wednesday,' although the name 'Sheffield Wednesday' was used in the home match programme as far back as 1905. In his book *Sheffield Wednesday a Complete Record, 1867–1987*, published by Breedon Books, my old friend Keith Farnsworth states that 'it was not until June, 1927, that the directors expressed the wish that the club be called Sheffield Wednesday, and the legal change of title was formally approved by the Football League in June, 1929'.

CHAPTER 3

Years of Big Changes

*Link with Derbyshire CCC severed –
Soccer crowds cause pitch problems – 'Inspired'
alterations at County Ground – Move to Baseball
Ground – Game of three halves – Limited company
formed – The original directors – Transfer fees in a
year: £70 – Scandal as secretary absconds – W.T.
Taylor sets long-service record*

T HE LINK-UP with their hitherto arch Midland rivals was not the only important step Derby County took in 1891. An even more momentous one came when they severed their connection with Derbyshire County Cricket Club. News of this breakaway, ending several weeks of rumour, was given in a report that the cricket club's committee submitted to their annual meeting during April that year. It stated:

> After the present football season, the football club will be separated from the cricket club, as the system of running them in conjunction with one another has been found of late years not to pay. The committee are prepared to let their ground at a fixed rent for football because they consider that it will be better to have a fixed sum coming in than having to depend upon whatever profits might be made.

It was revealed that although the cricket club had benefited by £586 from the football club over a period of six years, they had received no financial assistance from that source for the past two seasons because the soccer section had lost money. By splitting up, it was hoped to have an arrangement more suitable for both parties, but the break was soon to be made even more emphatic by the switching of the Rams' headquarters to the Baseball Ground in the Normanton area of the county borough.

Derby County had originally drawn a considerable advantage from having the cricketers' County Ground off Nottingham Road as their home venue, for at that time it was generally regarded as the best sports enclosure in the district. The football pitch there was then described as 'a magnificent piece of turf', on which were staged an international match, between England and Ireland, four FA Cup semi-finals, and the final itself.[1] The ultimate destination of the trophy was decided outside London for

---

1. The first FA Cup semi-final at the County Ground in Derby was between Queen's Park, the Glasgow amateur club, and Nottingham Forest, who drew 1–1 on March 14th, 1885.

(continued overleaf)

the first time in 1886, when Blackburn Rovers rounded off their hat-trick by beating West Bromwich Albion 2–0 in the replay at Derby after a scoreless draw at the Oval.

That replayed final was seen as an excellent yardstick by which to measure the growing enthusiasm for football, and there was an encouraging attendance of 16,144 (about 1,000 more than at the game at the Oval) despite the fact that, even though it was early April, snow fell heavily throughout the morning and did not cease until less than two hours before the kick-off.

The advent of regular football at the County Ground, however, was soon seen to be to the detriment of the cricket club, for, with soccer spectators encroaching towards the cricket square—especially for the major matches that took place so close to the cricket season—the ground suffered for the summer game from being trampled upon by thousands of agitated feet. Visions of large crowds (though not over-large by later standards) were not contemplated when the football club came into existence, and to begin with the only restraint between the players and the public was a stout rope fixed to stakes.

More formidable barriers were not erected until the bigger crowds were attracted by the major Cup games, but in those early years the cricket pitch—in marked contrast to the football one—still remained in bad condition, with the reputation of being the worst in England on which first-class matches were played. Consequently, Derbyshire (again in contrast to their soccer cousins) found it extremely difficult at that stage to build up an attractive, wider-ranging fixture list in the face of what amounted to a boycott by certain counties which, in any case, regarded them as opponents too inferior to be worth meeting.

One old account informs us that 'many a famous batsman carried away the marks of the punishment he received from rising deliveries at Derby'. Foremost among them was John Shuter, the Surrey captain, who was felled by a fast ball from the unpredictable George Walker, an unpleasant bowler to contend with at the best of times, and had to retire 'bleeding profusely' from an ugly head cut. The pitch that day was described as playing 'very queerly', though, in truth, the deplorable mishap could not be blamed to a great extent on the after-effects of football because it occurred the year before the first of the FA Cup semi-finals to be decided at the ground.

At that time, the cricket pavilion stood about a hundred yards from the main entrance off the Nottingham Road, a small gatehouse with two turnstiles near the canal bridge and the old Stores Road, and was almost directly opposite the racecourse grandstand. It provided practically the only shelter spectators could enjoy, and, according to another ancient account, 'on a bad day the plight of the crowd was almost pitiable'.

Queen's Park won the replay at the Merchiston Castle ground in Edinburgh by 3–0, but lost to Blackburn Rovers in the final at Kennington Oval for the second successive year. Other FA Cup semi-finals at Derby: At the County Ground—March 13th, 1886: Blackburn Rovers 2, Swifts 1; March 9th, 1892: Nottingham Forest 2, West Bromwich Albion 6 (second replay); March 16th, 1895: The Wednesday 0, WBA 2. At the Baseball Ground—March 30th, 1899: Liverpool 0, Sheffield United 1 (third replay); April 11th, 1901: Aston Villa 0, Sheffield United 3 (replay).

Strong protests more immediately applied to the state of the cricket square, however, and when these were put before the county committee they brought about 'an inspired moment' for one of its members, James Ragg, who had been a keen and successful cricketer particularly adept at the single-wicket game. At his suggestion, the pavilion was moved in 1886 to the site it was to occupy for nearly 70 years, alongside the far boundary facing the main entrance.

Most importantly, the pavilion, in its new position almost at right angles to the racecourse grandstand, which was then too far away to be used for cricket watching, was given a Janus-like front to face both ways,[2] and Derby County's pitch was marked out on the other side of it, well away from the cricket area. At the same time, the cricket square was relaid, and, safe from soccer's maltreatment, became one on which batsmen no longer had to tread warily for fear of injury. 'If not the best in England', as the local evening newspaper's readers were told, it was 'at least one on which the greatest batsmen of the time delighted to disport themselves'.

James Ragg shared the brunt of the expenditure on the improvements at the County Ground with George Henry Strutt, another influential figure behind the scenes. One of Ragg's friends, Samuel Walters, was quoted around that time as saying:

> At one of the recent football matches, a gentleman from Kent expressed, in conversation with me, his conviction that Derby had the finest racing, football and cricket ground in England, and that, with the addition of a cycle track and tennis courts, would be superior to any in the universe. Many assert this to be mainly due to Mr Ragg and his generosity, which has cost him something in the region of £1,000.

The gent from Kent undoubtedly overstated his case—and not only in his reference to the universe. Despite all the admirable efforts to raise the standard, the ground itself continued to be one of the least appealing on the county cricket circuit, tucked away at one end of the huge, uninviting expanse dotted with local club pitches, and around which horses raced until the 1930s. It remained quite enough of an embarrassing contrast to picturesque Queen's Park at Chesterfield long before the famed Australian all-rounder Keith Miller complained, after playing there on his third full English tour of 1956, that it was 'bleak and open, making cricket a grim prospect as the wind comes whistling in from across the northern moors'.

By the time of that match between Derbyshire and the Australians, the county cricket playing area at Derby had been moved across to the corner of the ground adjoining the Grandstand Hotel, but the line of tress which has since softened the outlook, along with other considerable improvements, had not had time to grow sufficiently tall either to provide shelter from the wind or hide the vast, unsightly acres of flat land the new pavilion faced.

Back in those far-off fledgling days of football, when a player without a moustache was almost as scarce as a spectator without a cap, the County Ground's environment

---

2. Janus was an ancient Roman god of gates and doorways, depicted with two faces looking in opposite directions.

Steve Sprints to Victory

About 1,500 people attended the first athletics meeting to be arranged by Derby County at the Baseball Ground on August 30th, 1897. The programme opened with a 100 yards professional sprint handicap, won by Steve Bloomer in 11.5 seconds ahead of Joe Leiper and Jimmy Methven. The professional footballers' mile handicap was won by John Boag (off 110 yards) in 4 min 48.5 sec, from John Burton (110), John Miller (120) and Bloomer (30).

Burton, an inside-forward signed from Derby St. Andrew's, played only ten times in Derby County's first team, scoring three goals, before moving to Chatham in 1899. Just over a year later he joined Tottenham Hotspur, for whom he totalled 57 appearances, mainly at wing-half, in the Southern and Western leagues.

Earlier athletics meetings, organised jointly by the Derbyshire County Cricket Club and the Rams, had been held at the County Ground, but the first of them on a scale of any importance, held on September 12th, 1885, had been marred by rain. Gilt clocks, valued at four guineas, were a popular choice for first-place awards. Entries were received from as far afield as Grimsby, Lincoln, Manchester and Sheffield.

was of much less concern to soccer fans than it was to their cricket counterparts, though the players certainly did not appreciate the carbon stoves in the dressing rooms which, from all accounts, gave out more unpleasant fumes than heat.

It was also said that the aforesaid Jimmy Trainer, then of Proud Preston, used to pack brown paper under his jersey to protect him from the bitter winds with which he had to contend on his visits to Derby.

In spite of the drawbacks, it was not because of any wish to seek more fitting, if not more salubrious, surroundings that Derby County, having quickly abandoned the cricket club's colours of chocolate, amber and pale blue in preference for the soberly contrasting black and white, completed their breakaway from the parent body by moving from Nottingham Road to the Baseball Ground. The reason was that the Derby Recreation Company, which leased the County Ground and racecourse from Derby Corporation, began to make it a less attractive proposition for Derby County to continue playing there, and an increasingly uncomfortable situation came to a head at Easter in 1895 when the Rams were unable to fulfil an attractive fixture with the Corinthians amateur team because of a horseracing meeting that was being held in the same week.

The County had already played a few games at the Baseball Ground owing to fixture clashes with horseracing, and their departure to that venue, which was to become so atmospheric over the years as stands arose around it amid a maze of terraced houses, was unanimously recommended by the football club's committee when the packed meeting that approved it was held at the Derwent Hotel. As part of the agreement with his new tenants, Francis Ley, the wealthy industrialist whose foundry was next door, undertook to increase his expenditure on improvements to the accommodation at the ground which took its name from the baseball contests he staged there after having his appetite for that game whetted on a visit to the United States of America.

Francis Ley, who was later knighted, founded his Ley's Malleable Foundries company in Derby in 1874. He built a large works institute for the recreation of his employees, and also provided them with a sports field for the playing of cricket and football. This was known as the Vulcan Ground, and stretched as far as Pear Tree Road in those days before the area was built up.

In 1878, representatives of the foundry industry in the United States came over to look around Ley's premises, and they were so impressed that they invited Sir Francis to make the visit that he paid there in 1880. It was during his tour of several of the American works in the autumn of that year that he became so taken with the game of baseball that on returning to Derby he made arrangements for land on his works sports ground to be used as a baseball pitch in the summer months.

When Derby County moved in, the Baseball Ground's dressing rooms were at the Osmaston end, the players entering the pitch from a hut situated near what was known as Catcher's Corner from the connection with the American game. The popular side was then completely open, consisting only of an ash bank with old railway sleepers for the spectators to stand on, and although the terracing there was eventually concreted, it was not until as late as the 1932 close season that £750 was spent on providing the increased, uneven cover that was such a feature of the ground until it was torn down to make way for what was first known as the Ley Stand after the regaining of First Division status in 1969.

Back in 1895, the addition of the small stands transferred from the County Ground, in addition to the improvements the owner organised, made room for crowds approaching 20,000. Only about half that number attended the first match to be played there after the permanent move from the county cricket club's home, but fears that attendances at Derby County's home fixtures would be adversely affected were dispelled as soccer forced baseball from the Derby scene in maintaining its popular appeal in the town. The only unwelcome aspect, as the superstitious saw it, was the spreading of that tale of the 'Gypsy's Curse.'

By coincidence, the first visitors to the Baseball Ground after it became Derby County's regular home, on September 14th, 1895, were Sunderland, who had also been the opponents there on the first occasion, towards the end of the 1891–92 season, when the County Ground had been unavailable for a League game. The Rams lost that earlier encounter by an only goal, but this time they scored twice without reply. Both goals, the clincher in the last minute, were credited to the legendary Steve Bloomer, who the month before had helped Derby to defeat Fuller's in the English Baseball Cup Final at the same ground, though John Goodall joined him in bundling Scottish international goalkeeper Donald Gow into the net with the ball for the first one.

This victory over Sunderland was some small compensation for the heavy defeats Derby had endured at Roker Park—by 5–1 and 7–1 on their first two visits in 1891, by 5–0 in 1893, and by 8–0 on the opening day of season 1894–95.

That eight-goal onslaught could really be reckoned as another 11-goal one, in what might well be considered to have been a game of three halves. For the Rams trailed by

3–0 after a first half in which the formidably-named John Conqueror deputised as referee for the appointed official, Tom Kirkham, who had missed his train, and when Kirkham arrived he gave the County's captain, John Goodall, the chance to start the match all over again. Not surprisingly, in view of the score, the offer was gratefully accepted, only for Sunderland also to end the new first half with a lead of three goals—to which they added five more with a gale behind them after the interval.

The year after their move to the Baseball Ground, Derby County announced another big change in their set-up with this statement in a prospectus issued on August 17th, 1896:

> The guarantors and committee of Derby County Football Club consider it desirable to incorporate the club under the Companies Acts, 1862 to 1890, whereby the liability of the members is limited. A company has been registered for this purpose, with a capital of £5,000, divided into 5,000 shares of £1 each.
>
> The company take over the goodwill and the whole assets of the existing club, which consist of stands, cinder heaps, iron railings, turnstiles etc., and which have cost upwards of £1,400. They also take over the benefit and obligations of the tenancy of the Baseball Ground, which is sub-let to the club by the Hon. W.M. Jervis, who holds it under a lease (for football seasons only) for an unexpired term of six seasons.

After pointing out that, in accordance with FA rules, the dividend payable to the shareholders would be restricted to five per cent, annually, the statement added that 'the directors have every confidence that in a few years a considerable sum can be set aside as a sinking fund for the purchase of the ground.' This, in fact, did not happen until July 4th, 1924, when negotiations for buying the Baseball Ground were completed at a cost of £10,000 not long after plans to move to the Municipal Sports Ground, off Derby's ring road, had been abandoned.

Two years later, with the club newly restored to the First Division, £16,000 was spent on a new main stand along the Shaftesbury Crescent side of the ground. This incorporated the third location for the dressing rooms, which had been beneath the Railway Stand (so called because it was close to the railway lines that ran into the Ley's works) that had been in use since a first-round FA Cup-tie with Aston Villa in 1896 which comes back into the story in more detail later. That stand at the Normanton end of the ground was replaced by a double-decker in 1935, two years after a similar one had arisen behind the opposite Osmaston goal.

Despite all that expense, there was further talk of ambitious plans for a new stadium, designed by the Wembley Stadium architect, on the Municipal Sports Ground site after the 1939–45 War, but, again, nothing definite materialised, and it was not until 1997 that a move was finally made, to Pride Park. Even then, the Baseball Ground has been retained for reserve games.

In 1896, the management of the new company was entrusted to a president, the Hon. W.M. Jervis, two vice-presidents, W.T. Morley and Arthur Wilson, and a board of nine directors, one-third of whom retired annually and were eligible for re-election. Those original directors were Samuel Bennett Junior, Arthur Brown, John Dean, Morgan T. Roberts, John Ryley, R.J. Smith, George Stevens, J.W. Thompson and Dr C.H. Taylor.

It was in this list of the club's officials in the prospectus that W.D. Clark, hitherto assistant secretary, was named as manager, with his address given as 42, Full Street,

Derby. He was not directly involved in the running of the team, however, and the directors still retained a big say in the selection of the side even after inviting the Liverpool-born Harry Newbould, a qualified accountant, to combine his duties as secretary with managership that put him in close touch with playing affairs, including the recommending of deals in the transfer market.

Not that there was much money to spare on new players. Indeed, the balance sheet presented at an ordinary general meeting of the club held at the Royal Hotel on June 15th, 1897 shows that transfer fees paid during the past year totalled all of £70! Cash in hand then amounted to £33 4s. Players' wages added up to £2,802 11s 9d and gate receipts reached £4,764 18s 7d—less the share to visiting clubs of £806 19s 5d, Total income was £4,709 11s 6d, and there was a loss on the year of £323 5s.

Harry Newbould began his connection with the club as assistant secretary to J.H. Richardson, whose predecessor and namesake, Sam Richardson, had caused the big scandal of the joint enterprise between Derbyshire CCC and Derby County by allegedly embezzling the funds of both clubs and absconding.

The discrepancies in the accounts had been revealed by Derbyshire's incoming captain, the Australian Frederick Robert ('Demon') Spofforth, in 1889, two years after the Hon. W.M. Jervis, in his only year as the cricket club's honorary secretary after ending his 15 years as president, had wiped out their debts of about £1,000 with the aid of Walter Boden and Jervis's successor as president, George Strutt. Boden, on whose initiative, backed by his brother Henry, Derbyshire CCC had been formed in 1870, had been honorary secretary for the club's first dozen years, and was to be their president for four years from 1895.

Sam Richardson, who had been Derbyshire's first captain and, briefly, also their first wicketkeeper, was assistant secretary of the cricket club for 16 years, and secretary of Derby County, until his sudden exit. He went to live in Spain, where he died, in Madrid, in March, 1938, at the ripe old age of 93.

His defection brought about a change in the cricket club's management. Instead of having an honorary secretary and an assistant secretary, the committee decided to appoint a full-time paid secretary. Their choice fell on William Barclay Delacombe, a commanding figure standing 6ft 5in, who held that post until 1907 and altogether took an active interest in the club's business for more than 30 years.

Delacombe, who was born at Ascension in 1860 and died at Derby in 1911, frequently accompanied the Derbyshire team to their away matches and kept the score. He also played occasionally for the county, and, in the words of *Wisden*, 'although he was not a great cricketer he was certainly a useful one.' For Incogniti against L.C.R. Thring's XI at Dunstable in 1897, he took all ten wickets in an innings, including a hat-trick. In the following year he become one of the original members of the Derbyshire Friars team.

As Derbyshire CCC secretary, Delacombe was followed, after R.S.T. Cochrane's short tenure, by William Thomas Taylor, who kept the job for 51 years and 149 days from August 4th, 1908 to December 31st, 1959, beating by 17 months the time in office of the previous longest-serving county secretary, Kent's A.J. Lancaster. What was more, Will Taylor maintained his link with the county right up to his death in 1976, in his 92nd year, for he was made an honorary life member and vice-president besides acting as honorary secretary from 1962 to 1972 and being a member of the committee from 1960 to 1973. He was offered the Lancashire secretaryship in the mid-Twenties, but, to quote *Wisden* again, 'Derbyshire was always his county'. On the eve of the 1958 cricket season, then aged 73, he was made an honorary life member of the MCC for his services to cricket. And to mark the 50th anniversary of his appointment as Derbyshire's secretary he was treated to a small private lunch during the county's match with Nottinghamshire at Trent Bridge that July.

In his younger days, Taylor, like Delacombe, often travelled with the Derbyshire team, acting as scorer and substitute. His intermittent appearances extended from 1905 to 1910, and until his death he was the county's oldest surviving former player. Yet his life was very nearly snuffed out in only his early thirties. On his forehead he bore the deep groove caused by a bullet while he was on active service with the Army, in which he reached the rank of captain, during the First World War.

For Taylor's predecessor in longest secretarial service with a county cricket club there was an alarming sequel in retirement. Lancaster, who had succeeded his father in the Kent post, lost his bearings on a short walking holiday in Westmorland and fell into a peat hole. Many other hikers passed by, but he did not have the strength to attract their attention, and he lay there for 70 hours before being rescued.

W. T. Taylor, who became cricket's longest-serving county secretary in holding that post with Derbyshire from 1908 to 1959.

CHAPTER 4

Into the Football League

Epic Cup win leads to League status as founder members – The Bromages of Derby – Medal for McQueen – Haddow goes to glory from Derby deluge – Contrast for Bunyan, five goals for winger McMillan, in record win against Wolves – Former Derby pair help Manchester United to promotion

IF THERE WAS one result above all others that first firmly established Derby County as a force to be reckoned with, then it was the epic FA Cup victory they gained over Aston Villa, winners of the trophy the following season, on November 14th, 1885.

That 2–0 win marked the County's first serious step towards the top-class status they were to achieve in being invited to embark upon only their fifth season as one of the Football League's dozen original members, even though, having also beaten a Birmingham club, St. George's, in the first round, they were to tumble at the next hurdle against another, Small Heath Alliance, forerunners of Birmingham City.

The draw decreed that Derby should meet the Villa at Perry Barr, where they had lost by the same score in a friendly match only a few weeks earlier, but those formidable opponents were so confident of a repeat success that they readily agreed to switch the tie to the County Ground 'for a financial consideration'. That they were then made to feel more like Aston-ished Villa was due to the thoroughness with which the Rams prepared—even to the extent of special coaching, with blackboard demonstrations, by full-back Haydn Morley.

Another key to the Cup shock was the bottling up by Jack Flowers, a centre-half from Darley Abbey, of Archie Hunter, the accomplished Villa centre-forward and captain who was among the first Scots to enter English football. Derby wrested the initiative after about half-an-hour, when 'Jammer' Smith, the inside-forward from Long Eaton, punished a mistake by goalkeeper Hobson to give them the lead, and George Evans, formerly of Derby Midland and St. Luke's, completed the scoring in the second half when the hapless Hobson was again at fault in allowing the centre-forward's shot to slip through his hands.

Derby County's goalkeeper that day was William Luntley, who had previously played in the competition for Nottingham Forest—one of three members of his family to do so. Edwin Luntley, a full-back, twice defended for England. It was after the season of the famous defeat of Aston Villa that Derby's goalkeeping position was taken over by Harry Bestwick, who then gave way to Joe Marshall for the first League season. Marshall's deputies after Bestwick were Reuben Pitman and John Bromage, with Bromage taking over as the first choice for most of the next 1889–90 campaign.

Bromage, member of another footballing family, helped Derby Junction to their eye-catching Cup win against Blackburn Rovers before joining the Rams, and he rejoined the Junction after being involved in another match in the knock-out competition that was equally memorable, but for a diametrically different reason. He it was who had the misfortune to face eager Everton when they piled up their 11 goals in that record Derby defeat of 1890. His County career foundered with that walloping, which came straight after a five-goal mauling in the League at Preston.

Two of the other Bromages who played football professionally also did so for Derby County. Harry Bromage, another goalkeeper, was limited to five League games over three seasons with the Rams around the turn into the 20th century after being signed from Derby Constitutional, but he then found more scope with Burton United and Leeds City. Enos Bromage was an outside-left in Lionel ('Spud') Murphy's shadow who managed only six senior games in four years on the Baseball Ground staff, but he shared in a small piece of the club's history when he was one of all five forwards who scored in a 5–2 home victory over Blackpool during the 1925–26 season in which the County were promoted back to the First Division under the new direction of George Jobey.

Burton United were in the Second Division, of which they were original members, when Harry Bromage joined them from Derby in 1901, but, soon after he had left them, four years later they failed to gain re-election and drifted to extinction. For Leeds City, whose own demise was the soccer sensation of 1919 as they were expelled from the League and disbanded by the FA after allegations of illegal payments to wartime guest

**Bill Bromage, one of five footballing
brothers in a Derby family.**

players, Bromage kept goal in just over 150 matches before his transfer to Doncaster Rovers in 1911.

Enos Bromage, who left Derby County for Gillingham and later played for Nottingham Forest, Chester and Wellington Town, reached the Rams from Sheffield United after starting with Stapleford Town. Bill Bromage, another of the five footballing brothers in the Derby family, sons of John, was with the Blades, too, but is best remembered for his many years, from 1918 to 1945, as a trainer with the Rams.

It was at the Baseball Ground that Bill made his debut for Sheffield United Reserves in September, 1904. This was how he recalled it:

> I was at outside-left that day, and Derby County had on trial a new right-back from the Birmingham district. I had a good game, and the only kick that full-back had was when he kicked me on the back of the head about 20 minutes from time. I was taken home in a hansom cab, and that night the talk of the district was that I had been brought home the worse for drink. The neighbours were wrong in their diagnosis, but the treatment for my concussion was almost the same. I was in bed for three days with my head on an ice pillow.

Having left Firs Estate School at 13 to work at the brickworks in Stockbrook Street in Derby, Bill Bromage had a spell in the Rams' reserve side before joining Gainsborough Trinity, then members of the Second Division, at about the same time as former Derby left-winger Hughie McQueen, but he left them for Whitwick White Cross, a Leicestershire club, because they could not afford to pay their players in the summer. It was from there that he went to Sheffield United. His next move was to Doncaster Rovers, whom he captained, playing in 132 consecutive games.

Hugh McQueen, who was among eight 'Macs' while with Liverpool.

He and his wife, formerly Nellie Orton, who was also born in Derby, celebrated their golden wedding anniversary in August, 1951, and spent most of their married life at a house in Stockbrook Street. For nearly 50 consecutive years they went to Skegness for their summer holiday. 'I've had a great life', he said when he retired as a Derby County trainer. 'If everybody enjoyed themselves as much as I've done, there would be far less grumbling'.

Hugh McQueen made his way to Gainsborough Trinity in the 1902 close season via Queen's Park Rangers, to whom he was transferred from Derby the previous year. He entered English football from Leith Athletic in 1892, signing for Liverpool along with his brother Matt, who twice played at wing-half for Scotland against Wales while with Leith but had an extended run in goal for Liverpool before losing his place to Harry Storer. Matt McQueen further demonstrated his versatility not only as a player, filling every other position on the field, but also behind the Anfield scenes as a director, then manager. On finishing playing, he even had a turn as a League referee before rejoining Liverpool as team manager, duties he resumed for a few more years, until his retirement through ill health, after having to have a leg amputated as the result of a road accident while returning from a scouting mission.

The McQueen brothers were among eight 'Macs' while clubmates at Liverpool, with whom they won Lancashire League title medals in their first season, 1892–93, and then promptly helped to become Second Division champions as Football League newcomers. A year later, Hugh McQueen's transfer to Derby coincided with the Rams' move to the Baseball Ground, where, nimble and nippy, he became one of their most popular players, but it is a solemn thought that he almost never had the chance to wear the County's colours with such distinction. While training with Liverpool, he had a narrow escape from drowning when he dived off the springboard at Southport Baths and was hauled out only with great difficulty. It was not until after that frantic rescue that he confessed he could not swim.

McQueen missed just one match in his first season with Derby County when they went close to the double as losing Cup semi-finalists and First Division runners-up. And in each of the next two he was an ever-present member of sides that again went close to top honours. In 1896–97, the Rams were third in the League and once more reached the Cup's last four; in 1897–98 they battled through to their first final, in which McQueen's display earned him a gold medal awarded by a football magazine to the best player on the losing side. His final years in football were spent as a trainer, first with Fulham, his last club as a player after leaving Gainsborough, and then with Norwich City. He was 76 when he died at Norwich in 1944, which was also the year of the death of Matt, some five years his senior.

For the first two of Hugh McQueen's six seasons with Derby County, the Rams' goalkeeper was Jack Robinson, first of the Derbyshire-born players who also guarded England's goal. Robinson, a Derby man signed in the summer of 1891 after assisting Derby Midland and Lincoln City, was absent from only 13 of almost 200 games the County played in his six seasons with the club, but, as will be recalled more fully later, the unfortunate circumstances of his departure tarnished the high esteem in which he was held as one of the finest goalkeepers the Rams have ever possessed.

Robinson's arrival introduced badly-needed stability to a position that had been causing considerable problems. Before he took over, the highest number of first-team appearances for the club in the League was a mere 18, by John Bromage. More importantly, Robinson's daring and agility stemmed the flow of goals in the 'against' column that surged into a positive torrent during the short-lived occupancy of the hapless David Haddow, a Lanarkshire product who let in nearly 70 behind a sieve-like defence in only 16 games as Derby headed for penultimate place in the final 1890–91 table. A total of 81 conceded compared most unfavourably with the 23 of runners-up Preston and 29 of champions Everton. Even the bottom club, West Bromwich Albion, had two dozen fewer than the Rams scored against them.

Haddow both began and concluded his short Derby career with a back-bending day on the receiving end of a Blackburn barrage. His debut on the opening day of that season was blighted by having five goals scored against him, three of them by Jack Southworth, though he did at least have the consolation of being on the winning side because the County, bolstered by a John Goodall hat-trick, countered with eight. In the return match, however, there was no such redeeming satisfaction. Far from it. On a waterlogged pitch at Ewood Park, to which Blackburn had moved only that season, Haddow was swamped as Rovers themselves piled up eight goals, with not one in reply from an already-weakened Derby team reduced to ten men for the last hour by an injury to Lew Cooper.

Between those Blackburn broadsides, the black days for Haddow in the County's goal included the leaking of six and seven goals in the two meetings with Everton, six more against both Burnley and Preston, and five at Wolverhampton. Yet the fact that the fault chiefly lay not with himself but with those in front of him was clearly indicated by the sharp upturn his career took after he had left Derby. Following a brief return to the club from which he had been signed, Albion Rovers, he gained a Scottish Cup winner's medal with Glasgow Rangers in 1894, played for Scotland in the same year

**Jack Robinson, one of Derby County's
finest goalkeepers.**

when they drew 2–2 with England in Glasgow, kept goal for Burnley on their way to the Second Division title in 1897–98, and then came out of retirement to be in Tottenham's Southern League championship side of 1899–1900.

For the last half-dozen matches of Derby's 1890–91 season that were played between Haddow's unhappy last game for the Rams at Blackburn and Robinson's first match (also lost, by the odd goal of three at Stoke) the following September, the man relied upon in goal was Charles Bunyan, who began the first of two spells at Derby a couple of years after having the demoralising distinction of being beaten 26 times in Hyde's record FA Cup defeat by Preston North End in 1887. With the County, he had the extremely contrasting experience of remaining undefeated as Haddow's replacement, a week after the eight-goal deluge at Ewood, while they ran up their own record of nine goals in a home League game against Wolves.

Having played in Chesterfield district soccer before going to Hyde, Bunyan returned to North Derbyshire by teaming up with Chesterfield Town, as the Spireites were then officially known, after losing his place in Derby County's senior side to Jack Robinson at the start of season 1891–92. From there, he went to Sheffield United, after which he returned to the Rams for just over a year in the mid-1890s, but without adding to his 11 first-team appearances.

He then prolonged his stay in his home county with Ilkeston Town, and finally wound up his playing days back in Derbyshire, at Ripley Athletic, by way of Walsall, New Brompton (now Gillingham) and Newcastle United. The rest of his time in football was spent coaching abroad—originally in Sweden before the First World War, during which he served for 16 months in the 17th Middlesex (Football) Battalion before being invalided out. He was on another coaching assignment in Brussels when he died in 1923.

Charlie Bunyan's son Maurice was an inside-forward with the Racing Club de Bruxelles, and he therefore provided what was then the unique case of an Englishman representing his country while with a club on the Continent when he was chosen for the national amateur team in the Olympic Games of 1920, at Antwerp. Norway knocked them out, by 3–1, but one of Bunyan's fellow countrymen still had a decisive influence on the final.

Referee John Lewis, of Blackburn, abandoned it after 25 minutes because of a massed Czechoslovakian protest against the ordering-off of one of their players. The title was awarded to Belgium by default.

In Derby County's record 9–0 victory against Wolves on the day of Charlie Bunyan's recall as the last line of their defence, five of the goals, the most ever scored in one game by a Derby winger, came from Johnny McMillan, three of them created by George Bakewell's centres from the opposite flank. The others to find the net were McMillan's partner, Sam Holmes, from the Derbyshire village of Crich, who got two, Walter Roulstone and John Goodall.

McMillan, whose son Stuart also played for Derby (but just the once in their first team) and was their manager when they at long last carried off the FA Cup in the first post-war final of 1946, was making only his seventh appearance for the Rams. He had arrived the previous month from St. Bernard's, an Edinburgh club from which they soon afterwards also acquired Jimmy Methven, a fixture at full-back for 15 seasons, and their manager, in succession to Harry Newbould, for a dozen more in the League. Methven features prominently in later chapters.

Johnny McMillan, a native of Port Glasgow, altogether scored an exact half-century of goals in his 126 games for Derby County, enjoying his most successful season, mainly from inside-left, by outscoring even the prolific Steve Bloomer with 21 goals, three of them in the Cup, in 1893–94. Bloomer ended one ahead of him in the League, but failed to score in any of the four ties the Rams played in the knock-out competition, including a replay against Leicester Fosse, before being well beaten by Blackburn.

It was to the Fosse, who changed their name to City in 1919, that Johnny McMillan moved from Derby after playing his last few games at centre-forward in the side which finished the 1895–96 season second in the table. By then, Hughie McQueen was unchallenged in the five-goal winger's original position of outside-left, solving a problem that had become so pressing since McMillan's switch to inside-forward that even the ace marksman Bloomer had been tried there.

Walter Keay, although essentially an inside-forward, might have filled the bill after his signing from Darlington, but he was tempted away by the higher wage Southampton could offer him as a club outside the regulations of the Football League, and he helped them to three successive Southern League titles.

From Leicester, Johnny McMillan moved to Small Heath to play an important part, with 13 goals in as many games, on their run-in to promotion from the Second Division as runners-up to Grimsby Town in 1901. They were immediately relegated, McMillan missing the crucial last match, at home to Notts County, in which they were held to a scoreless draw instead of gaining the victory they needed to stay up on goal average, but a year later he helped them to maintain their yo-yo existence by sharing in another promotion as runners-up, this time to Manchester City. He led the attack, but did not score, as they shook off Woolwich Arsenal's challenge in their final game by narrowly winning at home against Manchester United. The Gunners, who went into that last

Johnny McMillan, a five-goal winger.

day two points behind but with a slightly superior goal average, would have gone up if they had beaten their visitors from Leicester and Small Heath had lost. The Birmingham club's success dashed those faint lingering hopes, and, in any case, Arsenal could do no better than draw with the Fosse in a game of no goals.

There was the same result to Arsenal's last match of the following season, at home to Burslem Port Vale, but they did go up that time, second to Preston North End. Leicester Fosse, though retaining their place in the League, finished at the foot of the table,[1] heavily beaten in their final game by Manchester United, who had risen from the ashes of the debt-ridden Newton Heath only a couple of years before. United, whose first signing under their new name was Tom Arkesden, a Burton United forward who had been on Derby County's right wing in their 1899 FA Cup Final defeat by Sheffield United (his only Cup appearance for the Rams), just missed promotion in third place—as they also did a year later before finally making it in 1906 as runners-up to Bristol City, the club they defeated in the 1909 final.

Before his transfer to Derby County, for whom he completed a half-century of League games, Arkesden was with Burton's other club, the Wanderers, who had just ended their three seasons in the Second Division, voted out in preference to Luton Town despite finishing eight points clear of bottom-of-the-table Lincoln City, and were soon afterwards disbanded. Burton United, who started out in 1890 as Burton Swifts, were founder members of the Second Division in 1892, but they were not re-elected after finishing last in 1907, a few years after Arkesden had left them, and they also subsequently went out of existence.

During Manchester United's promotion season of 1905–06, Arkesden was joined in their team by another former Derby County player, Dicky Wombwell, who filled all five forward positions in making almost 100 appearances in his three seasons with the Rams. Nottingham-born, Wombwell was signed by Derby from Ilkeston Town the month after Sheffield United had inflicted the Rams' second consecutive Cup Final defeat, and after leaving the Baseball Ground he put in nearly another three years with Bristol City, then newly elected to the Football League, before going to Manchester. From there, he went into Scottish soccer with Hearts, picking up a Scottish Cup runners-up medal against Celtic in 1907, then made his way back to Ilkeston via Brighton and Blackburn.

---

1. There was, of course, no Third Division to which Leicester could be relegated in those days. They and the club immediately above them, Glossop North End, remained in the League, but Stockport County, who finished 16th out of the 18 clubs then in the Second Division, were voted out and replaced by Doncaster Rovers. Stockport returned after the following 1904–05 season, when the two divisions were both extended to 20 clubs. Bury and Notts County, the last two in the First Division, were saved from relegation and Chelsea, Clapton Orient, Hull City and Leeds United were elected to Division Two with Stockport. Doncaster, who had also failed to gain re-election in 1903, were voted out after finishing last, and they did not reappear in the League until the Third Division North was increased from 20 clubs to 22 in 1923. Their membership then lasted until they dropped into the Vauxhall Conference in 1998.

Arkesden's path from Manchester United took him to Gainsborough Trinity, who were then only a few years away from losing their place in the Second Division. Around the time of that move, Johnny McMillan wound up his playing career with Glossop North End, another club whose League days were numbered, after having first left Small Heath to become the newly-formed Bradford City's first captain for their entry into the Second Division.

From Glossop, where he ended trainer, McMillan returned to Birmingham, the name to which Small Heath had changed in 1905, also as trainer, before entering management with Gillingham in the 1920 close season. The Kent club, whose playing staff briefly included his son Stuart, had just been elected to the new Third Division along with most of the other members of the Southern League, but they finished their first season there at the foot of the table. Although McMillan was noted for the happy atmosphere he developed despite the lack of playing success, he lasted at their helm for only one more season, only slightly less fraught in the new Third South.

His successor, Harry Curtis, a former referee, went on to transform Brentford from a struggling Third Division side into one of the leading First Division clubs during the years leading up to the 1939–45 War. McMillan took the opposite path out of football, returning to Derby and becoming licensee at the Normanton Hotel not far from the Baseball Ground. He was just a few months past his 69th birthday when he died at Derby in 1941.

Formation of League Given Lukewarm Reception

The formation of the Football League in 1888 was given a lukewarm reception by several clubs, and was looked upon with some uneasiness by those members of the Football Association who had rather reluctantly agreed to the recognition of professionalism only three years before.

That adverse feeling, however, did nothing to deter the men who were farseeing enough to realise that the rapidly increasing number of clubs in the country would benefit from being gathered together in an organised competition. Under the enthusiastic guidance of William McGregor, a Scot who has gone down in the game's history as the 'father and founder of the Football League', they pressed ahead with their plans and took the first tangible step towards their aim by calling a meeting of interested clubs at Anderton's Hotel in London's Fleet Street on March 22nd, 1888.

Derby County's officials had shown a certain amount of interest in the scheme from the outset, but their delegate attended the meeting solely for the purpose

(continued overleaf)

of 'obtaining information'. Consequently, the Rams were not allowed to take an active part in the proceedings, and, although it emphasised how highly they had come to be regarded, they must have considered themselves fortunate to be elected after the seven other represented clubs had agreed that 'a league or union of 12 of the most prominent clubs' should be formed.

Preston North End and Bolton Wanderers, who were classed by McGregor with Aston Villa, Blackburn Rovers and West Bromwich Albion as England's most attractive clubs, agreed to be included despite showing such little interest in the preliminary arrangements that they did not send a representative to the meeting. The other clubs elected besides Derby County were Accrington (who dropped out in 1893 and were re-formed in 1919 under the name of Accrington Stanley), Burnley, Everton, Notts County, Stoke City and Wolverhampton Wanderers. No southern club was invited because there was no professional football south of Birmingham at that time.

A month later, another meeting was held, this time at the Royal Hotel in Manchester, and belated but unsuccessful applications for membership were made by the Wednesday, Halliwell and Nottingham Forest. It was then thought unwise to make any immediate additions, but Wednesday and Forest were admitted to the First Division with Manchester United when the League was extended to two divisions for the 1892–93 season.

William McGregor was elected as the League's first president, with Henry Lockett, of Stoke, as secretary. In framing the original laws, the members agreed that the clubs occupying the four bottom positions at the end of each season should retire and offer themselves for re-election. No changes were made in the membership after the first season of 1888–89, Derby County (10th out of the 12) being among those who survived. Stoke City dropped out in favour of Sunderland in 1890, but missed only one season before returning, in company with Darwen, as the number of clubs was increased to 14.

'Test' matches involving the bottom two clubs in the First Division and the top two in the Second were introduced for the 1892–93 season, but were replaced by the modern system of promotion and relegation for 1898–99.

CHAPTER 5

John All Good and the Strong Man of Football

Goodall brothers with so little in common – Invincibles near defeat at Derby – A triple hat-trick – Club record of consecutive games – Rams rally to escape relegation in 'test' with Notts County – Sharpe's 'proudest moment' – Five Hill-Woods for Derbyshire – Two who played for Derby the only ones to share a Leeds 'double' – What a surprise…after 15 years

THE GOODALL BROTHERS could scarcely have been more dissimilar, either in appearance or demeanour.

John, bald and more finely-boned, was known to his contemporaries as football's first Honest John. FA leaders called him John All Good, and he was described as 'quiet and gentle' by Ivan Sharpe, the England amateur international winger who played under his management at Watford before also assisting Glossop and Derby County, two of the old master's other clubs.

Archie, in direct contrast, was built on sturdy, robust lines. He was the Strong Man of Football, and, as the Rams were to be made well aware after he had been reunited with his brother in their ranks following his diversion from Preston to Villa for most of the 1888–89 season, he could be one of the game's most cussedly awkward customers to cope with, tempestuous and controversial in the extreme.

The many respects in which these brothers had so very little in common extended even to the countries for which they were selected at soccer. Their parents were Scottish, and they were both brought up in Scotland, but John qualified to play for England, whom he represented 14 times, through being born in London, at Westminster, and Archie won his ten caps with Ireland because he was born in Belfast. Those diverse birthplaces were due to the moves the family had to make owing to the postings of the Army regiment in which their father was a non-commissioned officer. Their sister, Margaret, was born in Edinburgh.

Exemplary of character and supremely gifted as a footballer, John Goodall was a pioneer of scientific soccer and the passing game, raised in the classic Scottish mould. He developed his exceptional ability from an early age, when, in common with other boys in the games in which he took part, he played in his bare feet, using a small ball. An immaculate leader of the forward line, but adaptable enough to settle effectively into other positions in the attack, he combined his ball-playing skills with sharp marksmanship, and he only once failed to score in his first ten games for England. He totalled a dozen goals in an international career that was spread over a decade from early 1888.

After leaving Kilmarnock, where he was employed as an iron turner, to enter English football with Great Lever, he soon emerged as a top talent amid the increasing number of players who were lured from Scotland by the money to be picked up from the game south of the border. From Great Lever, he progressed to Preston, where he became one of the North End 'Invincibles' who completed the first League and Cup double in the League's first season of 1888–89, finishing 11 points ahead of runners-up Aston Villa without losing a match, and carrying off the Cup without conceding a goal.

Archie, who was exactly a year younger (both were born on June 19th, John in 1863), reached Deepdale from Liverpool Stanley. In September, 1888, the month before Archie made his next move to Villa, the brothers were in the full-strength Preston side—John at centre-forward, Archie at inside-left—when North End went very close to losing that unbeaten record at Derby in only their fourth League game. Preston, like the Rams a club with cricket roots, swiftly fell behind to goals from Henry Plackett and L.G. Wright, who had displaced Isaac Monks at centre-half, but Jimmy Ross, the younger of another pair of brothers with the Lancashire side, reduced the deficit with a shot Joe Marshall should have saved, and he rounded off the visitors' recovery with a winning hat-trick.

Jimmy Ross also held centre stage on that October day in 1887 when Preston overwhelmed Hyde with their 26 Cup goals, scoring eight of them. One source over-indulgently credited John Goodall with 16 on that record day, but, in fact, he contributed just the one. Jack Gordon and Thomson each netted five, Fred Dewhurst three. There was one North End game, however, in which John Goodall did outdo Ross by going one over the eight, celebrating his return to Scotland for a friendly with Strathmore in Dundee by registering a triple hat-trick in another huge win, by 16–2.

John Goodall spent four seasons with Preston, the last of them the Football League's first, before leaving Lancashire to take over the Plough Inn at Derby. This led to his signing for Derby County on May 3rd, 1889, the day after brother Archie joined the Rams from Aston Villa. The deal that brought the Goodalls together again with Derby was arranged, it was said, by 'a well-known solicitor'—a classic example, it might also be said, of the old days' equivalent of the modern agent. It produced a double reunion for Archie—not only with his brother but also with the County, one of several clubs for whom he had played towards the end of the last pre-League season.

But half of that deal quickly threatened to backfire as the big difference in temperament between the brothers was made clear to Derby's officials for the first of many times. Rumours that both wanted to pull out of the arrangement were promptly discounted as far as John Goodall was concerned, for he had given his word and was not the sort to go back on it. Archie, on the other hand, did ask for his release, and it was only with great reluctance that he agreed to stay when his request was refused. To have done otherwise would have left him without a League club for the two years of the contract he had undertaken.

Unprepossessing as those circumstances made his signing, and as troublesome as he was to prove on so many other occasions (as will be referred to more closely in due course), Archie Goodall remained a Ram for a dozen seasons beyond those original two. In the process, he placed himself high on the list of Derby County's staunchest defenders in totting up 423 League and Cup appearances, an impressive total that was overtaken at the club only by Jimmy Methven and Steve Bloomer up to the outbreak of one world war, and then by only England winger Sammy Crooks up to the start of another one.

What was more, in five of Archie Goodall's 14 seasons with Derby he was an ever-present—a distinction matched only by Methven—and from October 1st, 1892 until October 2nd, 1897 he did not miss a match. That set up a club record of 167 consecutive games which would have been greater still but for a couple of Cup-ties with the Wednesday being declared invalid as the result of protests (as will be recounted later in detail). His remarkable run began with a 3–2 home defeat of Nottingham Forest in which he scored Derby's opening goal, one of just more than 50 for the club, and ended with a 1–1 draw away to Notts County.

The scholarly John Goodall's length of Derby service was modest by comparison, but none the less valued. He played what was to be the last of his 26 FA Cup-ties (nine goals) for the Rams on the right wing in the 3–1 semi-final defeat of Stoke City at

**John Goodall, a pioneer of scientific
soccer and the passing game.**

Wolverhampton that earned the 1899 clash with Sheffield United at the Crystal Palace, and he made the last of his 211 League appearances (76 goals) for the club at inside-right in a 4–0 beating at Liverpool a week before that year's final.

There was one other match, giving him a total of 238 for Derby, that he rated as 'the most vital and exciting in which I ever took part'. It was played against Notts County at Leicester on April 13th, 1895 and was one of the 'tests' which then had to be fought out, involving the bottom two clubs in the First Division and the first two in the Second, to decide promotion and relegation. The Rams finished next to last in the top section, only one point behind West Bromwich Albion and Stoke, despite defeating runners-up Everton 3–2 in their final game with two goals by Bloomer and one from John Goodall. On the same day, Stoke saved themselves with a 5–1 home win over Blackburn Rovers, and just over a week afterwards Albion dashed Derby's last hopes of avoiding the play-offs by crushing the Wednesday by 6–0, a result that raised not a few suspicious eyebrows.

So to the 'test' at the Fosse field, where Derby indeed seemed doomed to drop out of the League's upper strata for the first time when Notts County were still a goal to the good with only five minutes to go. The rallying call of limping skipper John Goodall was answered most fortuitously, however, when the ball, thumped long and hopefully upfield by Jimmy Methven, rebounded off Johnny McMillan's back and fell favourably for Bloomer to equalise. With excitement building to fever pitch, the Rams threw everything into attack, and in the last minute McMillan snatched a splendid winner from a third successive corner kick that was taken, most appropriately, by Goodall.

Two members of the Notts attack, centre-forward John Allan, and outside-left Fred Fletcher, scorer of the opening goal, had started that season with Derby County. Allan, formerly of Glasgow Thistle, had been an ever-present in his only full season with the Rams, 1893–94, mostly as a right-winger. Fletcher, a local player, had only three League opportunities with Derby before joining Notts in November, 1894, the month before Allan followed him to Trent Bridge.

John Paul, the Rams' left-winger in the 'test' match, was a former Hibernian forward who also played in English football with Bristol Rovers; Percy Francis, on the opposite flank, was a Derby solicitor (the one behind the deals for the Goodalls?) who made his occasional appearances as an amateur before serving for many years on the club's board of directors. He was also on the Derbyshire CCC committee.

Only the year before missing promotion so dramatically, Notts County made history by becoming the first Second Division club to win the FA Cup. In the final, played at Everton's new Goodison Park ground, they defeated Bolton 4–1 with a hat-trick from Jimmy Logan, a former Sunderland and Aston Villa centre-forward who returned to Scotland, with Dundee, in the wake of a heavy defeat by the Wednesday in the first defence of the trophy, shortly before the vital date with Derby. About a year later, following a fleeting stint with Newcastle on coming back to England, Logan was back in the Second Division with Loughborough Town (another club soon to lose League status) when he caught a chill after being drenched in a downpour during a match at Manchester. Pneumonia set in, and he died at the age of only 26.

David Calderhead, Notts County's centre-half, though widely acknowledged as one of the best defensive pivots of that era, was denied any additions to the one cap he had gained while with Queen of the South because of the aversion the Scottish selectors then had to Anglo-Scots. He soon had the satisfaction of making up for the disappointment against Derby, however, by captaining Notts into the top flight as Second Division champions—just as he had derived the pleasure of receiving the Cup only a few years after being in the team beaten in the final by Blackburn Rovers. After starting in management with Lincoln City, Calderhead was in charge at Chelsea for more than a quarter of a century up to the early Thirties, and, like Johnny McMillan, he had his son (later also manager of Lincoln) on his playing staff.

In 1895, Bury, to whom Notts had ended distant runners-up in Division Two, claimed the other place at stake alongside Derby by scoring the only goal of their 'test' at Blackburn against Liverpool, the First Division wooden-spoonists (one point behind the Rams) who were to get straight back through another play-off series after finishing at the top of the next Second Division table.

Early in that 1894–95 season which had such a gripping climax for his team, John Goodall took part, along with his brother, in another match to remember. At Perry Barr, Birmingham, they were in this Football League XI that met Aston Villa in a benefit game for William McGregor, the League's founder: **Reader** (West Bromwich Albion); **Somerville** (Bolton Wanderers), **Scott** (Nottingham Forest); **Perry** (WBA), **Goodall, A.** (Derby County), **Needham** (Sheffield United); **Bassett** (WBA), **Ross** (Liverpool), **Goodall, J.** (Derby County), **Wheldon** (Small Heath), **Schofield** (Stoke City). Jimmy Ross, who later partnered the Welsh 'wizard' Billy Meredith with Manchester City, had moved that year from Preston— at first reluctantly, and then only due to Liverpool's persistence. His elder brother Nick had expressed a dying wish that he should stay faithful to North End.

John Goodall scored twice in the League's 3–1 defeat of Villa, in front of a crowd of about 10,000. The other goals came from inside-left Gordon, for the club side, and Freddie Wheldon, who was to join Villa and help them to three League titles in four seasons—and to the double in the first of them, 1896–97.

John Paul, who played on both wings for the Rams.

Some 16 months after taking part in McGregor's benefit, John Goodall played in his own—on January 25th, 1896, when Derby County met a Gentlemen of England team at the Baseball Ground. The 5,000 or so people who braved bad weather saw the Rams edge to a 4–3 victory in the face of a brilliant display of goalkeeping by Oxford University's George Raikes, one of seven members of the visiting side who were capped by England.

Raikes was beaten three times by John Miller, a centre-forward from Clyde who was in the first of his two seasons with Derby before leaving for Bolton Wanderers, and once by Steve Bloomer, who also hit the woodwork. Goodall himself had a scoring attempt come back off the goal frame, as also did the Gentlemen's Robert Topham, a right-winger whose brother Arthur had been among his England team-mates against Wales.

After just over ten 'happy years', as he described them, with Derby County, John Goodall moved in October, 1899, to New Brighton Tower, who were embarking upon their second season in Division Two. From there, in February, 1901, he returned to Derbyshire with Glossop, then also a Second Division club, and two years later he ended some 15 seasons in the Football League by joining Watford as player-manager and helping to relaunch them in the Southern League.

He stayed there, latterly as manager only, until 1910, and during that time he also re-entered county cricket, which he had played at first-class level with Derbyshire, by representing Hertfordshire. He first added himself to the list of Derby County footballers who have played cricket for Derbyshire during the 1895 season in which the Peakites were readmitted to the County Championship after being banished to the second-class periphery. In a team that also included L.G. Wright, the brothers William and Harry Storer and William Chatterton, he was run out with only four runs to his name in his first innings, but he made a useful contribution to a notable 107-run defeat of Yorkshire at Leeds by making his side's third-highest score of 32 when he batted again. Derbyshire were again the winners when Goodall played his second, and last, game in their first team the next summer, beating Warwickshire by ten wickets at Derby despite the considerable absence of William Storer at the Gentlemen v. Players match, but on that occasion, once more well down the order, he made only two runs in his only innings.

On leaving the Watford club, John Goodall resumed playing soccer with Mardy, the Welsh club, in the Second Division of the Southern League, turning out for the final time against Swansea in January, 1913, when in his 50th year. He subsequently went back to live at Watford, and it was there that he died in May, 1942, aged 78.

Ivan Sharpe, the England amateur international winger who helped Derby County to the Second Division championship in the 1911–12 season, regarded John Goodall as 'one of my gods', and he considered it 'the proudest moment of my life' when the great man, while Watford's player-manager, looked in at the offices of the *Herts Advertiser and St. Albans Times* to seek his signature on amateur forms. Sharpe, who assisted clubs wherever his work as a sports journalist took him, was then what he himself called 'the self-styled Sports Editor, a youngster in the third year of his apprenticeship to journalism earning five shillings a week', and playing for his home team St. Albans Abbey. To be sought out by such a titan was an accolade indeed, at the end of Sharpe's season as an outstanding member of a team that won the Hertfordshire League championship and all the cups for which they competed.

After a year at Watford, Sharpe moved to the *Glossop Chronicle* and reversed the football route taken by Goodall by joining Glossop North End, the North Derbyshire club then on Derby County's fixture list in the Second Division. Built up by Samuel (later Sir Samuel) Hill-Wood at an expense estimated at more than £30,000 even though most of their players were amateurs, Glossop had won promotion to the First Division in their first League season of 1898–99, as runners-up to Manchester City immediately after the abolishing of the 'test' system, and, although they had been just as promptly relegated, they were to soldier on in the Second until the First World War enforced the closedown that led to their resignation. Archie Goodall was among the international players who wore their colours in addition to his brother John and Ivan Sharpe.

Sir Samuel Hill-Wood, a Derbyshire cricket captain as plain S.H. Wood, and the High Peak Division's Conservative Member of Parliament from 1910 to 1929, renewed his attachment to Association football by taking the chair on Arsenal's board in 1927, and he held that office until his death, aged 77, only a few days into 1949. One of his successors at Highbury was his son Denis, who, in common with his three other sons, also followed him at Eton College and in playing cricket for Derbyshire. Since 1982, the family's tradition in the Arsenal chairmanship has been carried on in the next generation by Peter Hill-Wood.

Ivan Sharpe, an England amateur international winger who helped Derby County to promotion.

Soccer was steadfastly Samuel's first love, but he holds an unusual place in cricket's record books even though he was no outstanding performer at the summer game. Aided by a short-lived trial of a 'net' method of scoring, he shares with Lancashire's A.N. Hornby (the man who, as already recalled, led his team off in protest at Derby) the record of scoring most runs from one delivery 10, for Derbyshire against the MCC at Lord's in 1900.[1]

Having benefited greatly from John Goodall's expert guidance at Watford, Ivan Sharpe maintained his development on Glossop's left wing to such a degree that he earned selection among England's leading professionals by touring South Africa in 1910 with an unbeaten FA party that included George Richards, the Derby County wing-half and former inside-forward who was soon also to be among his colleagues at the Baseball Ground. Sharpe went into that tour, in the early stages of which he celebrated his 21st birthday, fresh from winning the first of his nine amateur caps, if in a narrow defeat, against Denmark in Copenhagen. He was recalled against Switzerland in Berne, scoring in a clear-cut win, shortly before leaving Glossop for Derby in October, 1911.

Negotiations for that transfer were protracted because Glossop's manager, Bob Sutcliffe, was most reluctant to part. His regret at eventually agreeing to the deal must have deepened still further when, within days, Sharpe made his debut for the Rams in a home game with, of all teams, Glossop, and, though not among the scorers, played a prominent part in their 5–0 victory.

Glossop gained their revenge in the return match, during a bad start to the new year in which Derby went through half-a-dozen League encounters without a win, but there were no more defeats for the Rams as they progressed to promotion. Sharpe spent another season with them, totalling almost 60 appearances, and in 1912 he attained other footballing high points by playing for the United Kingdom—as the all-English British side was then labelled—in the Olympic Games in Stockholm, and taking part in a full international trial at Blackburn.

During the two seasons he spent with Derby, Sharpe found how slender could be the dividing line between cheers and jeers. In his book *40 Years in Football*, he recalled that when the Rams returned in the spring of 1912 from the match at Barnsley in which they made sure of getting back into the First Division, he was 'hauled out of a convenience and, along with other County players, carried shoulder-high for half a mile through the streets of Derby'. Just under a year later, during a home defeat by Aston Villa, he incurred the displeasure of one fickle fan who had read in his newspaper that Derby

---

1. The ground was enclosed on the normal boundary by a net two to three feet high. It was first decided that when the ball went over the netting the batsmen should score three runs, and that when it was stopped by the net two runs should be added to those run. This proved too clumsy to be practical, however, and the whole idea was abandoned after unsuccessful modifications. The Derbyshire player's 10 runs off one hit began with an all-run four, and he also gained the two-run bonus because the ball reached the net. The ball was then overthrown to the opposite net for a further bonus of two, and the batsmen crossed for another couple while it was on its way.

County had recently given Sharpe a piano as a wedding present. The cry rang out clearly round the Baseball Ground: 'Go home and play that _ _ _ _ _ _ _ _ piano!'

Sharpe's break with Derby County in the summer of 1913 resulted from his job outside football taking him to the *Yorkshire Evening News*. Leeds City were the club to take advantage, and he completed another half-century of matches with them before leaving several years ahead of their expulsion from the Football League over their alleged illegal wartime payments to players.

One appearance for that Yorkshire city's new team, United, in a comfortable home win over Coventry City in November, 1920, made Sharpe the first man to play for both Leeds clubs. There was to be only one other, Tommy Lamph, a wing-half who was sold to Manchester City during the demeaning auction of the entire Leeds City playing staff, but within a few months also found his way to Derby County and soon afterwards returned to Leeds with United. Lamph managed fewer than 50 appearances spread over his four League clubs, and the tragic circumstances of his premature retirement from football are recalled in Chapter 19.

Ivan Sharpe, having shared his other soccer between the English Wanderers, Brighton and Hove Albion (in the FA Cup) and the reserve sides of Nottingham Forest and Luton Town, hung up his boots to concentrate on his journalism, in which he was one of the most respected and authoritative writers on the game until his retirement some years before his death at Southport in 1968, in his 79th year. At the Football League's annual meeting in 1958, the management committee, on behalf of the clubs, presented him with an inscribed silver salver 'as a token of appreciation of his 50 years' association with the League as a player and a journalist'.

Speed was the main asset that inspired several unsuccessful efforts to persuade Sharpe to play his football professionally. At Derby, he was rated the Rams' fastest winger since Reg Hounsfield, a former Wednesday player who was also an amateur, and he won many prizes at athletics meetings in various parts of the country over distances ranging from the sprint to 300 yards. While with Glossop he ran regularly for Salford Harriers, and not long before he joined Derby he finished only a foot behind the winner, who clocked nine and four-fifths seconds, when he competed off the 2^1/2-yard mark in an invitation short-limit sprint at Royton. The then English sprint champion, F.L. Ramsdell, was beaten into third place.

National newspapers were Ivan Sharpe's employers from 1922. In that year, he went to the *Sunday Chronicle*, to which he returned after following the renowned Jimmy ('Tityrus') Catton in editing the *Athletic News*. In his book, Sharpe said that 15 years before succeeding Catton he had written to him for a job, but had received no reply. He described it as 'an ambition realised' when he took over from him in 1924, and added:

> But what a surprise followed! Catton had left a drawer full of odds and ends, and told me to keep or destroy what I pleased. In the process I found my application of 1909…unopened. Yes, the wheel had come full circle, and very pleasantly, as it was James Catton who had recommended me as his successor.

Olympic Games Gold Medallists

Three players who turned out for Derby County were gold medal winners at the Olympic Games—Herbert Smith and Horace Bailey in London in 1908, Ivan Sharpe in Stockholm in 1912.[1]

Smith, a full-back noted for the power he packed into his left foot, made just one first-team appearance for the Rams in a 1–0 home win against the Wednesday towards the end of the 1906–07 season in which they were relegated from the First Division for the first time. He was an Amateur Cup finalist with Oxford City in 1903, when they lost 1–0 to Stockton in a replay after a scoreless draw, and besides representing the United Kingdom in the Olympic Games he was capped 14 times by England in amateur internationals from 1907 to 1910, captaining the side on several occasions.

While with Reading in 1905 and 1906, Smith also played in four successive games for the full England side during which only one goal was conceded in victories against Wales (3–1 and 1–0), Scotland (1–0) and Ireland (5–0). His other clubs included Witney, Richmond and Stoke. He was later president of the Oxfordshire FA.

Bailey, who kept goal for Derby County in their last three Second Division matches of the 1909–10 season, also won full England caps without being on the losing side in big wins against Wales (7–1), Austria (6–1 and 11–1), Hungary (7–0) and Bohemia (4–0), all in 1908 while with Leicester Fosse. From 1908 to 1913 he made five further appearances for England's amateurs—four as a Fosse player, the last after joining Birmingham.

Winger Sharpe, who figures prominently in this chapter, played in 54 League games and three FA Cup-ties for Derby, scoring a dozen goals, and was a regular member of the team that won promotion in 1911–12. He won his nine amateur caps from 1910 to 1914, while with Glossop, Derby and Leeds City.

In 1908, the Great Britain team, entered under the name 'United Kingdom', defeated Denmark 2–0 in the Olympic final with this team: H. Bailey; W. Corbett, H. Smith; R. Hawkes, K. Hunt, F. Chapman; A. Berry, V. Woodward, H. Stapley, C. Purnell, H. Hardman.

The UK line-up for the 1912 final, in which Denmark were beaten 4–2, was: R. Brebner; T. Burn, A. Knight; H. Littlewort, E. Hanney, J. Dines; A. Berry, V. Woodward, H. Walden, G. Hoare, I. Sharpe.

Britain withdrew from the Association football competition after the Olympic Games of 1920 in Antwerp (where they lost by 3–1 to Norway in the first round and were succeeded as champions by Belgium) because of the broken-time payments made by some of the other nations. They did not compete again until 1936, when, as Great Britain, they were beaten 5–4 by Poland in the second round in Berlin after defeating China 2–0. Italy won 2–1 against Austria in the final, after extra time.

In London in 1948, in the first Games after the Second World War, GB reached the semi-finals by beating Holland 4–3 and France 1–0, but then lost 3–1 to Yugoslavia and were defeated 5–3 by Denmark in the play-off for third place behind Sweden, the winners, and Yugoslavia. Four years later—in Helsinki where Yugoslavia were again beaten in the final, by Hungary—Britain went out to Luxembourg in the preliminary round, losing 5–3 after extra time.

At Melbourne in 1956, the title 'Great Britain' was retained, even though only Englishmen took part. Once more, they failed at the preliminary stage, beaten 5–3 over two legs by Bulgaria (0–2 in Sofia, 3–3 at Wembley). Given a second chance when invited to make up the numbers because several countries withdrew due to the expense, they defeated Thailand 9–0 but met Bulgaria again in the second round and were knocked out by 6–1.

These days, Great Britain do not even take part.

---

1. Herbert Smith, born at Witney in 1879, died at Oxford in 1951. Horace Bailey, born at Derby in 1881, died in 1960. Ivan Sharpe, born at St. Albans in 1889, died at Southport in 1968.

CHAPTER 6

Archie the Arch Unsettler

An epic ride on horseback from Derby to Kilmarnock…and back – Everton's bunnies – Ten men trounced at Preston – An extra-time revolt – Rams captain suspended in build-up to Cup Final – Forest revenge sparks 'fix' rumours – Sheffield United recover to deny Methven honour at the Palace – Ben Hall an ideal replacement – Walking The Hoop earns medal

SOME IDEA of Archie Goodall's considerable strength can be gained from the fact that he could raise 150lb with one hand, and a barbell of 186lb with both hands. And he would think nothing of taking up a cue straight afterwards and running up a break of 70 to 80 points at billiards.

There was also a much talked-about occasion when he rode his bay cob the 300-plus miles from Derby to Kilmarnock (where he had started his soccer, as a centre-forward, with the Britannia junior club for which brother John also played) and made the return journey on the same horse in five days. The cob wore out four pairs of shoes, but one pair lasted for 300 miles and became one of Archie Goodall's most prized possessions.

While I was working on the Derby evening newspaper, I culled from a dusty back number this anonymous account:

> Archie Goodall yields to nobody in his love of a fine horse, whether for riding or driving; in the casting of a fly upon such a purling stream as the Dove (they do say that his brother John is the finest fly fisherman in Derbyshire); in shooting the tortuous rabbit, or in bringing down a wild duck; in the manly toil of cricket; in pedalling a cycle of 104 gear up hill and down dale; in the daintiest science of billiards; in the massive amusement of weight-lifting; and, above all, perhaps, in long country walks.

Yes, quite definitely, somebody exceptional. But, accomplished as Archie was at 'the manly toil of cricket', he had to give second best at that game to his brother, even if John did play only twice for Derbyshire in the County Championship.

Apart from the wide variety of his sporting interests, Archie Goodall was Mr Adaptability on the football field. The majority of his appearances were made at centre-half, but he also played in both full-back positions, centre-forward, inside-right and outside-left. It said much for his daunting stamina that, when in his late thirties, he was absent from only ten games over his last three seasons with Derby County, and the players who faced him were kept ever-appreciative of the consequences of his favourite 'I'll lean against you' warning. Ivan Sharpe tells us that 'when the pair played for Derby County Archie would say to opponents who barged into Johnny: 'What are ye trying to do, sonny? Play rough? I'll lean against you in a minute.'

The Irishman of the family was feared for his shoulder charging, though there was one unhappy occasion when he overdid the robust stuff to such an extent that he incurred a month's suspension. That was an absence Derby County could have well done without—as was the one with which he first inconvenienced them when he refused to travel for an away match against his old club Preston because of his wife's illness. Forced to field only ten men, the Rams tumbled to a 5–0 defeat.

There was another match, away to Everton at the end of the second month of the League's first season, for which Derby arrived a player short. The home club lent them one of their own reserves that October day, but he was as helpless as his temporary team-mates as the County went down 6–2. The Rams really were Everton's bunnies in those early years of League football, for apart from that record 11–2 Cup trouncing they scored only 11 goals against 43 in winning just one—and that by the slenderest of margins—of the first ten matches between the clubs before decisively breaking the spell with a double victory they began with a 7–3 home win in the 1893–94 season.

A fortnight after the game at Preston for which Archie Goodall's refusal to travel put Derby at a numerical disadvantage even before they had kicked off, John Goodall had to be pressed into service as an emergency goalkeeper for the whole 90 minutes at Wolverhampton, where defeat was limited to the odd goal of three. It was on the Saturday between those matches at Deepdale and Molineux (where Wolves were in their first season) that Everton enjoyed their double-figure passage into the Cup's second round. That joy, though, was not long-lasting. Derby's over-indulgent conquerors

**Archie Goodall, versatile and long-serving,
but at times an upsetting influence.**

promptly went out to Stoke City, who themselves fell at the next hurdle in the competition that ended with Blackburn Rovers' then record victory over the Wednesday team captained by Haydn Morley.

The Preston game for which Archie Goodall made himself unavailable was the only one he missed in his first two seasons with Derby County, but he caused further consternation by declining to take part in extra time when they met West Bromwich Albion in a championship decider between the winners of the East and West sections of the United Counties League. That competition was formed to fill gaps in the fixture lists, but was dropped after only two seasons as the demands of the Football League grew with its expansion into two divisions and the consequent introduction of promotion and relegation. Archie Goodall was the Rams' top scorer as they topped the East Division from Nottingham Forest, but despite his extra-time revolt—staged because he said his contract ended after the normal 90 minutes' play—they won the replay 2–1 after a 1–1 draw.

The upsetting influence of Archie's unpredictable behaviour also counted against Derby when they lost two successive FA Cup finals late in the 19th century. In 1898, he went missing to dispose of some tickets shortly before the kick-off against Forest at the Crystal Palace, and the flutter of uncertainty he aroused in the County camp before his belated reappearance did nothing to settle already-jangling nerves. A year later, by which time he had succeeded his brother as captain, he was suspended by the Rams during the build-up to the final against Sheffield United for 'insubordination and inattention to training.' He had been ordered by the directors to join the rest of the players in special training at Buxton, but, as reported at the time, he had 'absolutely declined to go on the grounds that his private business rendered it necessary for him to remain in Derby'.

The ban was lifted shortly before the final, only for him to ask to be omitted from the team. He said he would do his best if chosen, but, to quote again from a contemporary account, he preferred not to play 'in consequence of the many mischievous and idle rumours that have been in circulation since his recent unpleasantness with the club.' He felt so strongly about it that he was absent from the first four matches of the following 1899–1900 season before agreeing to re-sign.

On the Easter Monday of the week leading up to the 1898 final against Forest, Derby County defeated the Nottingham club by 5–0 at the Baseball Ground with the aid of a Bloomer hat-trick, but five of the visitors' players who faced the unchanged Rams at the Palace sat out that League game, ostensibly through injury, and they benefited by watching their opponents' style of play from the stand.[1]

One of those onlookers was Forest's captain, Johnny McPherson, scorer of the goal that sealed their 3–1 victory in the final. Others welcomed back by the Reds for the big game included Arthur Capes, who netted their two other goals either side of the lone Derby reply by Bloomer, from whose header, following a free kick by Joe Leiper, the ball bounced down over the line off the underside of the crossbar.

---

1. Seven years earlier, Forest's neighbours, Notts County, lost 3–1 in the final to Blackburn Rovers only a week after gaining a 7–1 away win over them in the League.

Among the deputies at Derby who were omitted from the final, full-back Jim Iremonger[2] was probably the unluckiest to be deprived of a winner's medal in having to give way to the veteran Archie Ritchie. Iremonger, who, like his brother Albert, the legendary Notts County goalkeeper, also played cricket for Nottinghamshire, made the most of his chance after the retirement of Ritchie and the Forest's other Cup Final full-back, Adam Scott, by reaching exactly 300 League and Cup appearances in 15 seasons with the club and winning England caps. Another brother, Harry, later played for Forest in goal—a position in which Jim was also adept, and to which he reverted over his last few seasons in attaining that third century. It was there that he had the quietest afternoon of his career in a Forest's record League victory, a 12–0 trouncing of Leicester Fosse in 1909.

Arthur Capes, known as 'Sailor', had been signed from Burton Wanderers only because his more-in-demand brother Adrian would not make that move without him. In the event, Adrian's career petered out through illness and injury, whereas Arthur played for England and made almost 200 appearances in Forest's first team before also assisting Stoke, Bristol City and Swindon. The Capes brothers made their Forest debuts together against Derby County, in a 1–1 draw at the Baseball Ground on the opening day of the 1896–97 season.

The scorer of Forest's goal in that match at Derby was Chas ('Sammy') Richards, another Burton product in their team for the 1898 final, whose cousin, George Richards, was to play more than 300 games for Derby County before the 1914–18 War. For their Palace revenge meeting with the Rams, Forest also fielded two men who had been snapped up on Derby's doorstep—Dennis ('Dan') Allsop, a former Derby Junction goalkeeper who had been born in Derby and still lived there at the time of the final, and Frank Forman, a member of a well-known Aston-on-Trent family, who teamed up again with his brother Fred at Nottingham after they had been given only a few games before being released by the County.

That was a double misjudgement by Derby, for both rose to international standard, becoming the last brothers to play in the same England team (three times in 1899) until Jack and Bobby Charlton did so in 1965 at the start of an international association that culminated in their country's first winning of the World Cup.

Frank Forman, whose long service on Forest's committee after ending his playing career extended a couple of years beyond their second FA Cup Final success of 1959 (he was 86 when he died in 1961), was the natural successor to Johnny McPherson as the club's captain. In receiving the 1898 English trophy from Lord Rosebery, McPherson completed a notable double, for he had gained a Scottish Cup winner's medal with Hearts seven years earlier—during the 1890–91 season in which he had also been given his solitary Scotland cap in a narrow defeat by England at Blackburn.

---

2. Jim Iremonger, generally regarded as one of the finest batsmen to play for Notts, was at the centre of an unusual incident during a game against the MCC at Lord's in 1902. White enamelled stumps were used for the first time in a big match, and because the enamel was not quite dry the bail adhered to a stump which was moved by a delivery Iremonger missed while he was batting. As the laws decreed that a bail had to be removed, he was allowed to continue his innings and completed a century.

Fred Forman exceeded 180 senior matches for Forest—75 fewer than his brother—but five days after playing at inside-left in the big victory at the Baseball Ground he was displaced by Capes for the 1898 final, in which Derby's defeat was so unexpected that rumourmongers claimed the game had been 'squared'. Sensible people dismissed that allegation as, to use the words of one of the Rams' shareholders, 'preposterous and scarcely worth considering'. Even so, the same shareholder referred to 'other reports which, if true, prove that the players, by their conduct, "gave away" their chance of winning'.

He went on to ask if it was correct that some of the Derby players were intoxicated during Easter week, and that they quarrelled among themselves before and during the game, adding that 'if there are any black sheep the public should know who they are'. Those remarks drew an emphatic denial from the County's secretary, J.H. Richardson, who declared that 'the insinuations are as unfounded as they are absurd.'

There was no doubt that Forest were worthy winners. They went close through Capes, whose shot was luckily blocked by Jimmy Methven, Tom McInnes and Alf Spouncer before Capes fired them in front after some 20 minutes following a free kick by Billy Wragg. Steve Bloomer's equaliser came a dozen minutes later, but just before half-time Derby's goalkeeper, Jack Fryer, blocked a shot from Richards, only for Capes to be left with a simple tap-in chance to restore Forest's lead.

Derby stepped up their attacks after the interval against a side reshuffled because of an injury to Wragg, who became little more than a limping 'passenger' on the wing, but Allsop saved well from Jimmy Stevenson and Jack Cox, and McPherson came to the rescue when the goalkeeper was beaten by Bloomer. Then, with about four minutes to go and the Rams tiring, McPherson fittingly applied the finishing touch after Derby's centre-forward, John Boag, dropping back to help out at a corner, had headed the ball off the line.

Unwelcome as they were, the unproven allegations that swept Derby after that upset, even when linked with the disturbing effect of Archie Goodall's disappearance beforehand, were minor blips compared with the distractions which dogged the Rams before their second successive Cup Final defeat. With the disgruntled Archie dropping out against Sheffield United in such an acrimonious situation, Jimmy Methven took over the captaincy that had been handed on by John Goodall, who was then nearing the end of his distinguished career with the County. Denied the opportunity of a fourth final (the first two with Preston), Honest John accompanied the Derby party to the Palace only as a reserve, along with wing-half Charlie Leckie, a signing from Dundee who did sterling duty in a number of defensive positions over the next few seasons, and Harry Linacre, of whom more later in the chapter about goalkeepers.

The inclusion of Glaswegian Bob Paterson, formerly of Clyde, as Archie Goodall's central defensive stand-in for the Palace clash with the Blades was one of six changes from the Derby side beaten by Forest the year before. 'Jonty' Staley, the doughty defender from Newhall who had been such a patient reserve for much of the time since his arrival from Derby Midland, retained the place he had regained as Methven's partner because of injury to Leiper; Paisley-born Johnny May, a former captain of Abercorn who was also to skipper Scotland after leaving Derby for Glasgow Rangers, replaced England wing-half Jimmy Turner, who had rejoined Stoke City; John Goodall was succeeded on the right wing by Tom Arkesden, the recruit from Burton Wanderers; and William MacDonald, who played for Dundee both before and after his short stay with the

County, formed a new left wing with Harry Allen, an 18-year-old local lad. Jimmy Stevenson, an inside-forward from Clyde, had moved to Newcastle, and left-winger Hugh McQueen was unfit.

McQueen was to remain a force in Derby's attack for the best part of two more seasons before his departure to Queen's Park Rangers. Allen, who was signed from the Alvaston and Boulton club with reserve right-winger Harry Oakden not long before the 1899 final, played only two more senior games for the Rams after it—the first of them also against Sheffield United in their last First Division match of the season a week after the defeat by the Blades at the Crystal Palace. Derby won that one, at the Baseball Ground, by an only goal, scored by Steve Bloomer.

As if Archie Goodall's disputatious exclusion from that year's final was not demoralising enough, there was another most undesirable incident, involving ace scorer Bloomer, along the path to the Palace. We shall be coming to that in the next chapter. For the moment, it can be recalled that, despite all the unsettling influences on his team's preparations, Jimmy Methven did have some reasonable hopes of being the first Derby captain to walk up to receive the trophy.

This was especially so when the Rams had the better of a first half in which they should have led by more than just the one early goal scored by John Boag, a centre-forward who, before being signed from East Stirlingshire, had played in his native Scotland for the Ashfield club which also produced two others who were with Derby

John Boag, gave Derby a deceptive lead in a Cup Final.

Johnny May, captain of Scotland after leaving Derby County, for whom he made exactly 200 appearances. One of the billiard halls he later owned in Falkirk and Glasgow was managed by John Boag.

during that period. They were Stevenson and Alex Maconnachie, a forward who spent only part of the 1897–98 season with the Rams before leaving for Notts County the month before the Cup Final against Forest.

Another encouraging indication that the fates might at last be favouring Derby, regardless of all their tribulations, was the fact that Sheffield United made such hard work of getting to the final. In all but the third round, in which they accounted for holders Forest by a single goal, they were taken to replays, and at the penultimate stage they defeated Liverpool only at the fourth attempt—and then again by just one goal, at the Baseball Ground.

After draws by 2–2 at Nottingham and 4–4 in the first replay at Bolton, the third game of that semi-final series, in Manchester, became known as the 'Fallowfield Fiasco'. Derby referee Arthur Kingscott had to abandon play, with Liverpool leading 1–0, because the crowd encroached onto the pitch. Proving that hooliganism in football is anything but new, it was reported that 'free fights were indulged in', and that 'Mr Kingscott had no alternative but to order the players to retire' with the match not much more than half over.

Contrary to their expectations, Derby County found that it was not Sheffield United's difficulty in dispatching their Cup opponents that season, but their sheer determination not to fold up in face of adversity, that had the decisive bearing on the final. Having eventually surmounted the Liverpool obstacle, United gave further evidence of their own exceptional resilience by staging a staggering recovery from their interval deficit against Methven and his men. Their defence—in which right-back Harry Thickett, who had only recently won his two England caps in defeats of Wales and Scotland, played throughout with two broken ribs heavily bandaged—held firm as Derby's disintegrated. The County let in three goals in little more than ten minutes, and another one near the end as the margin of their defeat was widened from the 3–1 against Forest to 4–1.

To add to the discomfiture of the Rams, who were disorganised by an injury to May that left them a player short, the goal that sent Sheffield in front for the first time, some 20 minutes into the second half, was scored by a Derbyshire man, Billy Beer, previously an amateur with Staveley and Chesterfield. The others came from Walter Bennett, a former England outside-right who partnered Beer, and the left-wing pair, Jack Almond (who had continued to play football professionally despite being left a £16,000 fortune) and Alf Priest, soon to win his one England cap against Ireland in Dublin.

The crowd of 73,833, nearly 12,000 up on the previous year, was the largest for a football match up to that time—'of such dimensions', wrote the *Sporting Sketches* reporter, 'as to be almost awe-inspiring'. He added that 'one poor fellow fell a distance of 30 feet from a tree and apparently sustained concussion of the brain'.

As we shall see, an even heavier defeat was in store for Derby County when they battled their way back to the Crystal Palace four years later, only two matches from the end of Archie Goodall's lengthy reign in their ranks. His departure to Plymouth Argyle in May, 1903, was part of the Devon club's build-up for their first Southern League season, but early the following year he moved again, joining the Glossop team his brother had not long left. Having played his last two games for Ireland while with the North Derbyshire club, he briefly reappeared in the First Division during the last few months of 1905 in a Wolverhampton side heading for relegation. This anonymous tribute was paid to him during that twilight time of his career:

> He is one of those men who are generally 'there' when wanted, and his placing is perfect. Somehow or other, he is always on the ball, and certainly it may be said of him that age has not withered, nor custom staled, his infinite variety.

To fill the yawning gap left by the temperamental Irishman's exit, Derby County found an ideal replacement in Ben Hall, whose immaculate ball control and accurate passing supplemented astute defensive qualities that gave them excellent service in nearly 250 League matches and two dozen Cup-ties over eight seasons. Hall, who hailed from Ecclesfield, a coal mining area of South Yorkshire, entered League football as an inside-right, making a scoring debut for Grimsby Town on the 12th day of the 20th century in their home defeat of Leicester Fosse, the club to which he was to be transferred from Derby. He also turned out for the Mariners in each of the other forward positions except outside-right, in addition to wing-half and full-back, before settling down into a most competent centre-half, but he was unable to help them to avoid relegation to the Second Division at the end of the 1902–03 season. Because of his keenness to continue in the top sphere, he did not need much persuading when the Rams made their approach. With his gentlemanly outlook reflecting his brain-before-brawn pattern of play, he quickly became one of their most popular players.

After playing for Hyde and South Shields as well as Leicester Fosse after leaving Derby, Hall returned to help the Rams in a few wartime games—one of them alongside his brother Ellis. After that, he was Bristol Rovers' manager for their first Football League season of 1920–21, then manager of Loughborough Corinthians, and later a scout with Southend United. He died in 1963.

Archie Goodall maintained his strong-man image after leaving football by touring the music halls and theatres with The Hoop, a huge steel wheel that he constructed in the workshop behind his home in Wolfa Street, Derby, and introduced to a greatly impressed public during the Aladdin pantomime at the town's Grand Theatre on January 19th, 1909. It had a circumference of 50 feet, a width of five inches, a thickness of three inches, and a weight of almost 200lb. On its outer edges were thin strips of steel, and the former Derby County 'man of might', wearing boots with clips that fitted the hoop, walked right round the inner circle with arms folded, stopping at various stages to pose. Ivan Sharpe recalled:

> The highlight of the performance was to halt, suspended head down from the top of the wheel, and swing from his teeth two (lightweight) female assistants. There was no catch in it. Archie Goodall was a genuine strong man. Football opponents could testify.

Presumably the assurance that there was 'no catch in it' referred to the validity of what was described as 'a real blood curdler', rather than to the fact that he never let one of those young ladies fall! Goodall spent four years perfecting the act, which he claimed to be 'one of the most sensational performances on the variety stage', and by the time he revisited Derby with it in the summer of 1917, at the Hippodrome, he had added another dramatic feature. The *Derby Telegraph* 's theatre critic wrote:

> When hanging upside down he holds trapezes on which three acrobats give a display. Only an athlete of the strongest physical proportions could attempt it.

A party of Derby County players who went to watch Archie walk the hoop for the first time also saw him presented with a solid gold medal by his business manager, Herbert Sidney, 'for his pluck in performing a feat in which pure muscular strength plays a chief part'. It was given by T. Allan Edwardes and Arthur Carlton, joint managers of the pantomime.

For all his superior strength, however, Archie Goodall was outlived by his more delicate brother by more than a dozen years. He was 64 when he died in London towards the end of 1929.

**Ben Hall, an ideal replacement
for Archie Goodall.**

CHAPTER 7

Quite a Peaceable Tyrant

The bowler hat trick makes a top-scoring match-winner – John Goodall's protégé – Derbyshire by adoption, but claimed by Worcestershire – Escape in disguise after six-goal farewell – 'Double deal' costs Cup victory – Oversight leads to Bloomer's debut – Robinson at centre of poaching allegation – Needham the 'Prince of Half-backs'

AN OLD BOWLER HAT on a stick enabled Steve Bloomer to acquire the art of first-time shooting that brought him so many of his goals. The use of those training props was introduced to him by John Goodall, the father-like figure who made him his protégé, and to whom, as he readily acknowledged, he owed most for his rapid development into the deadliest marksman of his time.

For the bowler-hat-on-a-stick routine, Bloomer took up a position about 15 or 20 yards away, and let fly at it with a first-time shot when Goodall threw the ball to him from all angles. This they did several times a week, and Bloomer developed a wonderful knack of hitting the ball on the half-volley, his foot following through with the toes pointed down like a ballet dancer's.

Goodall also taught Bloomer how to gather the ball while moving at speed, an asset that left defenders baffled by the pace at which he swung away and around them. He rarely used the feint of foot movement or body swerve to get into positions from which he was ever ready to try a shot. He operated on the simple principle that the more you shot, the more you scored. Sudden shooting was the key to his success, first-timers from nearer the toe than the instep—a method that regularly enabled him to stick to his maxim of 'getting there first', before defenders could intercept.

This would appear to indicate a great deal of self-interest, and it is true that he could be a difficult man to play alongside. One of the more illustrious of his international colleagues, G.O. Smith, certainly found that to be so. Edward Grayson, who based his book *Corinthians and Cricketers* on his lengthy correspondence with Smith, the much-admired amateur centre-forward he hails as 'my hero of classical sporting history', quotes this most famous of Corinthians as saying:

> Bloomer, like McColl, of Scotland, was a most brilliant individualist and always worth a place as a magnificent shot, but he was not easy to play with,

Steve Bloomer,

Derby County's ace marksman in his England kit.

and personally I would much sooner have played with other inside-rights. However, he was a match-winner if ever there was one.

On this subject, we can hear again from Ivan Sharpe, who played in the same forward line as Bloomer at Derby. He went as far as to describe 'our Stephen' as 'a tyrant', adding:

> He said what he thought, and if things were going wrong his partner had no pleasant Saturday afternoon. 'What d'ye call that? A pass? I haven't got an aeroplane!' This was a fair sample of a Bloomer explosion…If, after a breakdown in attack, one studied the crowd, the sky, or any other useful object out of the line of Bloomer's glare—as was the rule in the Derby ranks of that day—he would stand stock still, in the centre of the field, strike an attitude by placing his hands on his hips, and fix the offender with a piercing eye. If the glare, as was the rule, was still ignored, he would toss up his head, as if beseeching the recording angel to make a note of this most awful blunder, and stamp back to his position in a manner intended publicly to demonstrate his disapproval.

Such behaviour could not be condoned, of course, potentially damaging as it was to team spirit, but Sharpe made it clear that it conveyed a far from true picture by also commenting that:

> Those who knew Bloomer knew that he was really quite harmless, quite a peaceable person, who meant well and got the best out of the players because of his inspiring example, his great unselfishness, and his tremendous devotion to his team on the field of play. So harmless, in fact, that within a week or so of joining the ranks of the great Bloomer's club the budding juniors selected Bloomer for their dressing-room pranks. A curious personality, but genius runs that way.

There are other accounts that tell of Bloomer showing another side to his forthright and outspoken character by being quite a practical joker himself. It is also interesting to learn, in view of his own exceptional prowess as a goal scorer, that he was strongly opposed to what he termed the 'contemptible' practice of hugging—let alone kissing!—after the scoring of a goal. According to one old report, he was convinced that this unwelcome behaviour was introduced by, of all people, soldiers who served in France during the 1914–18 War.

Whatever the source of what has since spread worldwide far beyond the excesses upon which Bloomer frowned so severely, that was one of his opinions with which many must surely sympathise. And, cantankerous though he could be, and as intolerant as he was of the failings of others, he deservedly earned widespread admiration and respect for his approach to the game generally. There certainly can be no denying that he was the idol of Derby County's followers, warts and all. He was the one the older fans of my youth were always still talking about, the one they unshakeably regarded as the greatest of all the legions of players who up to that time had worn the club's colours.

The late Sir Frederick Wall, a former FA secretary, called him 'the greatest of the old-timers'. Another enthusiast, unidentified, said that he was 'the Napoleon of football', though a more apt role model could have been chosen considering what happened at Waterloo. In the *Sporting Life*, he was described as a player 'who has left a mark on the records of the game which will prove indelible', the writer continuing:

> Bloomer's methods are a sheer delight to all who can appreciate the real football. He goes through a back rather than round him, and by that I mean

his detours are kept within a remarkably narrow range. And his shooting! Well, some of the shooting of the maximum wage men today [that was just before the First World War] must make Bloomer tired.

'The Incomparable Steve', as one article on Bloomer was headlined during his playing days, was brought into this unsuspecting world on January 20th, 1874, at an end-terraced house, since demolished, in Bridge Street, Cradley, opposite the spot where a monument was unveiled in his honour 126 years later. He was often said to be a Staffordshire man, but while I was on the sports staff of the *Derby Evening Telegraph* we received a letter from a reader who, at second hand, claimed him for a neighbouring county. 'I was told by Joe Hemstock', wrote this informant, 'that a brook separated Worcestershire and Staffordshire near Steve's former home, and that Steve was born on the Worcestershire side'.

The above is a facsimile reproduction of a medallion which is printed on both sides alike on stout gold bevelled card and attached to every pair of our

STEVE BLOOMER

LUCKY GOAL SCORERS

by means of coloured cord.

The effect is very pleasing and is calculated to attract the prospective buyer of football boots.

That statement by Joe Hemstock, who joined Derby County with Bloomer from Derby Swifts but never played in their first team, has been confirmed to me by Bloomer's grandson, my old friend Steve Richards, but although the stretch of water that divides the counties there is as narrow as some brooks, it is, in fact, the River Stour.

Those who thought 'Our Steve' hailed from Staffordshire were therefore as much in error as the many who came to regard him as a Derbyshire man because he was brought up in Derby, to which he moved with his parents when only five years old. Despite the fact that he achieved his fame outside the Black Country, he remained fiercely proud of his roots. As his grandson has also told me, 'he was never slow to remind people that his cradle had been in Cradley, emphasising it was on the Worcestershire side of the Stour.'

Bloomer was educated at Derby's St. James's School for the six years from 1880. When it came to starting work, he fittingly—in view of the modern terminology for the footballing position in which he was to make himself a household name—joined his brother Philip and their father, Caleb, as a striker in the foundry at Fletcher's engineering works in Litchurch Lane. Another brother, David, was a butcher.

Football, fostered at school, was by then an all-consuming spare-time passion for Steve and Philip Bloomer. They both helped Derby Swifts, whose headquarters were at the Nag's Head public house in St. Peter's Street, to win the Derby Shield. Philip was also to join his goal-getting brother with Derby County, but was given only one chance in their League side—at left-back when Steve was among the scorers in a 3–1 home victory over the Wednesday early in the 1895–96 season that the Rams ended as runners-up to Aston Villa.

Steve's scoring feats naturally made him the Bloomer brother most in demand while he was still in local non-League soccer—especially after he had piled up 14 goals in one match for the Swifts—and he also played for Derby Wednesday and Tutbury Hawthorn before joining Derby County. The Rams signed him first as an amateur, then as a professional— at the princely weekly wage of 7s 6d (37p)—after he had scored four goals against Darley Dale in his first game for them. The most he ever earned a week, basically, was £5 10s, 550p in modern money and roughly equivalent to an annual salary of £35,000 nowadays.

He was taken onto the County's staff at the end of the 1891–92 season, after scoring all six goals by which Tutbury Hawthorn defeated Gresley Rovers to complete a double by adding the Burton Junior Cup to the Burton Junior League title. Many of the spectators waited to fete him, but he was then too shy to face the adulation to which he subsequently had to become accustomed, so he borrowed a frock coat and top hat from a local councillor and walked through them unrecognised.

A few days after Bloomer had signed the registration forms for the Rams, the secretary of Burton Wanderers tried to persuade him to throw in his lot with the brewery club. He declined, but he was again approached by the Burton official at a dance he attended at the beginning of the following week, and this time he was induced to change his mind. It was a decision he was soon greatly to regret, and one that was to be a costly embarrassment to both himself and Derby County.

In the first round of the next FA Cup competition, in January, 1893, Derby were drawn away to the Wednesday. With only about three minutes left for play, they led through goals by John Goodall and Bloomer, but Fred Spiksley, the Sheffield club's England left-winger, scored twice to force extra time and then completed an amazing hat-trick by snatching a late winner.

The FA, however, decreed that the teams must meet again at the County Ground at Derby in upholding the Rams' claim that Alec Brady, the Wednesday's inside-left, was ineligible. Brady, a Scot who had played for Partick Thistle, Burnley and Sunderland before helping Everton to win the League championship in 1890–91, and Glasgow Celtic the Scottish Cup in 1892, had been snared in some comical subterfuge after he and centre-forward Jack Madden had been lured to Sheffield from Scotland.

Incensed by the prospect of losing two of their best players in such dubious circumstances, Celtic had sent a Roman Catholic priest from Glasgow in an attempt to talk them into going back, and, on learning of this, the Wednesday had hurriedly arranged for both to go into hiding. The priest had been resourceful enough to find Madden, who had returned with him, but he had been unable to locate Brady, who had stayed. Brady, who was to gain a Cup winner's medal with the Wednesday three years later (Spiksley scored both their goals against Wolves in the final), had to stand down from the replay, which Derby County won by an only goal, with Goodall again a scorer. That, though, was where it could be said that the Rams 'went for a Burton' over a Bloomer.

Wednesday, having by then been made fully aware of Bloomer's indiscretion in agreeing to join both Derby and Burton Wanderers, pointed out that he had broken the laws by signing for two clubs and appealed for a second replay. His 'extreme youth' was cited as some excuse for his conduct under some 'undue influence' by the Burton secretary, but the FA ordered the clubs to meet again at the Wednesday's Olive Grove ground. Bloomer, who incurred a month's suspension, had to follow Brady out of the action, and his goal in the first match was expunged from the records.

Worse still for Derby, the Wednesday shrugged off another goal by Goodall—whose couple in the first two meetings were also wiped off, along with Spiksley's hat-trick—to get through by 4–2 at the third attempt. Having survived a further, but rather forlorn, protest by the Rams, they then progressed past Burnley (and yet another objection) before going out to Everton, the club Wolves defeated in the final. Objections and protests were very much the bugbear of the competition in those far-off days.

Derby's other goal in their eventual defeat by the Wednesday was scored by Tommy Little, who was Johnny McMillan's regular partner on the left flank of the attack in the second half of that 1892–93 season, but made few further appearances before leaving for the first of two short spells with Manchester City that were separated by an even briefer stay in the States with Baltimore. His later clubs included Swindon Town and Barnsley.

Steve Bloomer's first season with Derby County was the only one until the 17th and last he spent at the club (discounting 1913–14, when he made only half-a-dozen appearances before retiring as a player) in which he was not their leading scorer in the League. In 1892–93, his 11 goals left him two behind John Goodall; in 1912–13, he scored 13 to the 15 of Harry Leonard, a former Grimsby Town centre-forward who had been recruited from Middlesbrough, Bloomer's only other League club.

Bloomer, who was five times the First Division's leading marksman, altogether scored 422 goals in his first-class career—from September 24th, 1892, when he opened his account from a penalty in a 1–1 home draw with West Bromwich, to September 6th, 1913, when he netted a couple in a 5–3 defeat by Sheffield United, again at Derby. Of those goals, 352 came in 599 League games, 41 in 55 FA Cup-ties, 28 in 23 international matches, and one in that dramatic 'test' against Notts County. His total of 678 appearances began in a 3–1 win at Stoke on September 3rd, 1892, Derby's first match of that season, and ended with a 3–2 defeat for the County in a second-round FA Cup-tie at Burnley on January 31st, 1914.

No other forward scored as many goals as Bloomer in the Football League until Bill Dean, disliker of his popular nickname 'Dixie', took the record up to 379 in 437 games—349 of them in 399 matches for Everton in a career that started with Tranmere Rovers in 1923 and concluded at Notts County in 1939. Since then, both have been overtaken by Arthur Rowley, who shared his 434 between West Bromwich Albion, Fulham, Leicester City and Shrewsbury Town in 619 games from 1946 to 1965. Bloomer's tally has also been exceeded by Jimmy Greaves, who, unlike the others, notched all his League goals, 357 of them, in the First Division—in 516 matches with Chelsea, Tottenham Hotspur and West Ham United from 1957 to 1971.

Bloomer's number of appearances in the British Championship, and also his total of England goals, were both overhauled on March 13th, 1911, in the 3–0 defeat of Wales at Millwall's ground. Bob Crompton, the redoubtable Blackburn full-back and captain, then played his 24th game against the other home countries (the 31st of his final total of 41 including internationals against foreign teams), and Vivian Woodward, the celebrated amateur centre-forward who played for Tottenham and Chelsea, took his goals tally to 29—like Bloomer in 23 games, but, unlike Bloomer, not all limited to matches with Ireland, Scotland or Wales—as he lined up among England's professionals for the last time.

England played their first amateur international on the Continent in November, 1906, when they defeated France 15–0 in Paris, but their professionals did not start official fixtures with foreign countries until 1908, the year after Bloomer won his last cap. Ben Warren, of whom more later, was then Derby County's representative in two matches with Austria in Vienna, and two others against Hungary in Budapest and Bohemia in Prague—all four games played in eight days during June. Austria were beaten by 6–1 and 11–1 (four for Woodward), Hungary by 7–0, and Bohemia by 4–0. How times, and results, have changed!

Woodward, 15 of whose goals in full internationals were obtained against Continental teams that were much inferior to those of today, also played for England in 38 amateur internationals, scoring more than 40 goals. In addition, he captained the United Kingdom sides that won the Olympic soccer title in 1908 and 1912.

With England's senior matches now far more plentiful than they were while Bloomer was such a key member of the team, the appearances record has been taken into three figures—first by Billy Wright (105), then by Bobby Charlton (106), Bobby Moore (108) and, currently, Peter Shilton, who became Derby County's most-capped player by playing 34 of his 125 international matches while with the Rams. And the England goals record has since been raised to 30, by both Nat Lofthouse (in 33 games) and Tom Finney (in 76), to 44 by Jimmy Greaves (in 57), and to 49 by Bobby Charlton, who, like Finney, subsequently became a most worthy addition to the list of soccer knights. Gary Lineker reached 48 in 80 appearances.

In comparing those scoring figures, it has to be remembered that Bloomer and Woodward got their goals under the old offside law, which required an attacker to have three opponents, not two as now, between himself and the goal when the ball was played to stay onside.

Right at the start of his first-class career, however, Steve Bloomer needed a bit of luck, for he would not have got into Derby County's first team as early as he did but for an administrative oversight. He was given his first chance at Stoke to fill one of the vacancies caused by the failure to send in the registrations of three players—Sam Mills,

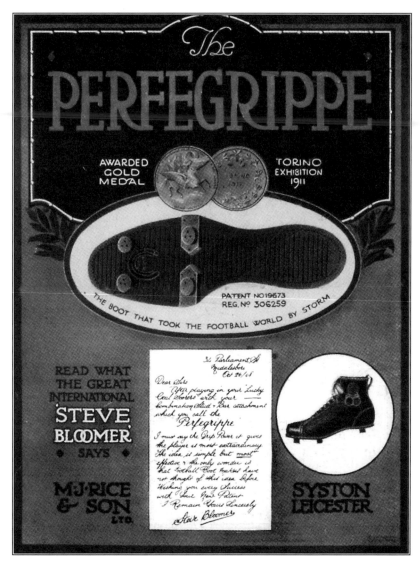

a former Derby Midland right-winger who went to Leicester Fosse, Jimmy McLachlan, an inside-forward who rejoined the Rams after a season with Notts County, and half-back Ernest Hickinbottom, the local product from Darley Abbey.

The two other players brought in were centre-half Henry Garden, another who was signed when the Midland club folded, and Fred Ekins, a forward from Chatham. That was Garden's only first-team game before leaving for Long Eaton Rangers. The further opportunities for Ekins were to be only a little more generous, but a few years later he did have the satisfaction of scoring Luton Town's first goal in the Football League.

Steve Bloomer, on the other hand, was in to stay—though at first his future did not look too good either. Indeed, with his pale, moon-like face and frail physique, standing only 5ft 8in, he made a most unfavourable initial impression on those Derby fans who found him more an object of amusement than an embryonic terroriser of the best defences in the land. If it is true that some of them actually laughed at and derided him, then they must surely have made as quick a conversion, to merge with his hordes of admirers, as he himself did in evolving into the highest scorer in the English game.

And it was not only sceptical supporters who were deceived. After that first match of the 1893 protest-ridden Cup saga against the Wednesday, a little group of county cricketers stood in the pavilion doorway at the Olive Grove ground discussing how they thought Bloomer would fare in the future. 'He's a good player', conceded one of them, George Ulyett, the Yorkshire and England all-rounder, 'but I don't give him more than five years at the most. He'll have all the steam knocked out of him in that time.'

It was an ill-fated forecast. Whereas Bloomer went on to last in League football for as long, some 20 years, as Ulyett did in county cricket (1893 was the Yorkshireman's last first-class season), that five-year term, sadly, was to relate to Ulyett's life. He was in only his 47th year when, having been in failing health for some time, he contracted a fatal attack of pneumonia while watching a match with Kent at Bramall Lane in the summer of 1898.

Covered in glory though so much of Bloomer's career was, however, he definitely did not find it all sweetness and light. The FA Cup competition, for instance, was to remain a particular stumbling block along his path. Having found his one goal far from enough in the final against Forest, he went into the Palace clash with Sheffield United a year later labouring under the distraction of an unresolved dispute in which he was the central figure.

This trouble flared up after Derby County's victory at Southampton in the third round of that season's competition. It was alleged that Bloomer had sworn to an affidavit stating that Jack Robinson, the Southampton and former Derby goalkeeper who was a current England international, had promised to give him £50 down to join the Hampshire club, with the additional undertaking that he would be paid £5 10s per week and be given an extra £50 for every season he remained with them.

Southampton's secretary denied all knowledge of the affair, but Derby's directors maintained that Robinson would not have acted as he was alleged to have done without official backing. Two years earlier, the Derby-born goalkeeper's transfer from the Rams to New Brighton Tower had been the subject of an FA Commission that had ruled it invalid until the Cheshire club had become affiliated to their county association. Now he was at the centre of another inquiry, and he proceeded to cloud the issue with several conflicting statements.

These ranged from a stout denial of being a tempter to the claim that it was Bloomer who had first broached the subject by asking if there was any chance of his joining Southampton. At one stage, Robinson, who that season helped Southampton to the first of the three Southern League titles they won while he was with them, even tried to pass the whole thing off as a practical joke. Yet, despite all that confusion—or, equally probably, perhaps because of it—the FA emergency committee who met to consider Derby County's protest about poaching decided that the charge was not substantiated.

But that decision was not reached until the month after the final, and there can be little doubt that Bloomer's off-day was partly attributable to the fact that he still had the uncertainty about the outcome hanging over him.

There were two other reasons why Bloomer was below his best against the Blades—and both were attributable to two members of the Sheffield team who, in addition to the aforementioned Billy Beer, had Derbyshire connections. They were the goalkeeping giant Willie Foulke, against whom Derby's hero found scoring difficult at the best of times, and Ernest ('Nudger') Needham, the 'Prince of Half-backs' who, it was reported in *Sporting Sketches*, 'found time to pay such attention to Bloomer that the famous crack was seldom able to get away'. On the rare occasions when Bloomer did, he either found Foulke's bulk too big a barrier or uncharacteristically wasted his chances. He lost a particularly good opportunity to increase Derby's lead early in the second half, when it was reported that 'he shot ridiculously wide' with the goal 'at his mercy'.

Foulke was at the reasonable weight of just under 13st for his height of 6ft 2in when, at the age of 20, he joined Sheffield United in 1894, but he became England's heaviest soccer international when he weighed in at about 19st with an 1897 cap in a 4–0 defeat of Wales at Bramall Lane. He was up to more than 22st, an awe-inspiring figure of gargantuan girth, by the time he cost Chelsea a £50 transfer fee in 1905, and he was near 26st when he moved to Bradford City after only one season with the London club—their first in League football.

Foulke had some alarming brushes with authority. One of them left even the famous Bolton referee Jack ('Jimmy') Howcroft, among the strongest and most respected of his time, admitting that it caused him the only really uncomfortable moments of his long career.

Ernest Needham, the 'Prince of Half-backs'.

Playing for Chelsea away to Burslem Port Vale, as they were then known, Foulke was in a strangely irritable mood. He groused his way through the game, then suddenly grabbed one of the home forwards round the midriff and hurled him into the Chelsea net. Howcroft promptly pointed to the penalty spot, whereupon the seething Foulke refused to take up his position for the kick. He did so only when Jackie Robinson, Chelsea's captain and player-manager, told him either to get back in goal or clear off, but he made no attempt to save the penalty. Instead, he stood stock still, glaring at the referee. Howcroft kept a respectable distance from the giant goalkeeper for the remainder of the match, and at the end of it he returned to his dressing room with unaccustomed haste.

When in less hostile mood, Foulke, as befitted his size, was quite a dab hand at saving penalties. In one game he stopped a couple of them. One foiled spot-kicker complained that 'he's got arms as long as a blooming gorilla'. Another protested that he filled so much of the goal there was 'nothing left to aim at'.

Howcroft had previously had a close-up of Foulke fury after the 1902 Cup Final at the Crystal Palace. Goaded by a goal awarded to Southampton which he claimed to be 'miles offside', Foulke missed the fact that the scorer had been played onside by a Sheffield United defender. After the match, which was drawn (United won the replay), he still felt so badly about it that he went in search of the referee, Tom Kirkham.

Howcroft, one of the linesmen that day, saw F.J. Wall, then the FA secretary, pleading with the big man, who was in his birthday suit, to go back to his dressing room, but to no avail. Bill, if not strictly out for blood, was determined to put his point of view most forcibly. So Howcroft shouted to Kirkham to tell him to lock the door of his cubicle, and the referee needed no second warning. Foulke was left frustrated, and Howcroft with this vivid memory:

> But what a sight! The thing I can never forget is Foulke, over 6ft tall and tremendous in size, striding along the corridor without a stitch of clothing.

Foulke's bulk earned him such nicknames as Little Willie, Fatty, Baby and Big Bill. He never objected. 'I don't care what they call me,' he said, 'as long as they don't call me late for dinner'. He fell on hard times after ending his playing career and he eked out a precarious living by turning himself into an 'Aunt Sally' in facing penalties at fairgrounds and on Blackpool sands. He was only 42 when he died in 1916 after catching a chill at the seaside.

Although born in Shropshire, Foulke grew up in Derbyshire at Blackwell. Needham hailed from the Newbold district of Chesterfield. They were among the footballers who also played cricket for Derbyshire—Foulke only briefly (four matches in 1900), but Needham in nearly 350 innings from 1901 to 1912 during which, as a left-hand batsman, he totalled more than 6,500 runs and hit two of his seven first-class centuries in one game against Essex at Leyton.

With Sheffield United, Needham was a member of the famed middle line completed by Rab Howell and Tom Morren (all three under 5ft 6in). He played in about 550 senior matches for the club, and helped them to win the First Division title in 1897–98. He also captained them to another Cup triumph at the Palace, in the 1902 replay against Southampton, the year after Tottenham had beaten the Blades at the second attempt, at Bolton, to become the only non-League winners of the trophy.

The Sheffield side again scuppered Derby's Cup hopes to earn that meeting with Southampton, and although injury kept Needham out of the second replay of their semi-final, at Nottingham, his deputy, Billy Parker, who had played in only one League game, not only kept Bloomer quiet but also shared in the build-up to Priest's winning goal. Derby led in both the original tie at West Bromwich and the first replay at Wolverhampton, but conceded equalisers through defensive errors.

On other occasions, Needham saw enough of Bloomer's best to describe him as 'the most twisting tormentor and wonderful shot I have ever faced'. He appreciated him as an England colleague too—most notably when Derby's hot-shot scored four goals the only time Needham captained his country, in a 6–0 defeat of Wales at Newcastle in 1901.

Billy Foulke, England's heaviest soccer international.

CHAPTER 8

Scourge of the Scots

*Bloomer at home with mentor in England debut –
Scores five goals against Wales – Three Rams players
capped together – Dispute points Turner to Derby –
The County's first caps – Police called to escort
O'Brien from Brooklyn ground – Ibrox tragedy –The
elusive Cup –Bloomer's full international details –
Record unbeaten run by England*

S TEVE BLOOMER had 80 games and nearly 40 goals behind him when he made his England debut towards the end of his third season with Derby—at his home County Ground in Nottingham Road, and alongside his mentor John Goodall, who had gained the distinction of being the first to appear in international football while with the Rams in winning the fifth of his 14 caps in a 4–1 win over Wales at Sunderland four years earlier.

Paradoxically, the call for Bloomer came, for the match with Ireland on March 9th, 1895, while Derby were under the threat of the relegation they had to play that 'test' match with Notts County to avoid, and after a scoreless spell of seven games for Bloomer during which they lost 6–0 at Bolton, 4–0 at Villa Park and 5–1 at Liverpool.

Stoke winger Joe Schofield, winning the last of his three caps, opened the floodgates to a 9–0 victory over the Irish with a shot deflected off Torrans, the Linfield full-back. Bloomer, Goodall and Preston's Frank Becton each scored twice, the other goals coming from Billy Bassett, Bloomer's right-wing partner from West Bromwich Albion, and Rab Howell, of Sheffield United.

Bloomer and John Goodall played together twice more for England after that demolition job at Derby—in a 3-0 win over Scotland at Everton's ground the following month, and in a 9–1 trouncing of Wales in Cardiff a year later. Bloomer scored 'only' one goal in that game against the Scots (there were to be seven more that made him their scourge in his nine other encounters with them), but he hammered in five at the expense of the beleaguered Welsh who were to suffer again when he faced them under 'Nudger' Needham's captaincy. The teams for that game in which 'Our Steve' went nap in the big win in the Principality on March 16th, 1896 were:

WALES: **Jones, S.** (Wrexham); **Arridge** (Everton), **Parry** (Everton); **Rogers** (Wrexham), **Chapman** (Manchester City), **Jones, J.L.** (Sheffield United); **Meredith**

(Manchester City), **Davies, Jos** (Manchester City), **Morris, A.G.** (Aberystwyth), **Morris, H.** (Manchester City), **Lewis** (Bangor).

ENGLAND: **G.B. Raikes** (Oxford University); **W.J. Oakley** (Oxford University), **Crabtree** (Aston Villa); **A.G. Henfrey** (Corinthians), **Crawshaw** (Wednesday), **Kinsey** (Derby County); **Bassett** (West Bromwich Albion), **Bloomer** (Derby County), **G.O. Smith** (Oxford University), **Goodall, J.** (Derby County), **R.R. Sandilands** (Old Westminsters).

England's other scorers were Smith (2), Goodall and Bassett. The lone reply was made by Chapman, who spent just that one season in Manchester City's Welsh contingent between his arrival from Newtown and departure to Grimsby Town.

Earlier that month, George Kinsey and Steve Bloomer had played in the 2–0 defeat of Ireland in Belfast, Bloomer sharing the scoring with Smith. Against Wales, with John Goodall restored to the attack in place of Everton's Edgar Chadwick, Derby County had three players in an England team for the first time.[1] That has happened on four occasions since then, though the Rams had as many as four men (Jack Barker, Tommy Cooper, Sammy Crooks and Ike Keen) in an international trial in the Thirties, and four more (Kevin Hector, Roy McFarland, David Nish and Colin Todd) in England squads in the 1970s.

George Kinsey, one of the three players Derby County had in an England team for the first time.

---

1. On April 14th, 1934, England 3, Scotland 0, at Wembley (Jack Bowers, Tommy Cooper and Sammy Crooks); October 17th, 1936, Wales 2, England 1, in Cardiff (Jack Barker, Crooks and Ike Keen); May 11th, 1974, Wales 0, England 2, in Cardiff (David Nish, Roy McFarland and Colin Todd); May 15th, 1974, England 1, Northern Ireland 0, at Wembley (Nish, McFarland and Todd).

Chadwick was on the losing side in only the last of his seven international appearances, by 2–1 against Scotland at the Crystal Palace in 1897. He won a League championship medal with Everton in 1890–91, but had the misfortune to be in the beaten team in three FA Cup finals (with Everton in 1893 and 1897, Southampton in 1902). He helped Southampton to win the Southern League title in 1901.

The 1896 match with Wales marked the end of George Kinsey's international career, despite the huge margin of victory and the fact that England won each of the four games in which he played. He gained the first two of his caps while with Wolverhampton Wanderers, for whom he excelled at left-half in their 1893 FA Cup-winning team against Everton. Burton-born, he joined Wolves after playing for Burton Crusaders, Burton Swifts and Mitchell St. George's, and he was a regular member of their side for three seasons before making an unsuccessful move to Aston Villa. After only three League appearances in his one year with the Villa, he followed the route to Derby taken only a few months earlier by left-winger Albert Woolley, who had been in the Claret and Blues' championship team of 1893–94. Woolley, sadly, was soon to be struck down by the illness that resulted in his early death, whereas Kinsey's fortunes revived as an ever-present in the 1895–96 season the Rams ended as First Division runners-up (to Villa) and losing FA Cup semi-finalists (against Wolves).

Shortly after the start of the next season, however, Kinsey lost his place at Derby to another England wing-half, Jimmy Turner, who won his three caps with three clubs— with Bolton Wanderers when he made his international debut in a 6–0 defeat of Wales at Stoke in 1893, with Stoke when he shared in the 9–0 win against Ireland on the day Steve Bloomer made his England debut at Derby in 1895, and with the Rams when the Irish were beaten 3–2 in Belfast in 1898.

From Derby, George Kinsey moved to Notts County, but he made only four League appearances for them before helping Eastville Rovers of the Birmingham and District League to convert themselves into Bristol Rovers of the Southern League. After several years in the West Country, he returned to his Burton roots and was reinstated as an amateur.

Turner, meanwhile, assisted Derby County into two more Cup semi-finals, and he earned his England recall the month before facing Forest in the first of the Rams' ill-fated finals. That Crystal Palace clash with those Nottingham neighbours was Turner's Derby swansong, for by the time the next season came round he was back with Stoke City, the club in his native Staffordshire he had originally joined from Bolton but had been driven to desert for Derby because of a dispute.

Ben Spilsbury's allegiance to Cambridge University at the time he won his three caps made John Goodall, though already a seasoned international, the first to play for England while with Derby County. Eight years later almost to the day, in March, 1899, brother Archie became the first to be capped by Ireland while with the Rams, in a 1–0 victory over Wales in Belfast, although there was another Derby player who was an Irish international before him. That was 'Toby' Mercer, an outside-right who took part in the last three of his dozen games for his country after ending a second spell with Distillery to cross the Irish Sea to the County in October, 1903. Negotiations for his transfer also had to be conducted with Leicester Fosse, who held his League registration.

John Thompson Mercer, to give him his full name, who helped both Linfield (1902) and Distillery (1903) to win the Irish Cup, made his international debut in a 1–0 win against Wales at Llandudno in February, 1898, and last played for Ireland when they lost 4–0 to Scotland in Glasgow in March, 1905. He was on the winning side in three other matches with Wales, and against the Scots in the 1903 Glasgow game, but he was also in the team thrashed 13–2 by England (four for G.O. Smith, two for Bloomer) at Sunderland in 1899. It was against England, in the defeat in Belfast when Jimmy Turner was last capped, that he scored his only international goal.

Mercer netted only once for Derby County too, in a 5–0 home defeat of Stoke City on Boxing Day, 1903, but injuries marred his short stay with the Rams after he had been a first choice in the team that put them into the Cup's last four yet again in 1903–04. On his return to his home city of Belfast he became a successful businessman, a director of the Glentoran club, and later chairman of the Irish League as well as Distillery. He was Glentoran's chairman when their ground was damaged by German bombers in 1941, and they might well have gone out of existence but for his casting vote which kept them in the Northern Ireland's wartime regional league.

While on the subject of Derby County's Irish international originals, it is worth recalling that the first Republic of Ireland cap to play for the Rams was centre-half Mick O'Brien, against Italy in April, 1927. He also represented Northern Ireland that month, in a 2–2 draw with Wales in Cardiff, but he made only three League and two FA Cup appearances for Derby between joining them at the advanced age of 33 in December, 1926, after an unhappy few months in New York with Brooklyn Wanderers, and leaving for Walsall in the summer of 1928.

Lured to the United States by a five-year contract and a weekly wage of £16, O'Brien came back to England under the uncertainty of an indefinite suspension imposed by an offended Brooklyn coach who had called the police to escort him from the Wanderers' ground. Derby County agreed terms for his transfer from Hull City, who had lost him to America, but his registration was accepted only after a Football League inquiry that resulted in the Rams and the Humbersiders being fined £100 each.

Michael Terence O'Brien, who was only 47 when he died in 1940, was a man of many clubs after his return from wartime service during which he took part in the Battle of Jutland following his switch from the Army to the Royal Navy. Having already been with several minor sides in the Tyneside area, and had trials in Scotland with Celtic and Alloa, he played for Brentford, Norwich and South Shields in the first post-war season of 1919–20. He then had a spell with Queen's Park Rangers before joining Leicester, from where he made his move to Hull after his transfer fee had been cut from £2,000 to £750 on appeal to the League.

Next came his brief connections with Derby and Walsall, followed by those only a little longer with Norwich and Watford before he turned to management with QPR, Brentford (assistant) and Ipswich. He was with seven clubs in playing ten times for Northern Ireland and four for the Republic, winning his last cap at the age of 38. A remarkable character.

Back now to Bloomer. The ace scorer of his era went without a goal in only one of his first 14 games for England (a 2–1 win over Scotland in Birmingham in 1899), and he alone was his country's successful marksman on each of the only two occasions he was on the losing side in his 23 international matches—both against the Scots. After the 4–1 defeat by the old enemy in Glasgow in 1900, he went through his last 11 England games over seven years in unbeaten teams (five wins and six draws).

His five-goal feat for England in 1896 had one precedent. Oliver Vaughton, of Aston Villa, had scored five on his international debut in a record 13–0 broadside in Belfast in 1882. Tottenham's Willie Hall, also against Ireland (at Old Trafford in 1938), and Newcastle's 'Super Mac' Malcolm Macdonald, in a European Cup qualifier against Cyprus at Wembley in 1975, were to follow.

When Bloomer was limited to a couple of goals as the Irish again leaked 13 (but replied with two) at Sunderland in 1899, there was a difference of opinion about the number credited to Gilbert Oswald Smith, the gifted amateur who stole the scoring limelight from him in living up to being generally recognised as the best English centre-forward of the late 19th century. Some sources claim a record-equalling five goals for G.O. that day, but others, the more reliable, restrict him to four—among them Edward Grayson, who was in such close touch with Smith.

Bloomer was twice given the England captaincy in succession to Smith after the Corinthian had made the last of his 20 full international appearances in a 2–2 draw with Scotland at Crystal Palace in 1901, but the first of those matches with Steve the skipper, later that year, was an unofficial one against Germany, and the other, against Scotland on April 5th, 1902, was reduced to that category because of a crowd disaster in Glasgow.

The Germans, now one of England's most formidable rivals but then an outclassed combination paying their first soccer visit to this country, were beaten 10–0 (three for Bloomer and four for Billy Wooldridge, of Wolves) in Manchester on September 25th, 1901—only a few days after they had lost 12–0 to England's amateurs at Tottenham.

The tragedy-hit game at the Ibrox stadium had to be abandoned as a 1–1 draw instead of counting in the British Championship. Wooden terracing the Rangers club had

Mick O'Brien, Derby's first Republic of Ireland international.

Toby Mercer, whose stay with the Rams was marred by injuries. He later became chairman of the Irish League.

installed to increase their ground's capacity collapsed under the strain as the crowd craned to watch Scottish winger Bobby Templeton, then of Aston Villa, speeding down the touchline, and a mass of bodies tumbled to the ground through the broken struts. The death toll mounted to 25, with 24 dangerously injured, 168 seriously injured, 153 injured, and 172 slightly injured—as classified by the police.

When the game was replayed in Birmingham early the following month, the result was another draw (2–2), enough to give the Scots the title. Bloomer did not score in either match, but at Ibrox he supplied the pass from which Jimmy Settle, the Everton forward formerly with Bolton and Bury, equalised the early goal scored for Scotland by Alexander Brown, who the previous season had netted a record 15 times in Tottenham's FA Cup-winning run.

'Sandy' Brown, a scorer in every round of the competition proper as Spurs, then of the Southern League, became the only club from outside the Football League to carry off the trophy, had to wait until two years after the Ibrox disaster, by which time he had moved to Middlesbrough, for what was to be his only official cap. Again he played against England, at Celtic Park, but he ended on the losing side as Bloomer grabbed the game's only goal to clinch the championship.

By then, Bloomer's own hopes of an FA Cup-winner's medal had foundered on his last two realistic chances of collecting one. It was ironic that, allegedly not wishing to damage his reputation by playing under an injury handicap in such an important game, he dropped out of the 1903 Final against Bury when there were those who unfairly felt that he could well have risked it, whereas Jack Fryer, the 6ft 2in goalkeeper from Cromford, did report fit when, as events emphatically proved, the general feeling was that he should never have even considered doing so. More about that in the next chapter.

What was to be Steve Bloomer's final advanced opportunity to claim a Cup-winner's medal went by the board the year after Derby County had been so emphatically Bury'd by the record six-goal winning margin for a Cup final. He scored five times as they reached the semi-finals for the seventh time in nine seasons, including the winning goals against Wolves (at Villa Park in a second replay) and Blackburn in the second and third rounds, but at Molineux neither he nor any of his team-mates could find the target against Bolton, then of the Second Division, who snatched the decider 15 minutes from time. In the final, Bolton lost by the same score to Manchester City, themselves producing no response after claiming unsuccessfully that Welsh wizard Billy Meredith's 20th-minute winning effort was offside.

The goal by which Derby knocked out Blackburn for the third successive year was about as late as Taylor's winner against them for Bolton. Bloomer was the scorer, but, filling the captaincy vacancy left by Archie Goodall's transfer to Plymouth, he surprisingly spurned an earlier excellent chance to hit the target by entrusting the taking of a penalty to Joe Warrington, a Macclesfield-born outside-right from Derby Wanderers who was briefly being tried at centre-forward. Warrington, soon afterwards transferred to Brentford, found the responsibility as unnerving as the traumatic experience he had shared in the final against Bury, and his shot from the spot was saved.

These were the details of those seven semi-finals, one of which went to two replays, during that period in which Derby County found the trophy so near yet so far, thrice winning through to the final only to retreat from London each time embarrassingly defeated:

March 21st, 1896: Derby County 1 (Bloomer), Wolves 2 (Malpass, Tonks)
(at Perry Barr, Birmingham. Att: 35,000)
March 20th, 1897: Derby County 2 (Goodall A., Goodall J.), Everton 3 (Chadwick, Hartley, Milward)
(at Victoria Ground, Stoke. Att: 25,000)
March 19th, 1898: Derby County 3 (Bloomer 2, Goodall J.), Everton 1 (Chadwick)
(at Molineux, Wolverhampton. Att: 30,000)
March 18th, 1899: Derby County 3 (Bloomer 3), Stoke City 1 (Maxwell)
(at Molineux. Att: 24,500)
March 15th, 1902: Derby County 1 (Warren), Sheffield United 1 (Hedley)
(at Hawthorns, West Bromwich. Att: 33,600)
March 20th, 1902: Derby County 1 (Wombwell), Sheffield United 1 (Priest)
(at Molineux. Att: 17,500)
March 27th, 1902: Derby County 0, Sheffield United 1 (Priest)
(at City Ground, Nottingham. Att: 15,000)
March 21st, 1903: Derby County 3 (Warren, Boag, Richards), Millwall 0
(at Villa Park, Birmingham. Att: 40,500)
March 19th, 1904: Bolton Wanderers 1 (Taylor), Derby County 0
(at Molineux. Att: 20,180)

Jack Fryer, mistakenly reported fit for final.

In both the intervening years, 1900 and 1901, the Rams went out in the first round—by 3–0 against Sunderland after a 2–2 draw; by an only goal at Bolton.

Derby yet again reached the semi-finals five years later, but by that time, as will be recalled in greater detail in Chapter 11, Bloomer was no longer with them. To the mortification of Rams fans, 'dire necessity' (to quote an old account's assessment of the Rams' financial situation) drove Derby's board to succumb to a renewed approach for him from Middlesbrough in March, 1906.

It was with the Boro that he won the last two of his England caps, brought back after a four-match absence for the 1907 games with Wales, at Fulham, and Scotland, at Newcastle. Both were drawn 1–1, Bloomer bowing out with the goal against the Scots. This was his complete England record in the British Championship:

Date	Result	Opponents	Venue	Bloomer's goals
1895				
March 9th	9–0	Ireland	County Ground, Derby	2
April 6th	3–0	Scotland	Everton	1
1896				
March 7th	2–0	Ireland	Belfast	1
March 16th	9–1	Wales	Cardiff	5
1897				
Feb 20th	6–0	Ireland	Nottingham	2
March 29th	4–0	Wales	Sheffield	1
April 3rd	1–2	Scotland	Crystal Palace	1
1898				
April 2nd	3–1	Scotland	Glasgow	2
1899				
Feb 18th	13–2	Ireland	Sunderland	2
March 20th	4–0	Wales	Bristol	2
April 8th	2–1	Scotland	Birmingham	
1900				
April 7th	1–4	Scotland	Glasgow	1
1901				
March 18th	6–0	Wales	Newcastle	4
March 30th	2–2	Scotland	Crystal Palace	1
1902				
March 3rd	0–0	Wales	Wrexham	
March 22nd	1–0	Ireland	Belfast	
May 3rd	2–2	Scotland	Birmingham	
1904				
April 9th	1–0	Scotland	Glasgow	1
1905				
Feb 25th	1–1	Ireland	Middlesbrough	1
March 27th	3–1	Wales	Liverpool	
April 1st	1–0	Scotland	Crystal Palace	
1907				
March 18th	1–1	Wales	Fulham	
April 6th	1–1	Scotland	Newcastle	1

The only match with Scotland that Bloomer missed, through injury, in his first eight seasons as an international player brought to an end an England record run of 20 games without defeat. Played in Glasgow on April 4th, 1896, it resulted in a narrow win for the Scots with goals by Lambie (Queen's Park) and Bell (Everton) to one by West Bromwich's Billy Bassett, John Goodall's partner on the right wing.

It was the first time Scotland fielded players with English clubs, Bell being joined by Doig (Sunderland), Brandon (Blackburn Rovers), Cowan (Aston Villa) and Hyslop (Stoke).

One of the players brought into a reshaped England attack was the subject of much criticism, for many thought that a seasoned professional should have been chosen instead of C.J. Burnup, an inexperienced 20-year-old amateur from Cambridge University who was painfully out of his depth. He was not capped again, but he did well enough for Cambridge to be a Blue from 1895 to 1898, and he also played soccer for Old Malvernians and the Corinthians.

As a cricketer, Cuthbert James Burnup played three times against Oxford University, and in eight of his 12 seasons with Kent, whom he captained, he exceeded 1,000 runs. He seldom bowled, but he has gone down in the record books in that respect for being the hapless MCC bowler off whom, as already recollected, Derbyshire's captain, S.H. Wood, 'netted' ten runs off one delivery at Lord's in 1900.

CHAPTER 9

Bury'd by Bury

Trio in three finals – Semi-final revenge over Everton
after defeat of Villa, holders and League champions –
Blades end Rams unbeaten run at Baseball Ground –
FA Cup stolen and design of its replacement pirated –
A 'Siamese Twin' makes his fortune in Canada –
Bloomer's century at cricket worth 52p – A car fit for
a Queen – Fryer folly in heaviest Cup Final defeat –
Consolation at Fulham

ONLY THREE PLAYERS, goalkeeper Jack Fryer, full-back Jimmy Methven and centre-forward John Boag, took part in all three of the FA Cup finals Derby County contested around the turn into the 20th century.

When I met Jimmy Methven shortly before his 84th birthday late in 1952, he told me that the game in which the Rams reached the first of those finals, the semi-final against Everton at Wolverhampton in 1898, was the most memorable of all those he played in—and there were just over 500 of them in League and Cup during his 15 seasons as the club's right-back. He was an ever-present in five of those seasons, missing only one match in the first four of them, and he was absent only 29 times altogether. It was his proud claim that he never played in the second team.

Everton were strongly fancied to repeat the win they had gained against Derby at Stoke at the same stage of the competition the previous year, but the County, who had already knocked out holders Aston Villa, extracted sweet revenge by beating them 3–1. As was so often the case, the trump card was dealt by Steve Bloomer, scorer of two of their goals. John Goodall got the other, Edgar Chadwick replying.

Bloomer also scored twice in the previous round, backing up a hat-trick by Boag in a remarkable 5–1 away win against Liverpool in a replay, but Derby had to battle through their first three matches of that Cup campaign without him because of injury. Hugh McQueen got the goal that ousted Villa in the first round, John Leonard, a former St. Mirren right-winger, was the matchwinner in an equally close game away to Wolves in the second, and Jimmy Stevenson, who was to be among the footballers killed in the First World War, netted in the drawn first meeting with Liverpool.

Leonard also scored on his League debut for Derby County, in a 2–1 home defeat by the Wednesday, but he made only three first-team appearance for the Rams in all. The other one was in the third-round home Cup-tie with Liverpool, after which he lost his place as John Goodall reverted to outside-right to make room for Bloomer's return as his partner. Leonard played just one senior game for his next club, Notts County, then joined Eastville (later Bristol) Rovers.

Derby County's victory over Villa was an achievement of special merit not only because the Rams were without their leading scorer but also because the Aston club were both Cup holders and League champions, having emulated Preston's famous double by romping 11 points clear of Sheffield United and Derby County (third on goal average) after defeating Everton 3–2 in the 1897 final.

It was Villa's second losing visit to Derby as Cup holders in three years. On the first occasion, on the first day of February in 1896 (the week after John Goodall's benefit match), memories of the epic 1885 Cup win against the high-riding men from Birmingham were revived by a 4–2 margin in the first Cup-tie to be played at the Baseball Ground. Villa, to whose champions Derby had finished third in 1894, arrived as First Division leaders by two points from the Rams, who had a game in hand, but they were comprehensively beaten despite rallying to score twice after all the home team's goals that glorious day—the day on which one spectator climbed into Derby soccer folklore by scaling a flagpole for a better view—had come in the first half, two each to Bloomer and John Miller.

On the following Saturday, Villa were back at the Baseball Ground for a League match, and they staged another two-goal revival to earn a draw that ended the Rams' run of 11 home wins since their move from the County Ground. That all-conquering sequence included five-goal onslaughts against Wolves and Burnley (there was also one away to Nottingham Forest), and an 8–0 whipping of Small Heath. Bloomer did the hat-trick in those games with Wolves and Forest, and he notched another when the double was completed over the Nottingham club with a 4–0 win at Derby. Against both Burnley and Small Heath, the ace marksman had to be content with just the one goal as the scoring honours were shared around.

**John Miller, shared scoring with
Bloomer in defeat of Cup holders.**

Preston were narrowly beaten in the Rams- next home match after Villa's 2–2 draw had ended their winning sequence, but, by 2–0 on March 14th, 1896, Sheffield United then became the first visitors to win at the Baseball Ground since the first fixture Derby County fulfilled there. That original soccer match at the ground, lost 1–0 to Sunderland almost exactly four years earlier, was the first of two for which the Rams temporarily switched from Nottingham Road before settling into their new headquarters. There was also only one goal in the other one, but Derby obtained it to beat Burnley.

The Rams therefore went through 17 successive games unbeaten at the Baseball Ground—14 in the League and three Cup-ties, and all won except the draw with Villa— before being blunted by the Blades. A week later they went out of the Cup, but they managed to finish second to Villa in the League despite winning only one of their remaining five matches. That lone victory was gained against third-placed Everton, from whom they took three of their last five points in their two meetings over Easter.

In going down at Derby when they first defended the Cup they had won in 1895, Aston Villa created a unique piece of soccer history by losing the trophy twice in the same season. A few months previously, on the night of September 11–12, 1895, the Cup they had claimed in April with a goal scored by Bob Chatt inside the first minute against West Bromwich Albion at Crystal Palace was stolen while on display in the window of football outfitter William Shillcock's shop at Newton Row in Birmingham. A £10 reward was offered, but that cup, 'a battered old relic' insured for £200, was never found. Villa were fined £25 by the FA, and for that modest amount a replacement of similar design was bought after a proposal that 'one of gold, the cost not to exceed £200' had been voted out by the FA Council.

Derby County remained in the running for the new trophy until their semi-final with Wolves at Perry Barr. Having equalised in a first half the Wanderers dominated, Bloomer had a goal controversially ruled out for offside, the referee deciding against awarding it after consulting a linesman, and soon afterwards the Rams suffered another demoralising setback when Bloomer went off injured.

Against ten men, Wolves regained an initiative that brought them a late winner, but in the final they lost by the same 2–1 score to the Wednesday, for whom Fred Spiksley scored the first of his two goals in barely 30 seconds. David Black, a left-winger who had been awarded his one Scotland cap seven years earlier, in a 7–0 defeat of Ireland, equalised in the eighth minute, but Spiksley regained the lead with the game still only 18 minutes old. That decider was struck with such force that the ball rebounded out of the net while Wolves' goalkeeper, Billy Tennant, deputising for the injured Billy Rose, was still wondering where it had gone. On seeing it lying in front of him, he kicked it upfield under the impression that it was still in play, and, failing to notice the kick-off from the centre spot, he ended the game believing the score was still 1–1. He took some convincing that there would not be a replay.

The new FA Cup that the Sheffield club's captain, Jack Earp, received in 1896 from Lord Kinnaird, who had been on the winning side in five of his nine finals as a player with the Wanderers and Old Etonians, was competed for until 1911, when it was given to his lordship to mark his 21 years as FA president.

Because the design had been pirated in Manchester, it was replaced by one, valued at the time at 50 guineas, which was competed for across more than 70 seasons until it was withdrawn through wear and tear. Its first winners, after a replay with Newcastle

United, were Bradford City, and therein lay a double coincidence. It had been made by a Bradford firm, Fattorini and Sons, and that remains the only occasion on which a Bradford team have played in an FA Cup Final.

The current Cup is the fourth in line, won for the first time by Liverpool in 1992. It has two identical replicas. One trophy is with the holders, one is used for promotional purposes, the other is kept in a bank vault.

After his misfortunes in the 1896 semi-final against Wolves, Steve Bloomer quickly gained personal and club revenge by doing all Derby's scoring as they narrowly won a seven-goal thriller when the Wanderers visited the Baseball Ground in the League early the following season. Billy Beats, who was to be England's centre-forward alongside Bloomer on the day of the Ibrox disaster, was twice on target for Wolves. Bloomer scored three more in a 7–2 home win over Bury a week later, gave the fans a Christmas Day treat by hitting another hat-trick when visitors from West Bromwich were beaten 8–1, and then provided the impetus towards a second successive Cup semi-final appearance with further trebles in the first two rounds of competition as Barnsley St. Peter's were dispatched by a repeat of the result against Albion, and Bolton Wanderers by 4–1.

Three of the Rams' other goals in those two Cup-ties were notched by one of the club's lesser-known players, Willie Fisher, inside-left deputy for his fellow Scot Jimmy Stevenson, who was himself a four-goal man in another big home victory in the First Division that season, by 6–0 against Blackburn Rovers. Fisher had the creditable striking rate of eight goals in only 15 senior matches, but before that year was out he was allowed to leave for Burton Swifts.

In 1899 he linked up again with three other former Derby players, George Kinsey, John Leonard and John Paul, in the newly-named Bristol Rovers team which entered the Southern League. That club came into existence as the Black Arabs in 1883, became known as Eastville Rovers from 1884 to 1897, then for one year as Bristol Eastville Rovers before the change to the present name.

Steve Bloomer also scored in the home defeat of Newton Heath that put Derby County into the Cup's last four of 1897, but at Stoke's Victoria Ground the Rams again fell at the penultimate fence, the Goodall brothers getting their goals in the 3–2 defeat by Everton. The breaking of the semi-final barrier in each of the next two seasons led only to those Crystal Palace calamities against Nottingham Forest and Sheffield United, and, after the ending of the club's interest in the competition in the first round for the intervening two years, renewed raising of hopes foundered amid the ruins of the failures in two semi-finals and one final over the following three seasons. No wonder so many supporters believed in the Gypsy's Curse.

In 1903, the semi-final with Millwall, who were to become original members of the Football League's Third Division 17 years on, provided a reasonably comfortable passage to the County's third final in six years after John Sutcliffe, a former rugby player who had kept goal for England and been a losing finalist with Bolton, had twice picked the ball out of his net in the first dozen minutes, but it was marred by a nasty injury to outside-left George Davis midway through the first half.

Davis, who played for his home team, Alfreton Town, both before and after his career with Derby County, stumbled, after being tripped, on a strip of the matting that had been laid down alongside the Villa Park touchlines for the linesmen's use and hit his head on the adjoining asphalt cycling track as he went sprawling. He was carried off concussed, but resumed for the second half despite, as one witness described it, 'looking fearfully bad'.

Though still feeling shaken, he returned to the side after missing a League defeat at Liverpool a couple of days later, and he retained his place for that most one-sided of cup finals against Bury. He also maintained his form sufficiently to play twice for England early the following year, scoring in a 3–1 victory in Belfast, and although further injuries considerably restricted his appearances over the next two seasons he again came back so strongly that it was quite a surprise when he left the Rams to rejoin Alfreton in 1908, shortly before his 27th birthday.

Four years after that, he did something else unexpected when he and his wife and their eldest son, also George, emigrated to Canada. He went out there to coach in Manitoba, but soon afterwards he entered the hotel business, in which he made his fortune and was followed by George Junior and their other son, Arthur. It was from Art (as he was Canadianised) that Bert Mozley took over the running of one of the hotels in the Davis chain, the Royal at Calgary, after the former Derby full-back and captain, having met the Davis family while on tour with the FA, had also travelled to a new life on the other side of the Atlantic in the mid-1950s.

I was especially pleased to meet George Davis Senior when he came back to England on holiday only a few months before Mozley left this country, for he was such a close friend of my step-father, George Richards,[1] whom he partnered in almost half of his 150 or so games on Derby County's left wing, that their team-mates dubbed them 'the Siamese Twins'. Jimmy Methven suggested, tongue in cheek, that they 'won enough money to set up a library from their phenomenal luck as partners playing [the card game] nap!'

Jimmy Stevenson, scorer of four goals against Blackburn.

---

1. My mother married George Richards several years after the death of my own father in a motor-cycle accident. Although, at the age of nine, I took a while to get used to this new man in my life, I could not have wished for a better step-father. He was always very kind and considerate, and, though most modest concerning his own achievements, he helped to develop my interest not only in Derby County FC and Derbyshire CCC, but also in football and cricket generally.

A picture sent to me from Canada by George Davis. It was taken of him
with his wife and their youngest son, Arthur, 'at our great Calgary
Stampede and Rodeo, which I consider the finest in the world'. He added
that Art, as he was known out there, 'had bestowed on him the title of
Chief Bear Paw, of the Stoney Indian tribe—a name given at one time to
Lord Baden-Powell and other celebrities on their tours through Canada'.

They first linked up on the football field at the City Ground, Nottingham, on May
3rd, 1902, when Derby County played a combined Forest-Notts County team in a match
arranged in aid of the Ibrox Disaster Fund. Their left-wing partnership would have
lasted longer but for the switching of George Richards from inside-left, where his
trickery earned him the nickname 'Corkscrew', to left-half, the position in which he
was capped in an 8–1 trouncing of Austria in Vienna in 1909 and went on the FA's

unbeaten tour of South Africa in 1910. He was also an England reserve against Scotland, and but for injuries—the most persistent of them a dislocated shoulder—he would almost certainly have gained more international honours during a career with Derby County that stretched from 1902, when he was signed from the Leicestershire club Whitwick White Cross in face of competition from the Wednesday, until his retirement from the Rams' staff in 1914, shortly before the outbreak of war.

Despite his enforced absences, George Richards exceeded 300 appearances for Derby, whom he captained for a time towards the end of his stay at the Baseball Ground, and when he left the club only three players, Bloomer, Methven and Archie Goodall, had played more League games for the County than he had. He guested for Queen's Park Rangers while in London on war work, then returned to his Castle Donington home to keep busy in the basketmaking trade and on his smallholding. Although then too old for top soccer, he did not finish playing cricket, with Castle Donington, until a few months after his 72nd birthday, in 1952.

In his hey-day as a cricketer, he shared in two unbroken double-century opening partnerships for the Darley Dale club—one with C.A. Ollivierre, the West Indian Test

Two players who turned out for Derby County, George Richards and Ivan Sharpe, are in this FA party that toured South Africa, unbeaten, in 1910. Back row (left to right): Benson (Sheffield United), Duckworth (Manchester United), Leeming (Brighton), Hayes and Wall (both Manchester United). Middle row: F. Hughes (S.A. manager), Silto (Swindon Town), E.G. Wright (Corinthians, vice-captain), Raine (Sunderland), Bulcock (Crystal Palace), Richards (Derby County), Sturgess (Sheffield United), D. Yeads (S.A. Trainer). Front row: A. Berry (Oxford University), Fleming (Swindon Town), Hibbert (Bury), Wedlock (Bristol City), C.J. Hughes (FA vice-president), V.J. Woodward (Tottenham Hotspur, captain), Lievesley (Sheffield United), Holley (Sunderland), I. Sharpe (Glossop North End).

batsman who played for Derbyshire, the other with the brother of W.T. Taylor, the county club's secretary. Richards himself would have represented Derbyshire if he had not had to refuse an invitation to join their party for three consecutive matches in the South of England because he was not qualified by either birth or residence. He was born at Bulwell, in Nottinghamshire, and lived in Leicestershire.

While with Derby County, he was among the Rams men who played cricket for the Ley's and Ewart's works team whose factory was adjacent to the Baseball Ground. The others notably included two prominent footballers we shall be coming to at greater length in a later chapter, Horace Barnes and Jimmy Bagshaw—and, on one particular occasion, none other than Steve Bloomer. Shortly before the 1914–18 War it was Bloomer who did most to upset Rolls-Royce's hopes of winning the Derby and District League title. He was awarded 10s 6d (52p) in appreciation of his not-out 112, his highest score.

The two George Henrys, Richards and Davis, met for the last time while the Alfreton man was back in England in the summer of 1954. Davis also called, suitably Stetson-hatted, to see us in the Sports Department of the *Derby Evening Telegraph* and aroused no little interest by his means of transport. For it was no ordinary automobile that he parked outside in Albert Street. Passers-by stopped and stared to admire the 20ft-long coupe, a Lincoln, in which millionaire George Davis had already travelled more than 4,000 miles, touring and looking up old friends. This was the limousine used by Princess Elizabeth during her tour of Canada with the Duke of Edinburgh before she became Queen. It had cost the retired hotel magnate £166 to bring this splendid vehicle over with him on his six-month holiday, and he had already had a number of offers for it.

It was back in England, at Wimbledon, that George Davis died in April, 1969, almost into his 89th year. George Richards was 79 when he died nearly ten years earlier, at Derby City Hospital at the beginning of November, 1959, having been suddenly taken ill earlier in the day. Their reminiscences during their last meeting were of the happiest with one outstanding footballing exception—the 1903 FA Cup Final defeat by Bury in which they were partners on the left flank of Derby County's attack.

For George Davis, at least, there was some consolation in Canada 19 years after that six-goal pounding at the Palace. In his 41st year, on what he looked back to as 'the happiest day of my life', and three years before he stopped playing, he gained a winner's medal with Calgary Hillhurst in the Dominion of Canada Cup Final.

Deserved as Bury's resounding triumph was, there were several mitigating circumstances as far as the crestfallen Rams were concerned—as indeed, as we have seen, there also were when they were beaten in their two previous finals. Jimmy Methven, who himself played after having been doubtful because of a chill, was particularly vehement in the view that Jack Fryer's own fitness was so uncertain that the goalkeeper should have given way to Frank Davies, who was on stand-by—especially as Davies had offered to give Fryer his medal. Fryer, whose groin injury had caused him to retire from an Easter Monday match at Middlesbrough in which the Rams had been reduced in a 3–1 defeat to eight fit men (wing-half Charlie Leckie also had to go off and Fryer's goalkeeping deputy, Charlie Morris, was limping), afterwards claimed, however, that Derby's directors and manager Newbould had influenced his decision to play.

The biggest blow to Derby's hopes of being third time lucky in a Cup Final was naturally the absence of Steve Bloomer, whose ankle injury had not mended sufficiently

George Richards wearing the England cap he won against Austria in Vienna in 1909, and making another basket in the workshop adjoining his home at Castle Donington.

(Derby Evening Telegraph)

for him to feel capable of playing. Bitterly disappointed as he must have been at missing another chance to help the Rams bring home the trophy, he did not want to let the side down through the risk of failing to do himself justice. There was also the strong possibility that he would be unable to last out the game and therefore leave the team a man short in those days of no substitutes. This was emphasised by the fact that when he aggravated

A post card George Richards received from a Derby County fan while he was the club's captain. It exhorts him to 'Wake Bentley up for a goalgetting effort'.

the injury on his return to the team for the Good Friday game at Newcastle (also lost) just over a week before the final, the ankle swelled to such an extent that he could not wear a shoe on that foot for the best part of two days and had to stay behind at Tynemouth over the weekend.

Furthermore, Bloomer, who had to take many hard knocks as a main danger-man, missed not only the Cup Final but also the Rams' last four League matches of the season—in the last of which the Birkenhead-born Davies made his only first-team appearance before moving to Glossop.

From having again been in line for the Cup and League double, Derby faded away to finish ninth in the First Division table. They were seven points behind champions Wednesday, the only team they defeated, with an only goal by George Richards, in their last eight League matches, six of which they lost in addition to their Cup Final thrashing. The game at Newcastle was the only one of the club's final dozen, including the Cup quarter-final, semi-final and final, in which Bloomer played.

The folly of Fryer's inclusion against Bury at Crystal Palace in defiance of his thigh and groin troubles was soon evident, but he was beaten only once during a first half in which Derby almost equalised when a shot from Richards was headed off the goal-line by the Lancashire club's 20th-minute scorer, skipper George Ross.

But what a different story it was after the interval. Within a few minutes, Fryer aggravated his injuries in unsuccessfully attempting to prevent Bury's second goal, and had to go off for treatment. He resumed, limping badly, after Charlie Morris, the Welsh international full-back who was again his stand-in, had made one fine save only to be beaten from the rebound, and he conceded the fourth goal before having to go off for good—never to play for Derby County again. As Fryer left the field he looked

George Richards and (right) George Davis, partners on the left flank of Derby County's attack who were known to their team-mates as 'the Siamese Twins'.

back over his shoulder to see the reinstated Morris let in No. 5—the fourth goal in the first 11 minutes of the second half—and Bury might have added more than the sixth one that completed the rout, twice hitting the bar.

They should also have had a penalty, for Morris, who several years later was to deputise in the Wales goal for the injured Dick Roose against England, swapped places with Jimmy Methven late in the game, and neither his fellow full-back nor skipper Archie Goodall informed the referee that the change was being made. Methven's explanation for escaping the award of a spot kick the first time he touched the ball as the second substitute goalkeeper was that 'the referee [Jack Adams, of Birmingham] must have felt sorry for us.'

The use of four goalkeepers in that one-sided final (the other one was Bury's little-needed Hughie Monteith) was repeated in 1908 during the match in which Charlie Morris filled that role in the Welsh emergency against England at Wrexham. Horace Bailey, then of Leicester Fosse and later briefly with Derby County, played throughout for England, who won 7–1. Morris switched from full-back to take over in the home country's goal when Dick Roose, one of the game's most gifted amateurs, was injured in the first half, but after the interval the Derby player was able to revert to his usual position because England agreed to the promotion from 12th man of Dai Davies, the Bolton Wanderers goalkeeper who had been capped against Scotland and Ireland four years earlier.

Leigh Richmond Roose, to give him his full name, became a man of many clubs through playing for those near where his profession as a doctor took him. He made his two dozen appearances for Wales while with Aberystwyth, London Welsh, Stoke City, Everton and Sunderland. He also turned out for, among others, Huddersfield, Aston Villa, Arsenal, Northern Nomads and Glasgow Rangers. Despite his occupation outside soccer, he was not unduly bothered about hygiene when it came to the cleanliness of the shirt he wore under his goalkeeping jersey. He was always reluctant to have it washed for fear that his good luck would be swilled away with the suds down the drain.

As far as Bury are concerned, there has been a lot of lost luck since their two winning FA Cup finals in the first four years of the 20th century. They have yet to get as far as the competition's last four for a third time, and from a highest First Division final placing of fourth in 1925–26 they have slipped as low as having to endure two spells in the old Fourth Division.

However, the 6–0 romp of 1903 at the Crystal Palace was a pinnacle of Cup achievement they could hardly have hoped to better in any case. They went through that season's five rounds without conceding a goal, beating Wolves, Sheffield United, the holders, and Notts County each by 1–0 before scoring three times without reply from Aston Villa in a Goodison Park semi-final. They also kept their defence intact in five of the eight games they played in lifting the trophy in 1900, beating Burnley 1–0, Notts County 2–0 after a scoreless draw, Sheffield United 2–0 after a 2–2 draw and Nottingham Forest 3–2 after a 1–1 draw, before sinking Southampton 4–0 in the first of two consecutive finals refereed by Derby's Arthur Kingscott.

Sickening as being so devastatingly Bury'd in Derby County's third final was for all those connected with the Rams, each of whose players had been promised a free new suit by one of the town's tailors if they had lifted the Cup, none could have felt more miserable than the troubled John Spencer Fryer. The depressing circumstances of his departure soon afterwards to Fulham provided a sharp contrast to the popularity he had enjoyed since being 'chaired' from the Wolverhampton pitch where his outstanding display against Everton had done so much to carry the Rams into the 1898 Cup Final in his first season with the club.

It was a sad end to a distinguished Derby career only one short of 200 appearances. And not for approaching half a century were Derby County again to get as far as the final—a long wait that was well rewarded with their extra-time victory over Charlton Athletic when the trophy was first at stake after the Second World War. Was it just a coincidence that the 'Curse' was lifted by the crossing of a gypsy's palm with silver during the build-up to that Wembley showpiece?

For Fryer, there were happier times ahead with Fulham before another injury caused him to miss the whole of the 1907–08 season and, after a brief comeback, forced him to give up playing in 1910. He kept a clean sheet when he made his debut for the Cottagers against Tottenham in his first game since the traumatic 1903 final, and he kept almost 40 more as a prominent member of the team that twice won the Southern League championship in successive seasons from 1905 to 1907.

CHAPTER 10

An Unexpected Departure

*Rams lose manager Newbould to Manchester City –
Nightmare start after mass suspensions – Five players
collapse with heat exhaustion – Eadie helps both City
and Derby to promotion – Morris, a full-back in the
classic mould, is Derby's first Welsh international – The
'Squire of Spondon' – Tragic end for Ben Warren, the
'manly son of Newhall'*

HARRY NEWBOULD caused quite a stir when he suddenly abandoned Derby County in the summer of 1906 to accept the secretary-manager's job at Manchester City. The men on the board at the Baseball Ground declared themselves both 'surprised and disappointed.'

It was not as if City were then a much more attractive proposition than Derby, even though the Rams had finished four of Newbould's six seasons as their secretary-manager in the bottom half of the First Division, with a highest placing of sixth (out of 18) in 1902 and a lowest of 15th (out of 20) in the campaign they had just completed.

True, the Manchester club had won the FA Cup only two years earlier—in the season immediately after Derby's debacle at Bury's hands—and they had ended second, third and fifth in the table since promptly regaining the First Division status they had lost in 1902. But there was one massive disadvantage. Those achievements had been newly sullied by a scandal that had left them in total disarray.

Tom Maley, the man Newbould replaced at City's helm, had just been suspended *sine die*, along with chairman W. Forrest, following an FA inquiry into payments made by the club, and two other directors and 17 players had been banned for seven months in addition to the imposing of fines. The club had to fork out £250, the players £900 between them. All this after Welsh 'wizard' Billy Meredith, the freescoring winger whose trademark was the toothpick he chewed, had already been suspended for the whole of the past season for allegedly trying to bribe an Aston Villa player.

The FA lifted Tom Maley's suspension in 1911. He managed Bradford Park Avenue from February that year until early in 1924, after which he had a short spell as manager at Southport before leaving the game. Two of his brothers were also soccer managers— Willie with Glasgow Celtic, Alex with Hibernian and Crystal Palace. Tom's son, Charles, was secretary of Leicester City and Bradford City.

For Manchester City, it was handicap enough to have been deprived of Meredith for the 1905–06 season, for he had been the key player in their Second Division promotions of 1898–99 and 1902–03, and their first FA Cup triumph of 1904. Now, just as they were preparing to welcome him back, they had to continue to cope without him—a loss that became an even bigger blow when neighbouring United made it their gain as soon as the Welshman was available again. Worse still from City's viewpoint, Meredith was joined in his move across Manchester by three of his fellow expelled colleagues, Bannister, Burgess and Turnbull, after they had served their suspensions. They made their United debuts on New Year's Day 1907, in a home win over Aston Villa gained with a goal from 'Sandy' Turnbull.

In the following season, all four helped United to win the First Division championship for the first time, with Turnbull the leading scorer. Then Meredith and Turnbull were in the first United team to carry off the FA Cup in 1909, Turnbull scoring the only goal of the final against Bristol City, and both again featured prominently in the club's second League title triumph of 1910-11.

To the 362 League and Cup matches he had played for Manchester City, scoring 150 goals, Meredith added 332 games and 35 goals for Manchester United before a dispute over wages led to his transfer back to City in the summer of 1921. He had already turned out again for City just over 100 times as a guest during the First World War, and although he made only 32 further League and Cup appearances for them he did not finally bow out until after he had played in a 1924 Cup semi-final against Newcastle (who went on to win the trophy) while in his 50th year. After that, with 29 years as a League footballer behind him, plus 48 full caps in a 25-year international career, he ran a public house in Manchester. He was 83 when he died in 1958.

'Sandy' Turnbull, who totalled 364 games and 160 goals with the two Manchester clubs, formed a highly profitable striking partnership with his namesake Jimmy Turnbull, a United signing from Clapton Orient, but had his career cut short by the war. He was killed in action in France, near Arras, in May, 1917. Burgess, a full-back from Glossop, and Bannister, a forward from Chorley, played less prominent roles, but both totted up more than a century of appearances in Manchester service.

Two of the players Harry Newbould had to bring into a largely remodelled Manchester City side when he began his daunting task of picking up the pieces left by the wholesale bans had Derby County connections. One was Frank Davies, the former Rams reserve goalkeeper acquired from Glossop North End the month before Newbould took over; the other was centre-half Bill Eadie, a Scot the new manager signed from Greenock Morton along with an inside-right named Grieve who played in an otherwise all-international attack. Eadie was to help both City and later Derby to promotion as Second Division champions, but his League career ended with the outbreak of the war that limited him to just the 1914–15 season in the Rams' defence.

Newbould inherited three of City's capped forwards, though it was not until a year after the manager had left Derby for Manchester that one of them, centre-forward Irvine Thornley, played his one game for England in a 1–1 draw with Wales at Fulham. The two others were right-winger George Stewart, who had first been chosen by Scotland while with Hibernian, and inside-left Lot Jones, who won 18 Welsh caps while with City and two more after moving to Southend United.

The fourth international forward in City's attack was Jimmy Conlin, an outside-left who gained his solitary England cap in a 2–1 defeat by Scotland, in Glasgow, only a few months before Newbould signed him from Bradford City. Conlin was another of the professional footballers who lost their lives in the Great War, killed in action while serving in the Army in 1917.

Newbould must have begun to doubt the wisdom of his sudden move from Derby when City got off to a start that was surely well beyond his worst fears. On the opening day of the 1906–07 season they finished a 4–1 home defeat by Woolwich Arsenal with only six men as one player after another collapsed with heat exhaustion in soaring temperatures. Two days later, a team showing only two changes despite those drastic effects of Saturday's sun suffered a 9–1 mauling at Everton.

Thirteen goals against were indeed unlucky for Davies as he then lost the place into which Walter Smith, signed from Leicester Fosse, settled for most of the nine seasons leading up to the war. Whereas Davies faded out, Eadie prospered after having the good fortune not to be brought in for his City debut until straight after that nightmare beginning to Newbould's reign at Hyde Road, where Derby County (beaten 4–0) had been City's first Division One opponents in 1899, and where City, formerly Ardwick FC, continued to be based until the switch to Maine Road in 1923. In making more than 200 appearances over eight seasons before his departure to Derby, Eadie proved a most worthy successor to the former Celtic pivot Tom Hynds, who was transferred to Woolwich Arsenal when he and the other banned City players were put up for sale at a Manchester hotel on becoming available again towards the end of 1906.

Newbould steadied the City ship with several other astute signings, but he literally had an up-and down existence in equalling the six-year managerial stint he had put in at the Baseball Ground before leaving to take over as secretary of the Players' Union, as the Professional Footballers' Association was then known. After his new club had gone uncomfortably close to accompanying his old one out of the First Division in 1907, they soared to a final third place a year later, themselves went down the season after that, then gained an instant promotion that was followed by two more narrow escapes from relegation. But for a late revival during which they dropped only three points in ten games, Newbould would almost certainly have left City back in Division Two.

Overall, however, he handled a difficult job with some expertise, especially in still having the ready eye for talent that had also enabled him to engage quite a number of outstanding players for Derby County. Among the men the Rams took on while their directors acted upon Newbould's recommendations were four who played for their country: Harry Maskrey, Charlie Morris, George Richards and Ben Warren.

Of that quartette, the only one not to play in the 1903 Cup debacle against Bury was Maskrey, then just a few months into a Derby career in which he became an admirable addition to the club's line of Derbyshire-born capped goalkeepers who get a later chapter to themselves. The side so shaken by the Shakers contained only four members of the team defeated by Sheffield United in the final four years before: Jack Fryer, who was Maskrey's almost direct predecessor, Jimmy Methven, Johnny May and John Boag. In addition to Morris, Warren, Archie Goodall and the left-wing pairing of Richards and Davis, the men who took over were outside-right Joe Warrington and Bloomer's deputy at inside-right, Charlie York.

Although the right wing was Warrington's best position, outside-left was the only other one he did not fill of the five the attack then comprised in making fewer than 40

League and Cup appearances for the Rams before his move to Brentford a year after the Bury humiliation. He put in further short spells with Portsmouth and New Brompton before returning to Derbyshire with Chesterfield in the autumn of 1907. Edinburgh-born York arrived in Derby from Reading as a centre-forward, but also had only restricted opportunities before moving to Sunderland midway through his second season at the Baseball Ground. His stay at Roker was even shorter, as was his next one back in Scotland with Hearts before he went south again to join Southampton.

Charlie Morris was a product of Chirk, the Welsh town that also included Billy Meredith among the many top-grade footballers it spawned. Before making soccer his full-time profession, Morris worked down a Welsh mine for eight years, and he was not even a regular member of the Chirk side when he was awarded his first Wales cap in February, 1900. It was a salutary experience, Scotland winning 5–2 in Aberdeen, but there were to be 26 more—the second in a 2–0 victory over Ireland at Llandudno a few weeks later, the third in a 1–1 draw with England in Cardiff the month before Derby County beat several rivals for his signature in April that year.

Joe Blackett, a former Gateshead and Loughborough Town full-back who arrived from Wolves the same month, started the 1900–01 season as Jimmy Methven's partner in the Rams' defence, and it was as a centre-half deputy for Archie Goodall that Morris made his League debut for the club in an away defeat by Manchester City towards the end of the following October. By then, however, Blackett's form was being affected by ill health and soon afterwards the decision to rest him from a home match with Blackburn Rovers gave Morris the chance of a recall in his usual position. He never looked back, giving a typically cultured display in a 4–0 win that paved the way to his becoming a

Charlie Morris, a full-back in the classic mould.

regular choice for more than 300 games over the next decade. Blackett, meanwhile, did the rounds with Sunderland, Middlesbrough, Luton Town and Leicester Fosse before being appointed Rochdale's player-manager.

Morris consistently showed himself to be one of the finest defenders Derby County have ever possessed, tackling with unerring precision and showing a marked aptitude for dealing capably with the ball from all angles. A full-back in the classic mould, he was among the best players in British football at his peak, an admirable successor to the County captaincy.

Although defence was naturally his chief responsibility, he did find time to score a couple of goals. Both came during the 1906–07 season in which the Rams, freshly under Jimmy Methven's management after Newbould's unexpected departure, lost their place in the First Division. He opened his account in their first home League match, a 2–2 draw with Manchester United; he completed it in the replay of a first-round FA Cup replay against Chesterfield.

Following a 1–1 draw in that all-Derbyshire tie at the Baseball Ground, Derby led 2–1 in the replay, in front of a then record crowd of some 14,000 for the Chesterfield ground, when play had to be abandoned because of bad light seven minutes from the end of extra time.[1] As the game had lasted for more than the normal 90 minutes, the FA ruled that the replayed replay should be on a neutral ground, and it was therefore at Trent Bridge, Nottingham, that Morris's final first-team goal sealed a 4–0 win for the Rams. Unfortunately for them, they failed to get past West Bromwich Albion in the third round, conceding two goals without reply at the Hawthorns after only narrowly knocking out Lincoln City, lowly visitors from Division Two.

Lincoln, founder members of the Second Division in 1892, finished the 1906–07 season next to the foot of the table but were saved from being one of the two clubs to drop out in favour of Fulham and Oldham Athletic because Burton United, the bottom club, lost their place in company with Burslem Port Vale, who resigned after ending 16th out of 20. Lincoln were voted out after finishing last the following season, re-elected a year later to the exclusion of Chesterfield, ousted by Grimsby Town in 1911, and brought back again in place of wooden spoonists Gainsborough Trinity in 1912. They were voted out yet again in favour of Cardiff City after being next to last in 1920, but became founder members of the Third North (along with Chesterfield) in 1921.

As Derby's first Welsh international, Charlie Morris missed only nine British Championship matches in winning 21 of his caps during his ten years at the Baseball Ground before moving to Huddersfield Town, then newly elected to the Second Division, in the 1910 close season. Though into his thirties by that time, he played his last three games for Wales during the one year he spent with the Yorkshire club before returning to his home country with Wrexham. He later went back to Chirk, where he died early in 1952, aged 71.

With Huddersfield, where his new clubmates included Ben Hall's brother, Morris made an impressive early reappearance at Derby in a 1–1 draw. The *Derby Express* described him as 'the schoolmaster of Huddersfield Town', adding:

---

1. The existing record attendance at Saltergate is 30,968, for a Second Division match in which Chesterfield defeated Newcastle United 2–0 on April 7th, 1939.

He is their coach and captain, and no side could wish for a better man. He not only knows the game from A to Z but his is also a model footballer. He has never tasted strong drink in his life, and his conduct, both on and off the field, is such that one wishes all players were like him.

Cricket benefited from Morris's expert touch, too. He was a successful opening batsman for Chirk and Denbighshire, and for several years after leaving Derby he was professional to the Duke of Westminster's team. He was also coach to Wrexham schools at the summer game.

Just as Morris was an ideal replacement for Derby County at left-back, so was Ben Warren for Jack Cox at right-half. Cox, who was known to his colleagues as 'the Squire of Spondon' (his birthplace on Derby's outskirts), was an automatic selection, making almost 250 appearances, over the eight seasons from his signing from Long Eaton Rangers in 1891 until 1899, when, shortly after being a losing Cup finalist for the second time, he preceded George Davis as an emigrant to Canada. He went into business as a painter and decorator in his adopted country, returning across the Atlantic to fight in the 1914–18 War, and he reached the ripe old age of 87 before his death in Toronto in mid-1957.

Cox had all the soccer attributes—an uncanny positional sense, strength in the tackle, accuracy in passing, and telling heading ability. He was well worth more than the single England cap he received in a 2–0 victory over Ireland in Belfast towards the end of his first full season with Derby County. In 1895–96, the season in which the Rams were runners-up to Aston Villa and progressed to the Cup's last four, he formed an all-international half-back line with Archie Goodall and George Kinsey.

Ben Warren, who hailed from Newhall, only a few miles from Swadlincote in the south of Derbyshire, first came to Harry Newbould's attention by chance. He was signed after giving an impressive display for Newhall Swifts in a match at Swadlincote which the Derby manager decided to watch only because the game he had originally planned to attend at nearby Stapenhill was postponed.

At that time, the wing-half positions in the Rams' first team were in the capable hands of Jack Cox and Johnny May, with Charlie Leckie, a forceful Scot from Alva, near Alloa, first in line to take over when Cox left. Consequently, Warren spent most of the 1901–02 season at inside-left, from where he was top scorer with eight goals, including a hat-trick at Lincoln, on the Cup run that Sheffield United ended in a second semi-final replay.

Warren also made occasional appearances at centre-half and centre-forward, but, with the faithful Leckie forced into the background after more than a hundred games, the 'manly son of Newhall' (as one paper described him) soon afterwards settled into the right-half berth that was best suited to the strong-tackling, direct and hard-working methods which made him such a great favourite among the Derby fans.

In his prime, Warren was widely regarded as the best wing-half in the Football League, boosted by a shoulder charge as fearsome as Archie Goodall's, and he would almost certainly have taken his total of League and Cup games for Derby County beyond the third century, instead of sticking on 269, but for the Rams' relegation to the Second Division for the first time in 1907. Having with some difficulty been persuaded to stay on for another season, he left, in August, 1908, to resume his First Division career with Chelsea, who paid £1,250 for him.

For much of the 1907–08 campaign, Derby looked set to regain their lost status at the first attempt, only to be beaten in each of their last five matches and fade away to sixth place. Three of those defeats were suffered by a lone goal, one of them most frustratingly away to Lincoln City, who were reduced to ten men and were heading for the League exit. The County finished six points behind runners-up Leicester Fosse, who went up with champions Bradford City.

Ben Warren's transfer to Chelsea brought him only a two-season reprieve in the top flight, for the London club were relegated with Bolton Wanderers in 1910. He helped them to third place in Division Two, just a couple of points away from immediate promotion, and also to reach the Cup semi-finals, during the 1910–11 season in which he increased his number of England caps to 22. The high degree of competence this zealous, but scrupulously fair, wing-half attained can be gauged from the fact that he did not miss any of the 19 matches England played from February 17th, 1906, when he made his international debut in a 5–0 beating of Ireland in Belfast, to the first day of June in 1909, when he scored his second goal for his country in an 8–1 crushing of Austria in Vienna. It was also against Austria, again in their capital, that he first scored

Jack Cox, the 'Squire of Spondon'.

Ben Warren, the 'manly son of Newhall', wearing one of his international caps.
(Derby Evening Telegraph)

for England the previous year. The margin on that occasion was 11–1, only two days after he had played a prominent part in the 6–1 defeat of the Austrians in England's first full international match on foreign turf.

The gulf that then existed between England and Continental teams was further demonstrated by the other big wins gained on those tours. Hungary, whose Magyar Marvels were to humble England so emphatically during the Puskas and Hidegkuti era of the 1950s, were beaten 7–0 in Budapest when England's team included Warren as a Derby County player in 1908, and by 8–2 when he went back there as a Chelsea man the next summer. Indeed, England in general enjoyed much mastery in those days, to such an extent that they lost just once while Warren was in their ranks—and that by only the odd goal of three on his third international appearance, against Scotland in Glasgow.

Warren won the first 13 of his consecutive caps while with the Rams, and it was back at the Baseball Ground that he was restored to the England team against Ireland in 1911 after his sequence had been interrupted for the three British Championship matches a year earlier while he had been out of action after undergoing an internal operation at St Thomas's Hospital. The Irish were defeated 2–1, and, after a more comfortable 3–0 win over Wales at Millwall, he played in what was to be his last international match, a 1–1 draw with the Scots at Everton. That was on April 1st, 1911, and after the first ten games of the following season he also dropped out of the Chelsea side that did go on to gain promotion—as runners-up to Derby County.

Warren's 361st and last League game (there were also 42 Cup-ties) was away to Clapton Orient on October 28th, 1911, when he severely damaged the muscles of his right knee. He would have resumed after recovering from that injury but for the breakdown soon afterwards of his mental health, a particularly tragic development for a man who had striven so intensely to keep himself in splendid physical shape. The strain of attempting to maintain fitness at the highest level after his operation, added to the pressures of travelling to and from Newhall, where he had insisted on continuing to live after his transfer to Chelsea, forced his premature retirement as a player after he had completed just over a century of games for the London club and quickly led to his early death.

The parlous state to which he had descended became obvious when he was found wandering in Derby's Nottingham Road, wearing only a collar and tie. Certified insane, he had to be admitted to the asylum in the Mickleover district of Derby, where he died in January, 1917, aged only 37.

Of the several benefit matches arranged on behalf of his dependants, the most successful was the one between North and South teams staged by Chelsea. It attracted a crowd of more than 15,000, which produced a welcome nest-egg for his wife, a niece of 'Jonty' Staley, the Derby County full-back. Their son Harry also played League football professionally, but, as a centre-half, he took part in only just over 30 first-team games with his four clubs before joining Folkestone as player-manager while still in his twenties.

Early in the Second World War, Harry Warren had the unusual experience of managing at the same time two clubs, Chelmsford and Southend (who then shared Chelmsford's ground). He altogether had 16 seasons in charge of Southend United before making a move he came to regret by taking on a difficult job at Coventry that soon led to his unhappy departure from soccer management. He was just of pensionable age when he died at Leigh-on-Sea in 1968.

CHAPTER 11

Bought by the Boro

An unpopular order to sell leads to FA inquiry – The first £1,000 transfer – Common penalty ends away drought – Curb on transfer fees fails – Six for Steve as record win is equalled – Sent off at Goodison – Boro and Bloomer banned – Signings stave off relegation for Boro, but Derby go down – Bailey answers emergency – More fines and suspensions at Ayresome

ONE OF THE LAST THINGS Harry Newbould did for Derby County was also the most unpopular. On March 15th, 1906, on the instructions of the Rams' directors, he sold Steve Bloomer to Middlesbrough. Financial considerations dictated this controversial transfer, which dismayed everybody devoted to the club—not least the player himself—and cast a cloud that swiftly brought the relegation Boro themselves were then struggling to avoid.

It was only at the second attempt that the Tees-siders secured the services of the man who will always stand high among the game's greatest goalscorers. A year earlier, Derby's rejection of their original bid, also made under the threat of demotion to the Second Division, had prompted Boro still to shake the soccer world by paying out the first £1,000 transfer fee for another England forward.

The player for whom that price tag, roundly and universally condemned as outlandish and foolhardy, has gained him a permanent place in the record books was Alf Common, of Sunderland. Four years before, he had left Roker Park for Sheffield United at a cost of £325, and had helped the Blades to win the FA Cup before being sold back to the Wearside club for the then record £520.

By one of those freaks of the fixture list, Common returned to Bramall Lane to make his debut for Middlesbrough—and, even more remarkably, they gained their first away win for two years as his goal from the penalty spot began the revival that ensured safety. Boro finished only two points clear of the drop, but, as it turned out, they would not have gone down anyway, for that was the season in which the bottom pair, Bury and Notts County, were reprieved by the extension of the First Division from 18 clubs to 20.

In 1905–06, however, Middlesbrough's plight deepened. So it was that, less than three months after being temporarily suspended by the Football Association for not paying a £250 fine that had been imposed for making irregular payments, they plunged back into the transfer market not only for Bloomer but also for Billy Brawn, an England winger who had been in Aston Villa's Cup-winning team against Newcastle the previous year, and Freddie Wilcox, also a forward, from Birmingham. The ban on Boro, in January, 1906, was lifted after their chairman, Lieutenant-Colonel T. Gibson-Poole, had cleared the fine with his personal cheque. But for that, they would have been unable to fulfil their League fixture at Derby on the following Saturday, when Bloomer and Common were the scorers in a 1–1 draw.

The fee Derby received when Bloomer reluctantly left to link up with Common was influenced by the fact that the FA had become so concerned about the principle of the transfer system since the record deal that they had decided 'no club shall be entitled to pay or receive any transfer fee or other payment exceeding £350 upon, or in respect of, the transfer of any player'. This amendment to Rule 29 had a serious defect, however. Although agreed to at a meeting of the FA committee at the end of March, 1905, it did not come into effect until the beginning of 1908. This gave the clubs plenty of time in which to devise ways of getting around the new regulation, and as a result it became so unworkable that the limit was withdrawn only just more than two months after its eventual introduction.

In Bloomer's case, the amount Middlesbrough paid was brought up to a more fitting figure than the FA proposed—somewhere between various estimates ranging from 'actually £700' to 'about £2,000'—by the inclusion as a makeweight of Emor ('Jack') Ratcliffe, a full-back who had made only 16 first-team appearances since joining Derby County from Loughborough Corinthians nearly four years previously. He was to make a mere nine more during his short stay with Boro.

Bloomer, at the other end of the transfer scale, departed with 419 games and 273 goals for the Rams behind him. He had three times broken the club's individual League scoring record for a season, raising it from the 15 of John Goodall in 1891–92 to 19 in 1893–94, 22 in 1895–96, and to 24 in 1896–97 (a total he again achieved in 1898–99 and 1900–01). He also twice set the record for all games in one season, from the 21 of Johnny McMillan in 1893–94 to 27 in 1895–96 and then to 31 in 1896–97.

Derby's individual record for League goals in a season was raised to 27 by Alf ('Snobby') Bentley in 1907–08, to 30 by Bentley in 1909–10, equalled by Harry Bedford in 1929–30, increased again, to 37, by Jack Bowers in 1930–31, and equalled again, by Ray Straw, in 1956–57. The club's scoring record for all matches in one season was raised to 32 by Bentley in 1908–09, to 39 by Bowers in 1930–31, and to 43, again by Bowers, in 1932–33.

Of Bloomer's 273 goals for Derby before his move to Middlesbrough, six came out of the nine the Rams scored without reply in equalling their eight-year-old record League victory against Wolves in a home game with the Wednesday on January 21st, 1899.[1] As already recalled, he bagged four goals in another match with Wolves, and there were 16 other occasions on which he scored three in a game before moving to the North-East. After his return to the Rams, of which more in its turn, there were two more, giving him another club record of 18 hat-tricks that has been most closely approached by Jack Bowers (11) and Harry Bedford (10). Bowers also had five fours,

---

1. Six goals in one game are still the Rams' individual record. Seven players have scored five: 'Sandy' Higgins, v. Aston Villa (home), December 28th, 1889; Johnny McMillan, v. Wolves (home), January 10th, 1891; Jim Moore, v. Crystal Palace (home), December 25th, 1922; Hughie Gallacher, v. Blackburn (away), December 15th, 1934; Dave McCulloch, v. Mansfield

Bedford three. In his second spell with Derby, Bloomer scored 59 goals in 106 matches, taking him to literally grand totals of 332 goals for the County in 525 appearances.

Apart from his suspension over the Burton Wanderers affair, the one big blot on Bloomer's record before his move to Middlesbrough was to be banned again, this time for 14 days, on being sent off against Everton at Goodison Park early in December, 1899. Already booked, he 'apparently kicked B Sharp' (as one report put it) during a melee in the home goalmouth, but it was said that 'the consensus of opinion was that he was led by the utmost provocation to forget himself.' Bert Sharp, a full-back, was the brother of the better-known Jack Sharp,

Alf Common, the first £1,000 footballer.

Steve Bloomer of England. His six goals helped Derby to equal their record League victory.
(Derby Evening Telegraph)

Town (home), January 9th, 1943; Roger Davies, v. Luton Town (home), March 29th, 1975; Kevin Hector, v. Finn Harps (home), September 15th, 1976. McCulloch's five were scored in a wartime cup qualifying competition, Hector's in a UEFA Cup-tie. The others came in League games.

an England international at both football and cricket, who scored one of the goals in Everton's 3–0 victory and was at one time unsuccessfully sought by the Rams.

Having left Derby, according to one anonymous pundit, 'with a heavy heart', Bloomer soon found himself once more in trouble with soccer's authorities. First, however, there was the task of trying to help Boro to preserve their threatened status, and he had the misfortune to make a start in complete contrast to Common's as his new club crashed to a 6–1 defeat away to leaders Liverpool, who were heading for their second Division One title. The first of the six goals he was to score in Middlesbrough's last nine games of the season soon followed, earning a point at Notts County, but although he was also among the scorers in big home wins over Stoke and Manchester City, the final day dawned with Boro still in acute danger of the drop. They and Bury were immediately above already-relegated Wolves, both one point behind Nottingham Forest. With Bury winning 3–0 at Sunderland, Forest losing 4–1 at Everton and Middlesbrough drawing 1–1 at Blackburn with a goal from Bloomer, these were the final positions at the foot of the table, Boro surviving on goal average as Forest joined Wolves in the dropping zone:

	P	W	D	L	F	A	Pts
Bury	38	11	10	17	57	74	32
Middlesbrough	38	10	11	17	56	71	31
Nottingham Forest	38	13	5	20	58	79	31
Wolverhampton W.	38	8	7	23	58	99	23

Middlesbrough had made themselves unpopular with their transfer dealings in twice so narrowly avoiding relegation, and the FA were forced to take action when rumours began to circulate that several clubs, wishing to see Bury go down instead, had assisted Boro in the purchases of new players they had made in their successful attempt to buy their way to safety.

In May, 1906, shortly after the season had ended, an FA Commission in Manchester examined Middlesbrough's books, and also questioned officials from Derby, Aston Villa and Birmingham. The findings were so unsatisfactory that Boro were fined £50, and, after further inquiries extending over the next year, a special Commission was set up to investigate the club's entire financial situation.

The Boro's chairman escaped censure by paying back the £500 it was discovered he owed the club through sometimes retaining the takings and paying the bills out of his own account, but manager Alex Mackie, who had resigned in the meantime and made his punishment academic by quitting soccer to go into the licensing trade, was suspended because of his involvement with the irregular payments to players. While with his previous club, Sunderland, Mackie had been suspended for three months by the FA after Andy McCombie, a full-back who also played for Newcastle, had claimed he had been given £100 to start a business. According to Sunderland it had been a loan, but an examination of their books had revealed irregularities.

The inquiry into Middlesbrough's affairs also brought Bloomer another fortnight's ban when it was found that he had received an unauthorised bonus of £10 to re-sign for the 1906–07 season. He returned from that third FA suspension to end both of his first two full seasons with Middlesbrough as their top scorer on 20 and 12 goals respectively—jointly on the second occasion with Sam Cail, a centre-forward from the Army who later played for Stalybridge Celtic. In the first of those seasons, while

Bloomer-less Derby County were relegated from the First Division for the first time (and Forest gained immediate promotion back to it), Boro rose to mid-table; in the second one, 1907–08, the Tees-siders attained their then highest final position of sixth.

That improvement was made under the first player-manager they appointed in filling the vacancy left by Mackie. The newcomer, who, for an outlay of £500, stiffened the defence besides also shouldering secretarial responsibilities, was Andy ('Daddler') Aitken, a captain of Scotland who had helped Newcastle to two FA Cup finals, promotion, and the first of their League titles—and whose sustained brilliance into his thirties was to earn him further caps while with both Middlesbrough and Leicester Fosse.

The upturn, if only temporary, in Boro's League fortunes was offset, however, by a distinct lack of success in the FA Cup. In the last three of their four seasons in the competition while Bloomer was with them they fell at the first fence; in the other one they went out in the second round, at Brentford, after two goals from the wily Steve had prompted a home win over Northampton. It was as if the hoodoo that had dogged Derby during his days at the Baseball Ground had followed him up to Ayresome, but George Allison, harking back to when he was a journalist on his native Tees-side before becoming a director and manager of Arsenal, offered a different explanation for the defeat at Brentford that came the Saturday after Bloomer had also scored twice in a home League win against Bury. In his book *Allison Calling*, he wrote:

> I remember vividly one result of a director being a little too over-enthusiastic. We were travelling to play a Cup match. Into the saloon came the director, for a word with Bloomer. 'Good old Steve', he said cheerfully. 'Keep it up! Two goals last week, two more tomorrow, boy! You're the fellow to pull us through! Have a cigar!' This apparent show of favouritism was much resented by the other players. 'No cigars for us, no goals for you', was what they told Bloomer. And sure enough next day there was abundant evidence in their play to prove that they meant what they said. We lost the Cup-tie.

A week later, Bloomer was back on the goal standard in a comfortable home victory over…Derby County, warnings of whose imminent descent had sounded when they had failed to score in six of their ten remaining games of the previous 1905–06 season following Bloomer's deplored departure—an ominous decline underlined by 6–0 and 7–0 crushings at Villa Park and Wolverhampton. A final position of 15th out of 20, after having started with five consecutive victories that included a Bloomer hat-trick against Preston, had left them only four points clear of the relegation zone they were unable to avoid a year later. Dragged down by a continued dearth of goals (they shared the division's lowest total of 41 with bottom club Stoke), their fate was sealed on April 20th, 1907, when a missed penalty led to a 3–1 defeat by Bristol City in their last home match.

With flickering hopes of escape faintly fanned by a sudden rush of blood that conjured up a 5–2 win against Everton at the Baseball Ground the Saturday before, the Rams had the chance to pull City back to 2–2 near half-time when Freddie Wheatcroft, an Alfreton-born England amateur international, was brought down in the penalty area. Ben Warren was usually to be relied upon from the spot, but goalkeeper Billy Demmery parried his shot and then fisted the ball out when he headed it back from the rebound. As it again ran loose, Warren charged in for his third attempt, only to concede a free kick.

Wheatcroft, a schoolmaster, was persuaded by Jimmy Methven to turn professional after twice helping Fulham to win the Southern League title, and after leaving the Rams he was with Swindon Town when they also twice took that championship. He was killed while serving as a lieutenant with the 5th East Surrey Regiment in France during the 1914–18 war.

The only goal Derby scored in losing to Bristol City came from right-winger Arthur Armstrong, a former circus acrobat who was making his League debut after playing in local football with Ripley Athletic and Bakewell. It was also the only goal he scored for the first team, in which he made just three more appearances before going into the Southern League with Brighton and Hove Albion. From there he made his way back to Derbyshire with Heanor Town by way of Pontypridd and Loughborough Corinthians.

A week after the failure against Bristol City, the season ended for Derby County with another defeat, by the odd goal in five away to Woolwich Arsenal. The Rams' marksmen that day were their joint top scorers in the League that season, George Davis and Jimmy Long, whose total of a mere eight apiece, both from 32 games, emphasised the main weakness that cost the club their place in the top section in their 19th season of League membership. Long, signed from Reading in the turbulent wake of Bloomer's exit, after having left Clyde to enter English football with Grimsby Town, was the leader overall with the addition of one Cup goal , and he just managed to reach double figures when he led the attack for most of his only other season with the club, their first in the Second Division.

The Rams went into that 1907–08 season without another player they had hoped could fill the Bloomer void. This was John Wood, whose first game, which resulted in a 1–0 home defeat by Bolton Wanderers, was also Steve's last before his transfer. Wood was a regular choice, mainly at inside-right, from then until near the end of the relegation season, but he scored only seven goals in his 40 games and was allowed to leave for Manchester City.

Wood, later with Plymouth Argyle, was the second player of that name in Derby's team during those difficult days. The other was Alf Wood, a defender of previous experience with Burslem Port Vale, Stoke City and Aston Villa who for two seasons was a determined left-half, in a middle line completed by the Bens Warren and Hall, before leaving for Bradford.

Left to right: Jimmy Long, Derby's top scorer in the first season after Bloomer's move to Middlesbrough, and the two Woods, Alf and John.

This was how the bottom six clubs finished the 1906–07 season of Derby County's descent:

	P	W	D	L	F	A	Pts
Liverpool	38	13	7	18	64	65	33
Bury	38	13	6	19	58	68	32
Manchester City	38	10	12	16	53	77	32
Notts County	38	8	15	15	46	50	31
Derby County	38	9	9	20	41	59	27
Stoke City	38	8	10	20	41	64	26

For most of the following season the Rams led the way in the Second Division, but they lost each of their last five matches and fell away to sixth place—six points behind Leicester Fosse, who went up as runners-up to Bradford City. A year later the Rams were fifth, but the gap widened to eight points; the season after that they finished fourth, only one point adrift of champions Manchester City and below runners-up Oldham Athletic and third-placed Hull City only on goal average. Promotion at last seemed assured until they slipped up against Bradford and Oldham during a demanding April run-in, and they arrived at the last day needing to win at West Bromwich to go up provided that Hull lost at Oldham (which they did, by 3–0).

As Manchester City were narrowly defeated at Wolverhampton in their final match, Derby would have been level with them on points in the second promotion place if they had beaten Albion, but they had to settle for a scoreless draw under the handicap of an early injury to Horace Bailey, a Derby-born England goalkeeper who was making only his third, and last, League appearance for the club after being hurriedly signed in an emergency caused by the unfitness of first-choice Ernald Scattergood.

Bailey had played for the Rams' reserves more than ten years earlier before becoming an amateur international and also winning five full caps while on Leicester Fosse's books besides gaining a gold medal at the 1908 Olympic Games in London. He courageously kept his goal intact against West Bromwich despite twice being knocked out after returning from attention to a damaged leg. And that defiance, typical of the whole Derby defence that day, was very nearly rewarded when, from a corner in the dying seconds, a header by inside-left Jimmy Bauchop skimmed the Albion bar.

Steve Bloomer, meanwhile, had entered his 37th year and become embroiled in another Middlesbrough battle against relegation. Without a manager in that 1909–10 season following Aitken's departure to Leicester which had been provoked by a clash of personalities with someone at Ayresome Park he diplomatically declined to name, Boro scraped just two points clear as Bloomer was sidelined after nine goals in 19 games had increased his overall tally since leaving Derby to 62 in 130. All but three of those goals came in the League, with four in a 5–3 home win against Woolwich Arsenal early in 1907 his biggest haul in one match for the North-East club.

In 1909–10, which was to be his final season on Tees-side, Bloomer played in only one of Boro's last 14 matches. Among those he missed was a 1–1 draw with Newcastle into which an FA-League inquiry proved inconclusive after the referee had alleged collusion between the clubs over the result.

Soon afterwards, Middlesbrough fell into still murkier waters. They were fined £100, and Andy Walker, whose arrival in the summer of 1910 filled their managerial vacancy more than a year after Aitken had left, incurred a four-week suspension for illegally approaching a player from his former club, Airdrieonians. Then, early in 1911, an FA Commission banned Walker and chairman Gibson-Poole permanently after upholding Sunderland captain Charlie Thomson's claim that Walker had offered him a £30 bribe to ensure that Boro gained the victory in the local derby that their chairman thought would favourably influence the voters at the election in which he was standing as the Tory candidate two days later. Gibson-Poole thought wrongly, losing by more than 3,000 votes, and he was seen as the main villain of the piece by more than 12,000 people who signed an unsuccessful petition for Walker's reinstatement.

All that happened after both Bloomer and Common had left. From being the costliest player in the game, Common was transferred to Arsenal on either a free transfer or for £100, depending on which source is to be believed, after agreeing to forgo a promised £250 benefit cheque because falling gate receipts compelled some cost-cutting. Bloomer, as will be recalled in greater detail in a later chapter, went back to his beloved Derby County—for £100.

Early in the 1912–13 season, Common left an Arsenal team heading for the Second Division to join a Preston side on their way up to the First. He ended his playing career a year later as North End slid straight down again in the company of Derby County, with whom they were to gain immediate promotion in 1914–15, and became a publican in Darlington. It was there, three years after his retirement, that he died in April, 1946, aged 66.

CHAPTER 12

Methven Takes Over

Aversion to Anglo-Scots costs deserved cap – Wife influences move to Derby instead of to Burton – Nicholas Senior concedes penalties that cost place in FA Cup Final – Chance meeting with Jack Davis – Bentley the 'pocket Hercules' breaks scoring records – Fatal sequel to last-gasp Cup victory – Banned for 30 years – The 'Busy Bees' – Not everything, notably a Rams deal for Buchan, comes to he who waits

I N ONCE MORE looking within their own ranks for a manager by choosing Jimmy Methven to follow Harry Newbould in 1906, Derby County pinned their faith in one of the most faithful servants they have ever had. Unlike his predecessor, Methven was not saddled with secretarial business, but he, too, was denied a free hand in team selection, and his ventures into the transfer market were zealously vetted before being authorised by the board.

Jimmy Methven, the player and manager. He solved Derby's right-back problem for more than 500 games over 15 seasons from 1891, then became manager until 1922.

Though born in Perth, Methven lived mostly in Edinburgh before his move to Derby. A consistent and clean-kicking full-back, he played a few games for Hearts and Leith Athletic, but it was through joining the Edinburgh St. Bernard's club, at the age of 17, that he found his way to Derby County in the May of 1891, the year after being a reserve for Scotland against England. The steady form he displayed for the Rams over the next 15 seasons must have made the County and their fans regard his failure to win even one Scottish cap as great a travesty of justice as was the overlooking of the club's wing-half Johnny McIntyre during the 1920s. The aversion the international selectors north of the border had to Anglo-Scots in those days was much to be regretted.

The offer to Methven to move to the Midlands came first from Burton Swifts, but he rejected it at his wife's prompting because it also entailed the running of a hotel. That was where Derby County stepped in, and they were luckier because Johnny McMillan, one of Methven's former team-mates with St. Bernard's, was already on their books. McMillan, signed the previous December, did not have too much difficulty in persuading this most dependable of defenders to rejoin him with the Rams.

Settling straight into the side on the opening day of the season before the one Derby started with Steve Bloomer as a newcomer—and, like the ace scorer, in a match at Stoke— Methven solved a right-back problem that had arisen since Arthur Latham's switch from player to trainer. During the previous 1890–91 season six men were tried there. These included Latham himself, and ranged from William Hopkins, formerly of Derby Junction, to William Roberts, a drummer with the Sherwood Foresters at Normanton Barracks who refused to be bought out of the Army when the Rams offered him a longer-term contract.

The others were Archie Goodall, John Baker and Archie Ferguson. Baker's limited chances were confined to the later stages of that season. Ferguson, formerly of Hearts, had been Latham's full-back partner for the Rams' first two League seasons, but soon after losing his regular place he left for Preston, then Ardwick, before going to the United States, where, like Tommy Little, he played for Baltimore.

Latham, who had previously played for St. Luke's besides Derby Midland, took his number of League appearances to just short of the half-century (which he exceeded with the addition of Cup-ties) before bowing out after a heavy defeat at Burnley in November, 1890, but he was to play one more game in an emergency getting on for a dozen years later. Having accompanied the team to Blackburn in April, 1902, as trainer— a role he also filled with England on several occasions—he had to stand in as goalkeeper because Tom Harrison failed to turn up after missing his train from South Normanton. The Rams lost 3–1, and Harrison, who had made his debut as Jack Fryer's deputy in a 2–0 win at Liverpool the Monday before, did not have another first-team opportunity.

From the time of Jimmy Methven's arrival until the beginning of the 1906–07 season, when he took over the managerial reins discarded by Harry Newbould, Derby County did not have to look elsewhere for a first-choice right-back. The breach was then admirably filled by William Joseph Nicholas, who since his signing from Staines a year earlier had been kept in a reserve role by the redoubtable Methven-Morris full-back combination. Nicholas, whose son Jack captained the Rams' Cup-winning team of 1946, totted up nearly 150 first-team games, mainly in harness with Morris, over four seasons, but, sadly, he is best remembered for being the man who conceded two penalties that turned Derby County towards defeat in a 1909 Cup semi-final against Bristol City.

The first of those spot kicks, for 'hands' by Nicholas Senior, who was also known as Jack, came in the dying seconds at Stamford Bridge and enabled Willis Rippon to wipe out the lead the Rams had gained through Ted Garry, a former Glasgow Celtic player who had stepped into Steve Bloomer's old place at inside-right.

The other, disputed penalty that helped to prevent the County reaching their fourth final gave Bristol City the lead a couple of minutes before half-time in the replay at Birmingham's ground four days after the 1–1 draw, Rippon again converting. Winger Jack Davis, a product of the Alfreton area that was such a happy hunting ground for League clubs, equalised soon after the interval, but the Bristol team, then a grade above Derby as members of the First Division, recovered to triumph 2–1 with a goal from Bob Hardy.

For the final, however, City were without both Rippon and another key player, Reuben Marr, through injury, and at the Crystal Palace they had no answer to a first-half score by 'Sandy' Turnbull that gave Manchester United, the previous season's League champions, the Cup for the first of many times, and Billy Meredith another winner's medal to accompany the one he had gained with Manchester's other big club five years earlier. Turnbull almost missed the match because of a knee injury, and was persuaded to play by his captain, Charlie Roberts, only shortly before the kick-off.

The knee injury that kept Rippon out, and for which he had to undergo an operation, was suffered in a 4–1 home League defeat by Blackburn Rovers on Easter Tuesday— an unlucky 13 days after the replay against Derby, and less than a fortnight before the final. Bristol City ended the season a respectable eighth in the table, but a year later they went into their last match needing the victory they gained to make sure of staying in the First Division, and the year after that they did drop out of the top section. They were not to return there for 65 years—and then only briefly as they incurred financial problems that very nearly put Ashton Gate off the League map.

The Bristolians' relegation companions in 1911 were Nottingham Forest, the club they had defeated with four goals from John Cowell in that vital game at the end of the previous season. As it happened, City would have delayed their descent even if

W.J. Nicholas, who conceded costly penalties in an FA Cup semi-final.

Jack Davis, as he was in the 1950s, about the time of my chance meeting with him on the road from Jacksdale to Codnor Park.
(Derby Evening Telegraph)

...and in his playing days.

they had lost, for Chelsea, who went down with already-doomed Bolton, were beaten at White Hart Lane on the same day by a goal scored by a player, Percy Humphreys, they had transferred to Tottenham only a few months before.

Mention of Jack Davis, Derby's scorer in the semi-final replay defeat by Bristol City, prompts me to recall the amazing coincidence of my meeting with him at the time in the 1950s when I was doing a series of interviews with Rams players of the past for the *Derby Evening Telegraph*. All I knew was that he lived in the Ironville area of Derbyshire, and after hopping off the Trent bus that took me out there from Derby one October evening (even senior reporters did not have their own cars in those days, and I was only a junior!), I was walking along the road from Jacksdale towards Codnor Park when I chanced to ask for directions to my destination from a man who suddenly approached from out of the lamplight ahead, briskly wielding a walking stick.

'Can you tell me,' I asked, 'where Mr Jack ('Pimmy') Davis lives?' Whereupon he drew himself up smartly and replied: 'I'm Jack ('Pimmy') Davis!'

This engaging character, who inherited the family nickname of 'Pimmy' by being the eldest of five brothers, was on his way to a meeting of the Jacksdale Pigkeeping Club committee (he had then been rearing pigs and poultry for some 45 years), but when he found that I was seeking him for an interview he readily suggested that we should return to his home in King William Street at Ironville for a little chat. Having not long retired from work down the pit, he was then a very sprightly 70—he was 81 when he died in 1963—and he was still a regular cricket umpire as Bulwell's representative on the Notts and Derbyshire Border League list.

His footballing days, in which he made more than 150 appearances on Derby County's wings after attracting their attention with displays that earned him an increase in his Somercotes United match fee from one shilling (5p) to five, ended at Codnor Park in the 1925–26 season by way of Ilkeston, Sutton, Heanor and Hucknall, but he continued playing cricket until the age of 63. A free-scoring batsman, he assisted Codnor Park and the Swanwick and Loscoe colliery teams, and was also given one County Championship game by Derbyshire, against Essex at Southend in 1920.

Unfortunately, that was the worst of all Derbyshire's seasons, in which the only one of their 18 matches they did not lose was abandoned because of the weather without a ball being bowled. No fewer than 40 players were called upon, and Davis, having scored only eight and one in his two innings, was among about a dozen of them who were not invited back. Two of the other newcomers did go on to make good in first-class cricket, and also to help the county to rise from those ruins to win the Championship 16 years later. They were wicketkeeper Harry Elliott and opening batsman Harry Storer Junior, who both played for England—Elliott at cricket, Storer at soccer.

All but three of the 11 goals Derby County scored in getting through to the Cup's last four against Bristol City in 1909 were netted by Alf Bentley, who, like Jack Davis, hailed from the Alfreton mining district of Derbyshire that produced so many outstanding footballers in those days. A 5ft 5in 'pocket Hercules' of an inside-forward or centre-forward known as 'Snobby', he joined Derby in a deal that demonstrated the astuteness Jimmy Methven so often showed in his quests for new talent.

Alf Bentley, a 5ft 5in 'pocket Hercules'.

On learning of Methven's interest in his sharp-shooting attack leader, Ernie Davis, Alfreton Town's secretary, gave his close friend Harry Newbould the first chance to sign him for Manchester City, but just as Derby's manager was preparing to increase his bid to all of £75, he learned that his predecessor was not interested, so he therefore saved the Rams a precious £15 by sticking to his original offer.

Bentley, a hustler rather than a 'general', fell just short of being a great forward, but City's loss was Derby's gain to the considerable extent of 112 goals in 168 games before he moved first, in May, 1911, to Bolton Wanderers, and then, two years later, to West Bromwich, by which time his price had risen to £650.

His start with Albion was one of the most explosive on record. Within ten minutes of the kick-off against Burnley at the Hawthorns on the opening day of the 1913–14 season he had a hat-trick under his belt; six minutes from the end he rounded off a 4–1 win by scoring again. In the first post-war season of 1919–20 he picked up a First Division championship medal, and he took his overall League and Cup goals tally beyond 160 before returning via Burton Town to Alfreton Town, with whom one of his last matches was an FA Cup qualifier lost by 8–2 to a Port Vale side that included a fair-haired full-back who graduated to the captaincy of Derby County and England, Tommy Cooper.

Bentley's initial season with Derby County ended in the relegation from the First Division that came so soon after Bloomer's departure, but, as already recalled, in the following one he broke the club's individual scoring record set by the great man for League goals in a season, raising it from 24 to 27. And in the next two of his three other seasons with the Rams he first increased the total for all matches in a season, to 32, then beat his own best for League fixtures alone with 30 in 1909–10. Three times he scored four goals in a game—at Barnsley and home and away against Leeds City—but the most memorable of all those he notched for Derby was the one that won a home third-round FA Cup-tie against Plymouth Argyle on February 20th, 1909.

The header with which he broke the stalemate by netting from a free kick by George Thompson, a Geordie winger previously with North Shields and Sheffield United, was nothing extraordinary in itself. What made it so special, and so controversial, was that it came a split second before the referee blew the final whistle.

The Plymouth players, at first under the impression that they had forced a replay with a scoreless draw, surrounded the referee in desperate protest when the award of the goal became clear, but all to no avail. Sections of the crowd invaded the pitch, from which the harassed official needed a police escort. More than 70 years later, I was at the Baseball Ground when Dennis Tueart, of Manchester City, put the ball into the net at the Osmaston end right on the whistle, but on that occasion he was the split second too late and it did not matter anyway. The Rams would still have won, by 3–2, if his 'goal' had counted, though they had left it too late to save themselves from dropping out of the First Division.

Plymouth's strong feelings about what they saw as a rough deal at Derby were also put into perspective, but tragically so. One of their players, Edward McIntyre, formerly of Newcastle United and Fulham, was arrested on a charge of manslaughter after allegedly striking Nick Wallis, Argyle's trainer, on the jaw, fracturing it, when a quarrel broke out over a game of cards during the journey back to Devon.

'Snobby' Bentley, who was only 54 when he died at Derby in 1940, scored in each of the four rounds the Rams played in reaching the 1909 semi-finals, but crucially failed to find the target in both the games against Bristol City. He began with three goals against Northampton Town, two of them in a home replay victory to which Jack Davis and Thompson also contributed, then converted a penalty in a win at Leicester that was sealed by the only first-team goal Ron Trueman scored for the County in the limited opportunities he was given after being signed from Macclesfield Town.

Next came Bentley's last-ditch winner against Plymouth, after which he did all the scoring with a hat-trick in a home quarter-final victory over a Nottingham Forest side reduced to ten men by the dismissal of centre-forward Enoch ('Knocker') West. That, regrettably, was but a minor blot on West's record compared with the manner in which his career ended.

Having given Forest a 100-goal dividend on their investment of a mere fiver for his transfer back to his home county (he was born at Hucknall) from Sheffield United, he moved to Manchester United and in 1911 helped them to their second League title in four years. In taking his total of goals for them to 80, he was also their top scorer in each of the next two seasons before being caught up in a plot to 'fix' the result of a game with Liverpool at Old Trafford, for betting purposes, early in April, 1915.

Manchester United, who were threatened with relegation, defeated Liverpool 2–0, but they won only one of their remaining seven matches and finished on 30 points immediately above the bottom pair, Chelsea (29) and Tottenham Hotspur (28). There was some suggestion that Chelsea had also been victims of a 'suspect' result, and for what were termed 'special reasons', they were saved from relegation when membership of the First Division was increased from 20 clubs to 22 for the first League season after the First World War. With Derby County and Preston North End promoted from the Second Division, that left one remaining vacancy. Logically, and by the 1905 precedent of a similar extension, it should have gone to Tottenham, enabling them to stay up too, but they were outrageously outvoted by their North London rivals Arsenal, who had finished only fifth in the Division Two of 1914–15, the last League season until the war ended.

The inquiry into Manchester United's home match with Liverpool found West guilty, along with three other United players and four from Liverpool, and he received the severest punishment of the lot—the longest suspension in Football League history. It lasted for 30 years, for not until November, 1945, was it lifted. He was then well into his 62nd year.

Before Steve Bloomer's return to the Baseball Ground from Middlesbrough, Alf Bentley formed with Horace Barnes and Jimmy Bauchop a thrustful Derby forward trio affectionately dubbed the 'Busy Bees'. Indeed, during the early years of the 20th century the Rams had a preponderance of players whose surnames began with the initial 'B', sometimes as many as seven in the same side. In addition to those three—and, of course, Bloomer—there were Bagshaw, Barbour, Boag and Buckley, plus the lesser-known Bradbury, Blessington, Bromage, Blackett, Ballwill, Barker, Bevan, Bailey, Betts, Bowler, Baker, Brooks and Benfield.

George Brooks, a former Manchester City, Bury and South Shields wing-half, and inside-forward Tom Benfield, who had been an amateur with Leicester Fosse, were both killed in action in 1918—Brooks on Armistice Day, Benfield the day before, November 10th. Both played their final games for the Rams in the club's last season before their closedown for the duration of the war—that of 1915–16 during which

Benfield also guested for the Fosse and Nottingham Forest in the Midland tournaments that replaced the suspended League programme.

John Hardman, a half-back who played in 14 League games and one FA Cup-tie for Derby County in the 1913–14 season, was also killed in the First World War, while serving in France in 1917. Formerly with Oldham Athletic, he joined the Rams from Pontypridd in August, 1913, and left them for Bristol Rovers in October, 1914.

Other former Derby players who lost their lives in the Great War were the amateurs Bernard Vann and Reginald Callender. Vann, previously with Northampton Town and Burton United, led the County's attack three times during their relegation season of 1906–07, travelling to the matches from Jesus College, Cambridge. Ordained in 1913, he became an officer in the Sherwood Foresters and, killed in action at Ramicourt in October, 1918, was posthumously awarded the Victoria Cross. He had already been honoured with the Military Cross and the French *Croix de Guerre*.

Callender, a Cambridge Blue and England amateur international, made five League appearances for the Rams at outside-left in the 1913–14 season, when they were again relegated. He had earlier played once in Glossop's first team.

There was also a tragically early death for Fred Barker, a local-born forward who scored twice in only four senior games for Derby County. He was still on the club's books when he was taken fatally ill towards the end of 1904.

But for one of the rare occasions when Jimmy Methven's overtures for new talent went awry, the list of Derby players whose surnames began with a 'B' would have included a famous forward who rose to stardom with Sunderland and Arsenal. Sammy Eaton, a Derby man who played for Leicester Fosse and Luton Town, tipped off the Rams about 'a great big gawky youth' who was an amateur with Northfleet in the Kent League. Methven was equally impressed when he saw Charlie Buchan in action, and several years later he recalled:

> I set off intending to do business, but, unfortunately as it happened, on the way I met an old Derby County player, George Lloyd, commonly called 'Sandy'. We naturally started talking football, and when my desire of bringing Charlie Buchan to Derby was mentioned 'Sandy' suggested, with a view to saving money for the transfer, that he should keep Buchan 'in tow' and save him for Derby County. It was near the end of the season, and, yielding to the temptation to save money, I arranged with 'Sandy' to hold Buchan for me.

But Lloyd, who was later a director of Gillingham, and whose baker's dozen of appearances in Derby's first team included the first replay of the 1902 Cup semi-final against Sheffield United, was unable to deliver his man. He had some excuse, for the competition was decidedly keen.

Bury, then of the First Division, made an approach through Bob Dunmore, who had just joined the Lancashire club after having been a trainer with Woolwich Arsenal while Buchan had briefly been an amateur in their reserve side. The future England forward declined their tempting offer, however, because at that time he still wanted to concentrate on becoming a schoolteacher and had no real thought of making his living as a footballer.

Then 'Punch' McEwen, a Fulham scout who had been Bury's left-back in their record Cup Final defeat of Derby County, persuaded him to go to Craven Cottage for an interview, but he also refused to sign for that club even though they were prepared to let him continue his training as a teacher. The weekly wage they offered him, half the

£3 Bury had been ready to pay, was not acceptable, and his request to increase it to £2 was rejected.

That was where Leyton successfully came into the reckoning. In May, 1910, Mick Busby, their right-back and part-time scout, told him they would pay him the £3 a week, and the balance tipped in their favour with the promise of an immediate first-team place—plus the fact that his home at Plumstead was only a few miles away. In all those circumstances, Derby County were never really in with a chance of signing him, and the disappointed Methven thus missed the coup of landing a player who developed into one of the greatest inside-forwards of his generation.

Leyton's player-manager in those days, Dave Buchanan, was distinctive in a most unusual way. He was so sensitive about being completely bald that he never appeared in public without wearing a black skull cap, even when playing football. Buchan recalled that 'not once during the many games I saw him play was the cap knocked off his head, though he was an expert at heading the ball'.

Tom Priestley, a Northern Ireland international inside-forward who played for Chelsea in the Thirties, was another professional footballer who wore a skull cap to conceal his baldness. Like Buchan before soccer claimed Charlie full-time, he was a schoolmaster, rising to be a headmaster at Londonderry.

Buchan might also have been a Chelsea player if the Stamford Bridge club had not baulked at paying the £800 transfer fee Leyton asked. Instead, for £200 more, it fell to Sunderland to have the good fortune to introduce him to the First Division. In ten seasons as a big favourite at Roker Park, excluding the war years during which he won the Military Medal in the Grenadier Guards, he helped them to a League title and a Cup Final before, at the age of 33, he figured in a transfer deal that attracted plenty of publicity for being very much out of the ordinary.

Arsenal were reluctant to meet Sunderland's asking price of £4,000 for a player of such advanced footballing years, but they eventually handed over more than that amount in agreeing to a £2,000 fee and £100 for each goal Buchan scored in his first season with them. In 1925–26, when Arsenal were runners-up as Huddersfield Town completed their First Division title hat-trick, he bagged 19 in the League and two more during a Cup run that ended at Swansea in the sixth round.

Yet Buchan could have been an Arsenal player for nothing more than the £10 signing-on fee if George Morrell, then their secretary-manager, had not refused to meet his claim for 11 shillings in expenses while he had been an amateur with the club 16 years before. It was a costly decision that led Buchan away to Northfleet, and, although he left without seeking to cancel his Arsenal registration, the League Management Committee ruled in his favour when the Gunners laid claim to him by challenging his move to Leyton. The official view was that his turning professional over-rode amateur agreements.

Despite paying more than they had originally intended, Arsenal could be well satisfied with the return they got for their money after Charlie Buchan's return to their ranks as a veteran. He again had the disappointment of being in a losing Cup Final team when, in 1927, Cardiff City became the first club to take the trophy out of England, but in 120 games for the Gunners he notched 56 goals before retiring at the end of the 1927–28 season to enjoy further distinction as a journalist and radio broadcaster.

Two of those goals were scored against Derby County—the first of them the winner at Highbury when the newly-promoted Rams played their first match back in Division

One at the start of the 1926–27 programme. The margin was 2–1, but there was a big doubt about the validity of Arsenal's opening goal, a second-half penalty converted by their right-back and captain, Tom Parker, that wiped out a lead gained by Harry Storer.

The ball did hit Derby's left-back, Tom Crilly, on the hand, but, as one reporter put it, 'that it was an accident was a unanimous opinion in the press box at least, for it was a break-back on the ball, as it dropped over the head of centre-half Thoms, that did the mischief'. The writer also complained that referee T.G. Bryan, of Willenhall, was not in a position to see exactly what happened, yet he promptly pointed to the spot without consulting a linesman.

Buchan's neat deciding goal came soon afterwards, and he and Parker (but not from a penalty) were also the scorers when the Gunners gained their first away win over the Rams, by 2–0, in the return fixture the following January.

Derby, however, emphatically reversed that double defeat in Buchan's last season with Arsenal, winning 4–0 at the Baseball Ground and 4–3 in London. They also had the satisfaction of denying Charlie another goal, for all three they conceded at Highbury were credited to centre-forward Jimmy Brain—a dubious hat-trick (two of his goals were disputed) that was countered by an unrefutable one from Jimmy Gill, the former Wednesday and Cardiff forward who was one of three players signed from Blackpool by George Jobey, one of Methven's managerial successors.

The first of those players was Harry Bedford; the other Georgie Mee, whose brother Bertie, who was later also with Derby, but without getting into the first team, managed Arsenal when they completed the League and Cup double in 1970–71.

Disappointed as Derby were not to land Charlie Buchan, they did have the extreme satisfaction years later of signing another gifted Sunderland and England forward who learned a lot of his craft as a schoolboy from standing behind one of the goals at Roker Park to watch his hero Buchan in action. That, of course, was Raich Carter, who will always hold a high place on the list of the many outstanding players who have graced the Rams' attack.

Some years before missing Buchan, back in the days when they were still to appoint a manager, Derby County lost another forward who became a big success elsewhere—but in his case they had only themselves to blame for letting him slip out of their clutches. They failed to spot Chesterfield-born Sam Raybould's potential when they gave him just a few games on their right wing, not his best position, and off-loaded him to Ilkeston Town for £10. Soon afterwards he was snapped up by Liverpool, with whom, mainly as a centre-forward, he proceeded to win two championship medals in the First Division, and another in the side promoted from Division Two. His 31 goals in the 1902–03 season set a Liverpool record that was not beaten for nearly 30 years.

Unlike Buchan, Raybould did not play for England, but he turned out three times for the Football League against the Scottish League. Like Buchan, he had Sunderland and Arsenal as his last two clubs.

CHAPTER 13

Flanders Leads Youth Parade

Bagshaw capped after 13 years with Rams – Bauchop
makes the wait worthwhile – Former Derby trio
clubmates at Bradford – Barnes health scare – £2,500
transfer causes uproar – Choice of 16-year-old sparks
protest – Buckley and Jobey, doyens of the game –
Derby's youngest players

T HE FIRST of the successful deals done for Derby while Jimmy Methven was their manager brought in wing-half Jimmy Bagshaw, a member of a family of eight, who was born at a house close to the Baseball Ground on Christmas Day, 1885, nearly ten years before the Rams made that stadium their home instead of the County Ground.

Bagshaw did not take up soccer seriously until he was 16, when he joined his local side, Graham Street Primitives, and also played occasionally for Fletcher's Athletic, the team run by the firm for which he worked in the lace trade before turning professional with Derby County in August, 1906. Just over 13 years later he was the longest-serving player then on the club's books when he played for England at the age of 33 in a 1–1 draw with Ireland in Belfast.

That was Bagshaw's only full cap, but he had been reserve against Scotland the previous year and had taken part in a Victory International against Wales. He lost the inscribed medal he received for facing the Welsh, but it was returned to him six years later. The finder had himself mislaid it within a week of picking it up.

Bagshaw, the player from whom Steve Bloomer took over the captaincy on rejoining the Rams from Middlesbrough, guested for Notts County during Derby's war-time closedown, and it was back to Meadow Lane that he went when he left the Baseball Ground early in 1920. Nearly two seasons later, he moved to Watford, but the climate there adversely affected his health and he soon returned to the East Midlands, ending his playing days with Grantham and Ilkeston United.

He then lost interest in football to such an extent that he did not watch a match for three seasons before deciding to end his exile by going along to watch his Nottingham works team, Raleigh Athletic, in an FA Cup qualifier. It was a chance return that was to bring him back into the game as a Notts County scout, for he was offered that job by their then manager, Horace Henshall, after recommending to him a promising young player who caught his attention in that Cup game. Later, he switched to scouting

**Jimmy Bagshaw, in his playing days and at his home in the Lenton district of
Nottingham near the Raleigh cycle works at which he was then employed.**
(Derby Evening Telegraph)

for Forest while Harold Wightman, a fellow former Derby County player, was their
manager.

During the 1939–45 war, Bagshaw also served Forest as trainer—and England, too,
on the day in 1941 when they defeated Wales at the City Ground with four goals from
Charlton's Don Welsh. Afterwards, he continued as a Forest scout, and he was altogether
with that club for around 20 years before retiring. He was only four months from his
81st birthday when he died at Nottingham in 1966.

The keen eye for talent Jimmy Methven showed in the signing of such reliable players
as Jimmy Bagshaw was not the only attribute of a successful manager that he possessed.
Just as he displayed a canny business sense and inside knowledge in restricting the
size of the transfer fee he had to pay for Alf Bentley, so he was prepared to combine
patience and perseverance to acquire a player he particularly wanted. This 'waiting
game' did not always work, as notably in the case of Charlie Buchan, but it did so to
special effect as far as Jimmy Bauchop was concerned.

This Sauchie-born son of Stirlingshire was Glasgow Celtic's understudy to Scottish
international Jimmy Quinn, after starting out with Alloa Athletic, when he first attracted

Jimmy Bauchop, for whom the 'waiting game' paid off.

Methven's attention, but Norwich City stepped in with a higher bid than Derby's—and that was how, instead, the Rams came to obtain Ted Garry from the Glasgow club. It took another two years for the pair to be reunited at the Baseball Ground as Methven finally got his man with Bauchop's arrival from Crystal Palace, the club he had joined from Norwich, and they were later clubmates again at Bradford—along with another ex-County colleague, goalkeeper Ernald Scattergood.

Garry was unable to live up to the hat-trick start he made with Derby in a 4–0 home victory over Lincoln City on the opening day of the 1907–08 season, only a dozen days before Bentley did all Derby's scoring in a 4–2 win at Barnsley, but he re-established himself after dropping back from inside-forward to wing-half. It was there that in 1911–12, along with Bauchop and Scattergood, he helped Derby County to a promotion from the Second Division in which he was also to share with Bauchop at Park Avenue in 1913–14 while the Rams they had left were once more being relegated.

With war then breaking out, Garry went back to the Dumbarton shipyards, where he had worked as a youth, and rejoined his home club, from which he had

Ted Garry the player—and in retirement.
(Derby Evening Telegraph)

progressed to Celtic via Ayr United. After the armistice, he coached in Barcelona (Steve Bloomer obtained a similar post in Spain at about the same time) before settling down back in Derby with his wife Bertha, who was born in the town. He worked at the Rolls-Royce factory and renewed his connection with the Rams as a member of the ground staff at the Baseball Ground, where he was the directors' steward on match days.

When I met him in the early 1950s he had only recently retired and, with the boating lake at Markeaton Park one of his favourite haunts, he was maintaining the interest in model yachts that dated back to his boyhood. He was 70 when he died at his home in Drewry Lane, Derby, near the end of May in 1955.

Derby County's signing of Jimmy Bauchop came soon after Bentley's solving of the centre-forward problem that had persisted since the departure of another Scot, John Boag, to Brentford the year after the Cup crash against Bury. William Hodgkinson, whose brother Albert was capped by Wales while with Southampton after failing to break into the Rams' first team, showed some promise in his second spell with the club from Hinckley Town, doing the hat-trick in a 7–2 home win against Sunderland, but was soon allowed to leave for Plymouth. Tom Paton then moved in from Glasgow Rangers, only to slip off to Sheffield United after managing only four goals in 38 games.

Altogether, nearly a score (not the most appropriate word in the goals context) of players were tried at the head of the attack after Boag dropped out, defenders Ben Warren, Ben Hall and John May among them, before Bentley was moved from inside-forward to become a regular choice as leader of the line. Of the others, the most successful was Fred Bevan, although the number of positions he filled—all but outside-left in the attack—was almost as varied as the clubs of his career. He reached Derby after assisting Millwall Athletic, Manchester City, Reading, Queen's Park Rangers, Bury and Fulham. Afterwards, he rounded off his playing days with Clapton Orient, completing his stay there as coach for the first few years after the 1914–18 War.

It took the blending of the 'Busy Bees' to put the buzz back in Derby County's forward line. When James Rae Bauchop was brought into his favourite inside-left position alongside Bentley, Methven had a twin spearhead that produced almost two-thirds of the Rams' 72 League goals (Bentley 30, Bauchop 21) in their first season together, the promotion near-miss of 1909–10.

Allied to that fire power there was Horace Barnes, possessor of one of the fiercest of left-foot shots. He preceded Bauchop at inside-left and, after also filling three of the other then recognised forward positions (outside-right was the exception), he also followed him in that position when the Scot made a short-lived move to Tottenham before his transfer to Bradford.

Bauchop, who spent his last League seasons with Doncaster Rovers and Lincoln City after helping Bradford into the First Division, left the Rams with the creditable total of 72 goals in 135 League and Cup games. It was at Bradford that he died in 1948, aged 62.

Barnes, a Yorkshireman from Wadsley Bridge, near Sheffield, made a scoring debut for Derby as an amateur in a 2–2 draw at Blackpool only two days after impressing in a trial run with the reserves against Ripley Athletic in October, 1908. He turned professional at the end of that month, but after he had completed the season as the club's second highest scorer, with 10 goals to Bentley's 32, doctors told him that he could endanger his life by continuing to play professionally because he had an enlarged heart. Such fears, fortunately, proved unfounded. As Jimmy Methven recalled it:

> The Derby directors sent Horace to Blackpool for a month or two to see what ozone could do for him, and when he returned to Derby he looked strong enough for anything. But the directors did not want to run any risks, so they instructed me to take him for examination by an eminent heart specialist in London. After giving Horace a thorough overhaul, the specialist said the player's heart was as sound as a bell, and accounted for the doubts regarding his health by saying that he had been gaining in height too quickly for his muscle development.

Although competition for forward places hotted up as Bentley's exit was offset by the signing of Harry Leonard and Ivan Sharpe in the wake of Bloomer's return, Barnes played his part in the winning of promotion before ironically enjoying his most successful season as a scorer with two dozen League goals, and another in the Cup, while the Rams once more fell back into Division Two in 1913–14. With such a good return in a struggling side, increasing his overall total for the club to 78 in 167 appearances, he became, at 24, one of the most eagerly-sought forwards in the game, and this, coupled with his natural desire to continue playing at the top level, made his departure inevitable.

From a chasing pack that also included Woolwich Arsenal, Newcastle United, Liverpool and the Wednesday, Manchester City emerged as the front-runners, but to clinch the deal in May, 1914 they had push the transfer fee record up to the 'exorbitant height' (as one shocked observer called it) of £2,500. Leslie Knighton, who was then City's manager, recalled in his book *Behind The Scenes in Big Football*:

**Horace Barnes, whose £2,500
transfer caused an uproar.**

Oh, the uproar that £2,500 transfer caused! Agitated people wrote to the papers saying it was the end of sport in football—it would just become one horrible gamble. Men argued with each other in pubs up and down England, not about the looming menace of the Kaiser's steel-helmeted hordes, but about the price paid for Horace Barnes.

In City's colours, Barnes struck up a flourishing striking partnership with Tommy Browell, a £1,780 signing from Everton whose nickname 'Boy' originated from an autumn day in 1910 when, at the age of 18, his hat-trick for Hull City had inspired a journalist to write that 'ten men and a boy beat Stockport'. Barnes was also to have a special reason, if an unpalatable one, to remember Stockport, for during the First World War he was fined by Manchester magistrates for absenting himself from his work in a munitions factory to play against the Cheshire club (he scored one of City's goals in their 3–1 win).

In 235 League and Cup games for City, Barnes scored 125 goals, yet neither he nor Browell, who netted 139 for the club in 247, gained a full England cap. Although Barnes represented the Football League, he was to have no second international chance after being in the team beaten 3–0 by Wales in a Victory International in Cardiff in October, 1919, whereas a week later Jimmy Bagshaw helped to defeat Wales 2–1 in another Victory celebration game at Stoke and was retained for England's first full post-war match in Belfast the week after that.

Three of Barnes's goals for Manchester City deserve particular mention. In March, 1921, he got two of them in the 3–0 win that ended Burnley's record-breaking run of 30 games without defeat. And on the opening day of the 1923–24 season he obtained the first to be scored at Maine Road, in a 2–1 victory over Sheffield United, following the City's move from Hyde Road.

Including the war years, during which he scored 73 goals in as many games, Barnes was in his 11th season with Manchester City when, in November, 1924, he moved to Preston North End. A year later, he was still effective enough as a 35-year-old to command a fee of £1,250 when transferred to Oldham, for whom, as with both Derby and City, he scored on his debut. As also in his first game for the Rams, Blackpool, beaten 3–2, were the opponents.

Barnes netted one of the goals in Manchester City's 3–1 home win when he first played against Derby County in the November of 1919, but both he and his team failed to score on his three reappearances at the Baseball Ground. The first two of those games were while he was with City, who, after a scoreless draw there in the immediate return match of the first post-war season, were one of only five sides to lose in the League (by 3–0) to the relegated Rams of 1920–21. The third and last game back at Derby for Barnes was the one in which the County clinched their return to the First Division with a 1–0 defeat of Oldham in their final home fixture of 1925–26.

In 46 League and Cup games for the Latics, Barnes totalled 20 goals before being transfer-listed towards the end of his second season at Boundary Park. He then ran into another rich scoring vein outside the League with Ashton National, getting 240 goals for them in four seasons before injury finally brought his playing career to a close.

That concluding period, which took him into his forties, included his greatest gush of goals in one game—six of them in the first half-hour of a match in which he played against Port Vale for the Rest of Cheshire. In retirement, he lived on until the autumn of 1961, nearly into his 72nd year.

As he made clear in recommending to his directors that Horace Barnes should be plunged straight into League football as a raw, untried 18-year-old, Jimmy Methven was not reluctant to take a chance on youth, but in an extreme case in that respect considerable controversy was aroused by the selection of full-back Fred Flanders for a home game with Birmingham on October 15th, 1910.

About a dozen of the Rams' supporters signed a letter of protest to the selection committee on the grounds that the club's position in the Second Division table, after they had gained only two wins in their first seven matches of the season, was 'too critical to afford an experiment with so young and inexperienced a player.' Flanders, captain of the only Derby Boys side to have won the English Schools' Shield (they defeated Oxford Boys by 2–1 in the 1908 final), made that first-team debut at the tender age of 16 years and 287 days, thus becoming Derby County's youngest player in League football up to that time.

This former pupil of Gerard Street School, who had also skippered England in a junior international match against Wales at Aberdare, was captain of Shelton United Reserves when he joined the Rams in May, 1910. Despite the fears that he had been given his

Fred Flanders, whose selection at 16 provoked fans to protest because they thought him too young.

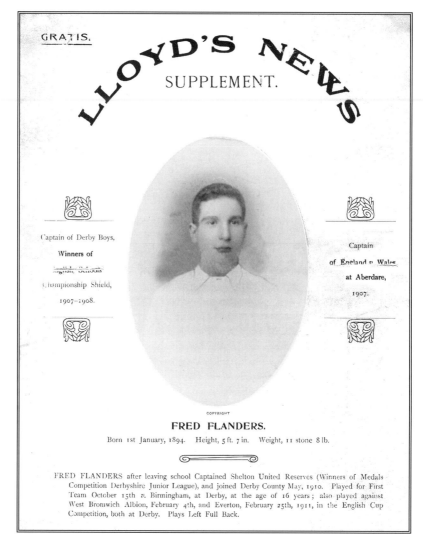

GRATIS.

LLOYD'S NEWS
SUPPLEMENT.

Captain of Derby Boys,

Winners of

~~English Schools~~

Championship Shield,

1907–1908.

Captain

of England v Wales

at Aberdare,

1907.

COPYRIGHT

FRED FLANDERS.

Born 1st January, 1894.   Height, 5 ft. 7 in.   Weight, 11 stone 8 lb.

FRED FLANDERS after leaving school Captained Shelton United Reserves (Winners of Medals Competition Derbyshire Junior League), and joined Derby County May, 1910. Played for First Team October 15th v. Birmingham, at Derby, at the age of 16 years ; also played against West Bromwich Albion, February 4th, and Everton, February 25th, 1911, in the English Cup Competition, both at Derby. Plays Left Full Back.

chance prematurely, he produced a commendable performance at left-back in the defeat of Birmingham. The only goal of the game came when Frank Womack, Flanders's opposite number, deflected into his own net a shot from Horace Barnes that would otherwise have been well covered by the goalkeeper. Barnes missed an opportunity to extend the margin of victory when he had a penalty kick saved. These were the teams:

Derby County: Scattergood; Barbour, Flanders; Garry, Hall, Bagshaw; Grimes, Bloomer, Bauchop, Barnes, Donald.
Birmingham: Dorrington; Bonthron, Womack; Corbett, Buckley, Daykin; Millington, Freeman, Jones, Draper, Lowe.

Fred Flanders, then the youngest to play for the club in League football, is second from the right among the players on the back row in this Derby County group picture of 1910–11. Those on his right (from left to right) are George Richards, who rarely played that season because of injury, Jack Atkin, Jack Nicholas, Ernald Scattergood and George Lawrence. Steve Bloomer is third from the left on the front row, with Alf Bentley and Jimmy Bauchop to his left, Billy Grimes on the extreme left, and Horace Barnes on the extreme right. In the middle row trainer Arthur Latham is on the left, manager Jimmy Methven on the right, and the first-team men are Tommy Barbour (third player from the left), Ted Garry, Ben Hall and Jimmy Bagshaw.

Frank Womack never scored for his own side in setting up a Birmingham record of 515 first-team appearances, 491 of them in the League, before ending his 20 years with the club he had captained into the First Division by leaving in 1928 to become player-manager of Worcester City, whom he guided to the Birmingham League title in his first season. In 1930 he was appointed manager of Torquay United, then led Grimsby Town into the First Division (1934) and within one game of an FA Cup Final (1936) before also piloting Leicester City to promotion as Second Division champions in 1937.

During the Second World War he managed Notts County, where he had much to do with the development of Leon Leuty, a centre-half who made good with Derby County, and after a barren spell with Oldham Athletic he rounded off his days in charge by returning to Blundell Park for the first few months of 1951 to deputise in the absence through illness of Charlie Spencer. When Spencer, who had been one of the game's first stopper centre-halves with Newcastle United before becoming Grimsby's longest-serving manager, resigned on medical advice, Womack bowed out with the appointment from Carlisle of Bill Shankly, the former Preston and Scotland wing-half who went on to make himself a Liverpool legend after also managing Workington and Huddersfield.

Birmingham's centre-half when Fred Flanders made his League debut for Derby in the autumn of 1910, Franklin Charles Buckley, was transferred to the Rams the following May, and, as Major Frank Buckley, preceded Shankly as one of soccer's most dynamic, newsworthy managers while with Wolves through the years leading up to the 1939–45 War. His three seasons with Derby County were the most successful of a playing career he began in April, 1903 at Aston Villa (with whom one of his five brothers, Chris, was both player and chairman) and continued with Brighton and both Manchester clubs before joining Birmingham.

Flanked mainly by Jimmy Bagshaw and George Richards in the middle line, this tough, uncompromising defender helped Derby to the Second Division championship in his first season with them, 1911–12, and although they were relegated again the month before he left for Bradford City in May, 1914, he performed well enough amid his team's adversity to become an England international. Unfortunately, the cap he gained against Ireland at Middlesbrough on February 14th, 1914 was his only one. And it coincided with England's first home defeat by the Irish—by 3–0 a year after they had lost in the Emerald Isle for the first time, by 2–1 in Belfast.

For five years Billy Wedlock, the tubby little Bristol City player known as 'Fatty', had made England's centre-half position his own with 25 consecutive appearances, and when that sequence ended Buckley found Tommy Boyle, of Burnley, and Joe McCall, of Preston, ahead of him in the queue to take over.

As Buckley was in his 32nd year when he did get his chance, age then counted against him besides the call for changes after the disappointing defeat by Ireland, and only three players—goalkeeper Sam Hardy, of Aston Villa, and Blackburn's Bob Crompton and Danny Shea—were retained for the match in which Wales were beaten in Cardiff a few weeks later.

Wedlock was recalled for that game, stepping off the international stage with a goal in the 2–0 win, and McCall was brought back in the Bristolian's place for the only other

Frank Buckley, an uncompromising
defender who became one of the most
newsworthy managers.

George Jobey, a canny Geordie.
(Derby Evening Telegraph)

match England played, lost by 3–1 to the Scots in Glasgow in April, 1914, before the Great War broke out. Having fought in the Boer War, Buckley was commissioned in the 17th Middlesex Regiment, the Footballers' Battalion, given command of the serving professional players, and promoted in 1916 to the rank of major he used for the rest of his life.

The leadership qualities for which he was so noted in addition to his vigorous enthusiasm for hard work were admirably suited to that wartime role, and were also to stand him in good stead on the managerial side of soccer to which he turned with the return of peace. A commanding figure, six feet tall and neither a smoker nor a drinker of alcohol, he set those around him an excellent example of dedication to the cause, and Steve Bloomer was firmly of the opinion that Buckley, not himself, should have been captain of the team that took Derby County back to the First Division in 1912.

From having seven clubs in a dozen seasons as a player, the major was to have seven more in 33 as a manager. He started out again after the war as player-manager of Norwich City, then members of the Southern League, with whom he was rejoined as trainer by Arthur Latham, who had been serving Derby County in that capacity since retiring as one of their full-backs. It was too late, however, for the then 36-year-old Buckley to make a sustained comeback as a player, especially as he had been wounded in the war, and he turned out only once for Norwich before concentrating on management.

His stay in East Anglia was destined to be short too, for at the end of his only full season with the Canaries, 1919–20, he resigned amid the throes of a crisis that also caused the resignation of six directors and the departure of several players. For the next three years he was out of football, working as a commercial traveller, before Blackpool brought him back as the game's highest-paid manager. He was unable to fashion a promotion-winning team during his often controversial four seasons with the Second Division Seasiders, but Wolves saw him as just the man under whose direction they could continue the climb back to the top flight they had started as Third North champions while George Jobey had been in charge.

Jobey, a canny Geordie who had played for Newcastle in a Cup Final and scored Arsenal's opening goal in their first game at Highbury, had sprung the big surprise of the 1924 close season by suddenly leaving Molineux the month after they had clinched that promotion to Division Two. Like Buckley, he had a spell out of soccer, running a hotel for a year, but he was then recalled to it by Derby County and, again like the major, was one of the foremost managers in the First Division throughout the Thirties.

Neither of them chalked up a top honour, but they went very close. Buckley pointed Wolves to promotion in 1931–32, six seasons after Jobey had done the same for Derby, and in 1939 the Wanderers had genuine hopes of pulling off the coveted League and Cup double then achieved only by Preston and Aston Villa. As it was, they finished runners-up in both competitions, second in the First Division for the second successive year and comprehensively beaten by down-table Portsmouth in one of Wembley's biggest upsets. Under Jobey, Derby were also twice Division One runners-up, in 1930 and 1936, and in 1933 they were strongly fancied for the Cup until unexpectedly coming unstuck in a semi-final against Manchester City at Huddersfield.

Besides achieving high standards on the field, Buckley and Jobey were both noted for being disciplinarians who commanded the greatest respect. Furthermore, they were the doyens of their profession in their final years in the game, Jobey leaving his last post in sight of his 69th birthday, Buckley following him out in the mid-Fifties when nearing his 73rd.

But for both there was also a downside. Jobey's near-15 years at Derby ended in his suspension, and that of five of the club's directors, after an FA-League Commission had uncovered illegal payments made to players since his appointment. His ban, originally for life, was lifted after four years, but he had to wait another seven before obtaining his final managership, at Mansfield, from which he was dismissed after only one full season (1952–53) for 'neglect of duty'. It was an accusation, arising from his failure to attend a sub-committee meeting of which he was unaware, that he strenuously refuted. Buckley surrendered his last job, at Walsall, a couple of years later, having failed in his other post-Wolves posts at Notts County, Hull City and Leeds United to reproduce the success at Molineux that he had combined with exceptional income from outgoing transfers in pursuing a prolific youth policy. Plentiful sales and even more plentiful team changes were sore points with supporters of clubs he managed.

Buckley, who was born at Urmston, Manchester, in November, 1882, died at Walsall on December 22nd, 1964. Jobey, born at Heddon-on-Tyne in July, 1885, died at Derby on March 9th, 1962, after spending the last years of his life in straitened circumstances at his Bangor Street home in the Chaddesden district of Derby.

The longevity of Buckley and Jobey in major football was in complete contrast to the time Fred Flanders spent at that level. After his debut against Birmingham, the former Derby Boys skipper made only 15 further appearances in Derby County's senior side before leaving for Newport County in August, 1913, but he returned to make almost a dozen more as a wartime guest. Flanders, who finally had a spell with Hartlepools United in the early Twenties, remained the Rams' youngest League debutant until September 6th, 1952, when Roy Patrick, also a full-back, played the first of his 50 first-team games for the club in a 2–1 defeat at Sunderland at the age of 16 years, 277 days.

Patrick, a former South Derbyshire Boys player from Overseal, near Swadlincote, who was later with Nottingham Forest, Southampton, Exeter City and Burton Albion, was himself succeeded as Derby County's youngest newcomer when Steve Powell, like Flanders Derby-born, played in a 3–2 victory over Stoke City in the first leg of a second-round Texaco Cup-tie at the Baseball Ground on October 20th, 1971, aged 16 years and 30 days. Three days later, Powell made his League debut, as a substitute during a 2–1 home First Division win against Arsenal.

Powell's father, Tommy, also first played in Derby's first team at the age of 16 (and 257 days)—against an RAF XI on Christmas Day, 1941, in the first match the Rams played when they resumed their activities in the 1939–45 War. Discounting Tommy's 87 wartime games, the Powells between them made 826 senior appearances (Tommy 406; Steve 420, including 11 as substitute). This put their aggregate 300 ahead of Derby County's next-best father-and-son pairing of W.J. Nicholas (143 games) and Jack Nicholas (383).

Sticklers for Fitness

*Methven foils Arsenal to sign Barbour – Egyptians in
English football – And Atkin's brother came too –
Gawky youth becomes one of Derby's fittest players
under Warren's influence – Rare goal starts escape
from relegation – Down again with worst record –
Barracking prompts protest – 'Jekyll and Hyde'
Leonard – Profitable move for Burton*

D URING THE SUMMER of 1908, some three months before Horace Barnes was so
suddenly introduced to League football as Derby County's inside-left, Jimmy
Methven pulled off another of his astute pieces of business by snapping up Tommy Barbour
in the face of keen competition from about a dozen other top-class clubs—Woolwich
Arsenal, Sunderland, Hibernian and Glasgow Rangers prominent among them.

George Morrell, a qualified referee who had taken over as Arsenal's manager earlier
that year after helping to revive the fortunes of both Glasgow Rangers and Greenock
Morton, had particularly high hopes of doing a deal when he came to an arrangement
with officials of Kilbirnie, the Ayrshire junior club for which Barbour was then playing.
Methven, however, nipped in to thwart his fellow Scot by completing negotiations
with the aid of Tommy's brother, and when Morrell arrived back north of the border
expecting to make the signing he found that Barbour had accepted Derby's terms.

When recalling this coup, Methven emphasised that Morrell took his disappointment
'like a true sportsman'. It was but one of many setbacks Morrell experienced during
his difficult years with Arsenal, who were then among soccer's poor relations under
the handicap of the declining support that eventually prompted their move from
Plumstead to Highbury. He was compelled to part with several key players because
of the Gunners' financial problems, and, unable to reproduce the sure touch that had
rescued Morton from heavy debt, he had the added misfortune to become the only
manager of a relegated Arsenal side before his resignation was enforced by the club's
closedown at the end of the 1914–15 season owing to the war.

Barbour joined Derby County as a wing-half, his favourite position, but he was
switched to full-back in an emergency with such successful results that he played the
majority of his 300-plus games there before departing to Darlington in time to be a
member, also at full-back, of the first side they fielded in the Football League—in a 2–0
Third Division North home win against Halifax Town in August, 1921.

Tommy Barbour, whose transfer to Derby disappointed Arsenal.

Tommy enjoys a game of dominoes at the Jolly Colliers Inn at Heanor, where he was the licensee.
(Derby Evening Telegraph)

Sticklers for Fitness

*Methven foils Arsenal to sign Barbour – Egyptians in
English football – And Atkin's brother came too –
Gawky youth becomes one of Derby's fittest players
under Warren's influence – Rare goal starts escape
from relegation – Down again with worst record –
Barracking prompts protest – 'Jekyll and Hyde'
Leonard – Profitable move for Burton*

D URING THE SUMMER of 1908, some three months before Horace Barnes was so
suddenly introduced to League football as Derby County's inside-left, Jimmy
Methven pulled off another of his astute pieces of business by snapping up Tommy Barbour
in the face of keen competition from about a dozen other top-class clubs—Woolwich
Arsenal, Sunderland, Hibernian and Glasgow Rangers prominent among them.

George Morrell, a qualified referee who had taken over as Arsenal's manager earlier
that year after helping to revive the fortunes of both Glasgow Rangers and Greenock
Morton, had particularly high hopes of doing a deal when he came to an arrangement
with officials of Kilbirnie, the Ayrshire junior club for which Barbour was then playing.
Methven, however, nipped in to thwart his fellow Scot by completing negotiations
with the aid of Tommy's brother, and when Morrell arrived back north of the border
expecting to make the signing he found that Barbour had accepted Derby's terms.

When recalling this coup, Methven emphasised that Morrell took his disappointment
'like a true sportsman'. It was but one of many setbacks Morrell experienced during
his difficult years with Arsenal, who were then among soccer's poor relations under
the handicap of the declining support that eventually prompted their move from
Plumstead to Highbury. He was compelled to part with several key players because
of the Gunners' financial problems, and, unable to reproduce the sure touch that had
rescued Morton from heavy debt, he had the added misfortune to become the only
manager of a relegated Arsenal side before his resignation was enforced by the club's
closedown at the end of the 1914–15 season owing to the war.

Barbour joined Derby County as a wing-half, his favourite position, but he was
switched to full-back in an emergency with such successful results that he played the
majority of his 300-plus games there before departing to Darlington in time to be a
member, also at full-back, of the first side they fielded in the Football League—in a 2–0
Third Division North home win against Halifax Town in August, 1921.

Tommy Barbour, whose transfer to Derby disappointed Arsenal.

Tommy enjoys a game of dominoes at the Jolly Colliers Inn at Heanor, where he was the licensee.
(Derby Evening Telegraph)

He never gained the Scottish cap for which he was at one time in the running, but he made several appearances in Army internationals during the 1914–18 War, in which he served with the Derbyshire Yeomanry in Egypt, Greece, Italy and France. It was in one of those matches, against the Egyptian Army, that he first met Tewfik Abdallah, a forward nicknamed 'Toothpick' who, with the help of his recommendation, became the second Egyptian to play in English League football when he was given a few games with Derby County in the 1920–21 season. The first one was Hassan Hegazi, a Cambridge Blue who had one game with Fulham in 1911. Not surprisingly, Abdallah, lacking pace, found it hard going in a disjointed side heading back to the Second Division, and he soon had to try his luck elsewhere, first at Cowdenbeath and then with Hartlepools United, before going to the United States.

Tommy Barbour was 32 when he resumed League football with the Rams after the war, and, although he was to have one more season as a first-team regular, it was around that time that he wisely safeguarded his future by taking over the Maypole public house in Brook Street, Derby. That remained his home after his transfer to Darlington, and he spent only a year with the Feethams club because he was then refused permission to continue training in Derby. Instead, he went into the Birmingham League with Burton All Saints, whose goalkeeper was his former County colleague Harry Maskrey, then also a publican.

After nearly a dozen years at the Maypole, Barbour moved to the Jolly Colliers Inn at Heanor, and he was in retirement at adjoining Marlpool when he died at 80 in 1967. A keen walker, this hardy Scotsman from Largs was cast somewhat in the Shankly mould, and he was still remarkably fit when I met him at his Heanor pub while he was in his sixties. His only physical drawback from his playing days was a right arm that would not straighten fully because of a split bone ('my only break') he suffered back at the Baseball Ground, playing for the publicans against a police team.

For much of his time with Derby County, Barbour formed a redoubtable full-back partnership with Jack Atkin, who also exceeded 300 appearances for the Rams, his only League club. Atkin was captaining his home team, Newhall Swifts, when he was recommended to Jimmy Methven by Jack Warde, a referee who later became a Derby licensee.

Here again, Derby's manager had to make a smart decision to get his man. When he made his approach with the offer of a 15-shilling weekly wage, Atkin refused to sign unless his brother Harry went with him. So, although Harry was not a first-team prospect, Methven agreed to take both players—and the 15 shillings were equally divided between them.

The Swifts, who also parted with right-winger Fred Riddell to the Rams around that time (he soon moved on to Bristol Rovers), reached the last qualifying round of the FA Cup in Atkin's final season with them before losing narrowly to a Glossop side from the Second Division that included former Rams player Johnny McMillan.

The Jack Atkin of those days, in 1907, was described as 'a gawky youth of 22', but, as befitted someone who spent more than 30 years working on his Sunnyside Farm at Newhall before going into retirement, he quickly developed into one of the fittest players on Derby's books through paying painstaking attention to his physical condition. He was so diligent in that direction that throughout his 15 years with the Rams he was excused from training with his team-mates, so certain were the club's officials that he could keep himself in tip-top trim at home.

The man most responsible for the cultivation of that admirable trait in Atkin's character was his Newhall neighbour Ben Warren, then Derby's captain, who was such a real stickler for fitness. Warren set an example that the young full-back, in whom he took a special interest, was only too ready to follow, and they regularly trained together at Newhall even after the England wing-half's transfer to Chelsea.

Jack Atkin, happily, enjoyed a far fuller life span than the ill-fated Warren. He told me that his health was 'as good now as it ever has been' when I had the pleasure of meeting him the month before his 70th birthday towards the end of 1952. He then had his home at Midway, a village not far from where he had lived at Newhall until retiring from his farm four years earlier, and he was still occasionally giving a helping hand in the haulage contracting business run by his eldest son, Stanley. He was in his 79th year when he died at Midway shortly after Christmas in 1961.

Jack Atkin, who readily followed Ben Warren's fitness example.

Jack with his wife at their Midway home, near Burton, in the 1950s.
(Derby Evening Telegraph)

Because he was so well 'toned up', Atkin rarely suffered injury or loss of form, but he never had a real chance to gain the international caps that might otherwise have come his way, such was the strong grip held by Blackburn's Bob Crompton on England's right-back position during his best years. He had to be satisfied with an appearance, late in his career, against Cambridge University in an FA team that also included West Ham's Syd Puddefoot, Ilkeston-born Alf Baker, of Arsenal, and the Tottenham left-wing pair, Bert Bliss and Jimmy Dimmock.

In the 1913–14 season Puddefoot scored five goals, including a hat-trick in seven minutes, in West Ham's 8–1 defeat of Chesterfield, then members of the Midland League, in a first-round FA Cup-tie. He played in three of the 1919 Victory internationals, but did not win his two full caps until the 1925–26 season, when he was with Blackburn Rovers after a spell with Falkirk, who paid the then record transfer fee of £5,000 for him after first having his services as a guest player during the war. He rejoined West Ham nearly four years after helping Blackburn, who paid £4,000 for him, to win the 1928 FA Cup Final. After ending his playing career he managed Northampton Town for two years in the mid-Thirties in between coaching in Turkey. He played several times for Essex in county cricket.

It was in one of Jack Atkin's last seasons, after returning as strong as ever from wartime service with the Army in France, that he gave what he rated his best-ever display, in a scoreless draw at Chelsea in April, 1920. Less than a fortnight previously, on Easter Monday, he also experienced what he described as his biggest footballing thrill in a home match with Everton. With the scores level, and only a minute to go, relegation-threatened Derby forced a corner taken by Alf Quantrill, then a new England winger, who told me what happened next in these words:

> When I placed the ball and looked up to see where I could put it to the best advantage, I saw Jack running up from the halfway line as hard as he could go. He was patting the top of his head with his hand, indicating that he wanted me to send the ball there. And I couldn't have placed it better, for Jack reached the right spot as the ball came over and headed it firmly into the net. What excitement! And what a grand captain Jack was, on and off the field.

That goal, which gained a 2–1 win, was Atkin's first for the club, in his 285th game. It avenged a 4–0 Good Friday defeat at Goodison and also marked the start of a late revival run that enabled the Rams to preserve the First Division status he had twice helped them to regain. In the following season he scored four more in consecutive matches. He obtained two of them from penalties—in a 1–1 draw with Bradford City in the club's last game of 1920, and in a 2–1 win over Huddersfield in the first of 1921, both at home—but put the other two into his own net.

Less than three months later, Atkin lost his place as Derby failed to pull off another escape act, making his final League appearance, his 308th, in a 3–0 defeat at Sunderland. The Rams ended that 1920–21 season next to the bottom of the table, two points above their relegation companions from Bradford with only five victories—an unwanted club record to set against their 21 defeats, and with the lowest number of goals, 32, among the 66 clubs then in the League. These were the final positions at the foot of the table:

	P	W	D	L	F	A	Pts
Oldham Athletic	42	9	15	18	49	86	33
Sheffield United	42	6	18	18	42	68	30
Derby County	42	5	16	21	32	58	26
Bradford PA	42	8	8	26	43	76	24

Only five victories, from 38 games, were also gained in the 1990–91 season which Derby County ended at the foot of the First Division. By contrast, when they were promoted from the Second Division in 1914–15 they equalled their record for a League season of 23 wins that had been set in achieving promotion in 1911–12 (both also from 38 matches).

That record was raised to 25 wins, but from 42 games, when Derby again regained First Division status, as runners-up, in 1925–26. They also won 25 of their 42 matches in claiming the Second Division title of 1986–87, but by then the record had been increased to 28, if from 46 fixtures, in the Third Division North of 1955–56.[1] The club's champions of 1956–57 (Third North) and 1968–69 (Division Two) both gained 26 victories from 46 and 42 games respectively.

With Carlisle-born Bert Chandler, who had been recommended to the Rams as a forward, settling in at right-back—a position he was to hold down for four seasons—Jack Atkin had only one more chance in the first team after his final League game at Roker. It came in a first-round FA Cup-tie at Villa Park that repeated the 6–1 scoreline, in favour of the home side, of a second-round match in which he had taken part at the same ground a dozen years earlier.

In 1910, Atkin had to play a one-back game against a goal-hungry attack, in which Harry Hampton did the hat-trick, because of an early injury to his partner, the senior Nicholas. In 1922, at the age of 38, he manfully stepped in to fill a gap caused by the unfitness of Chandler's partner, Archie Ritchie, but, to quote a contemporary account, he 'painfully failed to cope' as another Villa and England forward, Billy Walker, scored three of the goals. It was a sad end to a fine career.

That season of 1921–22 was Jimmy Methven's last as Derby County's manager. They finished it 12th in Division Two, with only three fewer defeats than they had suffered in being relegated in 1921 with their worst League record up to that time, and at one point the barracking became so bad that their players were goaded into making a public protest in the *Derby Daily Express*. That was the evening newspaper which went out of independent existence some ten years later, with the *Derby Daily [Evening] Telegraph* surviving, as part of the truce in the financially costly provincial newspaper 'war' between the Allied and Northcliffe groups of Lord Camrose and Lord Rothermere. In Bristol and Derby the Camrose paper was incorporated into Rothermere's; vice versa in Newcastle.

By the time of the protest against barracking, Derby County were having to labour on without not only Steve Bloomer, whose return to the Rams' attack (recounted in the next chapter) had ended with the war, but also Harry Leonard, the big, bustling and assertive centre-forward who had followed Bloomer from Middlesbrough to fill the gap left by the loss of 'Snobby' Bentley.

---

1. Derby County won 33 of their 45 matches in 1944–45, but that was a wartime season.

Henry Droxford Leonard had his critics, one of whom described him as a Jekyll and Hyde type of footballer ('when he is good he is very good, but when he is bad he is chronic'), but he left the Rams for Manchester United with the very praiseworthy record, including wartime games, of 98 goals in 184 appearances. He signed off most appropriately with the winner against Newcastle on the last day of the 1919–20 season. It had been in Newcastle's reserve side that he had gained valuable experience after coming to the fore in his home town with Sunderland Boys and Sunderland West End.

Leonard's scoring exploits for Grimsby Town after leaving Newcastle, first in a struggling side voted out of the Football League and then with the Mariners' Midland League champions who earned an immediate return to the Second Division, encouraged Middlesbrough to beat Derby County for his signature with a bid of £500 about a year after Steve Bloomer had rejoined the Rams from Ayresome. Leonard's four hat-tricks for Grimsby included a five-goal flourish against the reserves of Leicester Fosse during their Midland League exile.

Ill health, however, restricted him to an unlucky 13 games for Boro as he did not find the North-East climate to his liking, and in a matter of months, in October, 1911, Derby were successful with a renewed approach for him after failing to secure the transfer of Alf Toward, whose goals had helped Oldham Athletic into the First Division in 1910 as runners-up to Manchester City, but who had recently yielded his first-team place to Welsh international Evan Jones. Leonard lost weight because of his illness, but he still tipped the scales at 12st, and after an uncertain start he regained both form and fitness in settling down as Bentley's successor to enjoy his best days with Derby as his goals twice helped them to promotion.

Seventeen of them came in 27 games when the Rams went up in the 1911–12 season, 19 in 32 when they again reclaimed a First Division place in 1914–15. In between, his importance to the team was emphasised when injury kept him out for most of the first three months of 1914 as relegation again reared its ugly head.

First impressions, however, gave little indication of Leonard's true value, and Derby fans must have had serious doubts when a second successive scoreless draw coincided with the debut day, at home to Barnsley, that he shared with Charlie Betts, a full-back from Newcastle United who gained an early chance to establish himself for a couple of seasons alongside Jack Atkin because of an injury to Tommy Barbour. During that period Betts produced such consistent form that Barbour, when fit again, played mainly at right-half before he was able to resume his partnership with Atkin. Betts, who was born at Scunthorpe, put in two spells with Gainsborough Trinity as well as playing for North Lindsey and Watford before joining the Rams. He moved again, to Hull City, shortly before the First World War, and concluded his career back home with Scunthorpe United.

In his second game for Derby at Bradford, where Jimmy Bauchop scored the winning goal, Harry Leonard was again such a shadow of his most dangerous self that he was considered 'hardly fit enough to turn out at all' in one match report, the anonymous writer adding that 'his play in the circumstances was exceptionally plucky'. Yet it all suddenly came good for him at the third attempt. On the following Saturday, in his second home appearance on the eve of bonfire night in 1911, he put on his own firework display against Fulham. He had the ball in the net twice in the first five minutes, and in the second half he added two more goals as Derby coasted to a 6–1 win.

With the chief exception of a hat-trick against a Gainsborough Trinity team already doomed to last place in the Second Division and an unsuccessful application for re-election, Leonard got most of his other goals for the Rams in singles before the war halted League soccer. He was seen at his most dependable after missing the first six matches of the 1914–15 promotion season through injury, netting 17 goals in failing to score in only four of 18 consecutive matches on the way to his second championship medal. While he was out of the team, the front line was led by Norman Fordham, an emergency recruit from Ashford in the Kent League. Fordham, a brother-in-law of Frank Woolley, the Kent and England cricketer, helped to set the pattern for that quick return to the First Division with a hat-trick in a 7–0 home win over Barnsley on the opening day.

In wartime competitions, Leonard hit hat-tricks against Nottingham Forest, Bradford City and Hull City, and, with the inclusion of the 1919 Midland Victory League, he altogether scored 25 goals in 34 games before First Division football returned to the Baseball Ground with the resumption of the Football League's activities for 1919–20. His dozen goals in that first post-war season made him Derby's joint leading scorer in the League with Noah Burton, who had played for Bulwell St. Alban's and Ilkeston United before joining the Rams as an amateur near the end of 1915, but neither of them was to remain a Derby player for much longer.

Leonard made his move to Manchester United only a few weeks into the following season, but he played in just ten first-team matches for the Old Trafford club, scoring five goals for a career League and Cup total of 108, before winding up with Heanor Town. In Derby, he continued to be a familiar figure as a publican—first at the Albert Vaults in Whitecross Street, then at the Lord Nelson in Curzon Street, and finally at the Douglas Bar in Normanton Road for the last 18 years before his death at 65, after a long illness, late in 1951.

Noah Burton, who was born in Nottinghamshire, at Old Basford, guested for Nottingham Forest during the First World War, and he scored the lone goal by which they defeated Everton on Merseyside, following a scoreless draw at home in which the visitors missed a penalty, to win the Victory Shield in May, 1919. Several clubs sought his signature after that success, but he returned to the Rams and spent the first two peacetime League seasons with them before yet another relegation led to his transfer back to Forest during the summer of 1921.

That was a most profitable move for him. He missed only one match as it took him straight back to the First Division in a side also bolstered by the signing of another wartime guest, Sam Hardy, one of England's finest goalkeepers, from Aston Villa. Although then well into the veteran stage, having celebrated his 38th birthday the day before he first played for Forest in the League on August 27th, 1921, Hardy had gained his second FA Cup winner's medal, and also the last of his 21 international caps, only the previous year. There is more about him among the references to Derbyshire-born goalkeepers in Chapter 16.

Forest lost 4–1 away to Crystal Palace in Hardy's first game as one of their own players, but he was a key figure as, largely on the strength of their defence, they warded off the challenges of Stoke City and Barnsley to carry off the 1921–22 Second Division championship. They kept a clean sheet in 22 of their 42 matches and the number of goals they conceded, 30, was the lowest in the top two sections. They finished four points clear of their two closest rivals, Stoke accompanying them up instead of Barnsley on goal average.

Life in the First Division was anything but rosy for Forest, however. In 1923, they ended immediately above the relegation zone but were four points clear of dropping straight back with Stoke. A year later, they were again 20th out of 22, surviving only by having a fractionally better goal average than Chelsea. And the season after that they did go down, as wooden spoonists, after losing Hardy early on through an injury that forced his retirement at the age of 41. Not for 32 years did they return to the top flight, even spending two of the intervening seasons in the Third Division South shortly after the Second World War.

Despite being involved in the decline in the club's fortunes that set in so soon after he had helped them to promotion, Noah Burton was generally regarded as Forest's most popular player throughout the second half of the 1920s. Though somewhat ungainly in build, and not a prolific scorer (in 320 League and Cup appearances he added only 62 goals to the 18 he had registered in 61 games for Derby), he was a willing worker in all five of the then standard forward positions as well as wing-half, exploiting his prowess as a noted sprinter and showing not a little skill. He was also a heartening influence in the dressing room, the possessor of a fine singing voice and a keen wit.

Apart from missing much of the 1923–24 season through injury, he was a constant choice for a decade, and it was not until shortly before Christmas in 1931 that he last played in the League, on the day after his 35th birthday. He hung up his boots at the end of that season, but retained a prominent place on the Nottingham scene behind the counter at the tobacconist's shop he owned. He continued to live in the city after his retirement, and it was there that he died in July, 1956.

Harry Leonard, 'a Jekyll and Hyde type of footballer'.

Noah Burton, who made a profitable move from Derby to Nottingham Forest.

CHAPTER 15

Return of the Conquering Hero

No joke in chance meeting – Welcome home from huge crowd – Five ex-Rams help Fosse to promotion – Scoring comeback against Lincoln – Second Division champions in second season of Bloomer's second coming – Crowds pack Derby streets to acclaim return in triumph from Barnsley – Halse scores five against Rams – Cup Final dream comes true for Villa

IT WAS A CHANCE MEETING between Jimmy Methven and Steve Bloomer at a railway station, while both were returning home from a match, that led to England's freescorer rejoining Derby County from Middlesbrough at the venerable footballing age of 36. The man who was again to become 'Our Steve' took some persuading that the Rams manager was not joking when he asked him if he would like to return to the Baseball Ground, but once he realised that the offer was genuine he jumped at it.

Methven recalled:

> I could see by the expression on Steve's face that he was under the impression I was pulling his leg. When it dawned on him that I really meant business, I never saw a happier countenance in my life.

Bloomer's old club had progressively improved by finishing sixth, fifth and fourth in their three Second Division seasons since being relegated the year after his departure, but they had made a faltering start to their 1910–11 programme in winning only one of their first five matches—and that by just the odd goal of three at Wolverhampton between defeats by Chelsea (by 4–1 at home on the opening day) and Clapton Orient (by 1–0 in East London). Their next two games before Bloomer's comeback were both drawn—by 1–1 at home to Blackpool; 2–2 at Glossop.

A huge crowd gathered at Derby's Midland station to welcome their favourite home, and on October 1st, 1910 the band played *See the Conquering Hero Comes* as he took the field again as a Rams player, restored to the captaincy, for a home game with Lincoln City.

He had last played for the club in a 1–0 home defeat by Bolton on March 10th, 1906, in this team: Maskrey; Methven, Morris; Warren, Hall, Wood (A.); Fletcher, Bloomer, Cleaver, Wood (J.), Lamb. The line-up for his return, with the attendance doubled to 12,000, was: Scattergood; Barbour, Atkin; Garry, Hall, Bagshaw; Grimes, Bloomer, Bauchop, Barnes, Donald.

The wingers on that former, farewell occasion were local products, as also was centre-forward Fred Cleaver, who went straight into the side from Ashbourne Town but had only a dozen games, scoring three goals, before finding his way to Watford after a trial with Preston.

Tom Fletcher, a Heanor-born forward signed from Derby Nomads, had no wish to turn professional, but for a couple of seasons he made fairly regular appearances for the Rams, all along the front line, and he also toured America and the Continent with amateur teams. He was a useful cricketer, too, and in the 1906 summer he added his name to the list of Derby County footballers who played for Derbyshire when he faced H.B.G. Austin's West Indians, scoring 28 runs and sharing in a win by six wickets.

Sam Lamb was one of the Alfreton Town products. In the absence through injury of another one, George Davis, he displaced Frank Middleton on Derby's left wing for most of the 1905–06 season, but was then himself ousted when Davis became available again. Middleton, who, like George Richards, had been signed from the Leicestershire club Whitwick White Cross, found the competition less daunting in moving to Leicester Fosse, in whose Second Division promotion team of 1907–08 he was one of five players who also turned out for Derby County. The others were Horace Bailey, Joe Blackett, Jimmy Blessington and Tommy Shanks.

Blessington, an inside-forward summer signing in 1899, had only a couple of League games in his short stay with the Rams, but he enjoyed considerable success in Scotland before first entering English soccer with Preston North End. He won four Scottish caps while with Glasgow Celtic, whom he helped to three League titles and two Cup finals in four seasons. His path from Derby to Leicester took him to Bristol City and Luton Town, and after ending his playing career he was briefly the Fosse's manager before going to Ireland to coach Belfast Celtic. Shanks, Wexford-born, travelled to Derby from the opposite direction, and in his case international honours came not before, but after, he also failed to establish himself at inside-forward with the Rams. He gained his first two Irish caps while with Woolwich Arsenal, and a third during a second spell with Brentford that preceded his transfer to Leicester. From the Fosse he went back to London—first with Leyton, then Clapton Orient.

Whereas there were two home-grown wingers at the end of Steve Bloomer's first stay with Derby County, the players who occupied those positions when he began the second one came from much further afield. Billy Grimes hailed from Hitchin, in Hertfordshire, Davie Donald from Coatbridge, in Strathclyde, only a few miles outside Glasgow.

Grimes graduated from Hitchin Town to Watford, the club he rejoined late in the First World War after also playing a few games for Tottenham Hotspur on ending his connection with Derby County in 1916. His stay with the Rams dated back to March, 1910, when, having first played in Derbyshire for Glossop North End following his initial spell with Watford, he was signed from Bradford City. For the ensuing five seasons before the war halted League football, he solved a right-wing problem that had caused eight players to be tried there since the switching of Jack Davis to the opposite flank after the departure of George Davis, and, although scoring was not his strong point (only 11 goals in his 169 League and Cup games), he played an important part in the winning of the two Second Division titles during that period.

After leaving Watford for the second time, Grimes spent the 1919–20 season with Luton Town, the Hatters' last in the Southern League before their election to the new

Third Division of the Football League. He then retired from the game to resume his trade as a bricklayer, and he was still in that part of the country, near Biggleswade, when he died in January, 1936.

Although George Thompson, the Geordie signed from Sheffield United, was the most frequently used player among Derby's selection of outside-rights, the man from whom Billy Grimes directly took over, for an away match with Clapton Orient won with two Bentley goals, was Arthur Tinkler, a Mancunian with a job outside football, as a schoolteacher, who soon afterwards quit the Rams to join first neighbouring Heanor, then Ilkeston. He had only two first-team games with Derby, but when he re-entered the League with Birmingham he totted up just over 100 at half-back, mainly as pivot, before moving to Burton United early in the war.

Davie Donald, formerly of Albion Rovers and Bradford and later of Chesterfield, Watford, QPR and Hamilton Acadamicals, was the successor to Jack Davis at outside-left, but was replaced by Ivan Sharpe almost exactly a year after Steve Bloomer's comeback game.

The rousing reception Bloomer received on his return against Lincoln was so prolonged that the kick-off was delayed. After 20 minutes' play more pandemonium reigned as he scored the opening goal. He netted another, from a penalty, in the second half, and, with Jimmy Bauchop (2) and Horace Barnes also on the mark, the Rams romped to a 5–0 victory. It was undoubtedly one of those great Baseball Ground occasions to relish.

Derby, however, once more fell short of promotion that season, finishing nine points off the pace in sixth place despite several other clear-cut victories.

**Billy Grimes, a key player in
two promotion teams.**

Very fittingly, Bloomer was their top scorer with 20 goals in 28 League games (plus four in a Cup run that ended in the fourth round at Newcastle), and it was by only a very close decision that he was denied an England recall when Harold Fleming, of Swindon Town, gained preference for the game in which Ireland were beaten 2–1 at Derby on February 11th, 1911.

Bloomer's last international appearance therefore remained the 1–1 draw in which, at the age of 33, he had scored the equaliser against Scotland at Newcastle four years earlier. An extraordinary decision by referee Tom Robertson deprived Bloomer of another goal on that occasion. Receiving a pass from Vivian Woodward, he beat two defenders before putting the ball into the net, but was given offside. To quote from one report: 'Only a referee's error prevented England taking victory. The error was so clear that Bloomer may be forgiven his breach of etiquette.' The draw cost not only Bloomer a winning farewell but also England the British Championship, which went to Wales for the first time. As the then record England scorer, however, Derby's hero had the honour of being presented with a portrait of himself by the FA.

In addition to Bloomer, double-figure goals totals for Derby County in the 1910–11 season of his return to the Rams were reached by three of the club's other B-men— Bauchop, Bentley, who missed Steve's first game back because of suspension after being sent off against Glossop, and Barnes. Bauchop, who had a few games at wing-half before reverting to inside-left when Bentley resumed, altogether netted 21 goals. Bentley, in his last season with the club, totalled 15, and Barnes, switched to the left wing in place of Donald for several matches, contributed a round dozen.

Bloomer once more led Derby's scoring, with 18 in 36 matches, when they did go up at the next attempt. He also scored their only goal from a penalty in a home Cup defeat by Blackburn after the previous season's 4–0 reverse on Tyneside had been avenged by a 3–0 win against Newcastle, gained with goals by Bauchop, Richards and Leonard, at the Baseball Ground in the opening round.

The Rams faded from a run of 14 games without defeat up to the end of 1911, during which they gained 25 points out of 28, to go through their first six League matches of 1912 without another win, but they beat Chelsea to the championship on goal average in avoiding any further reverses in their last dozen fixtures.

The unbeaten sequence up to New Year's Day ended at Stockport—as also did an even better one of 16 League matches during the 1914–15 season in which Derby were again promoted. That latter run was interrupted, however, after the record-equalling 14th game by a narrow home Cup reverse against Leeds City, and, excluding 17 consecutive fixtures without defeat in the transitional season of 1945–46, the club did not again go 16 League matches unbeaten until they made their best start to a season in 1948.

In the Bloomer-led promotion success of 1911–12, a home victory in early April over the Rams' main rivals from Chelsea proved crucial, Harry Leonard scoring twice without reply. Even so, with five games then still to go, Derby's climb was not clinched until their final match, in which they won by the same 2–0 score at Barnsley with goals from Buckley and Bauchop.

For the Yorkshire club, who finished sixth, it was an ill-timed encounter. As if they had not already run into enough fixture congestion with three replays of their Cup quarter-final against Bradford City and another in their semi-final with Swindon Town, they had to receive the Rams only two days after they had played a scoreless draw

TELEGRAPHIC ADDRESS,
6, TEMPLE.

3, HARE COURT.
TEMPLE. E.C.

May 31/10.

Dear W. Richards,

Permit me to say how sorry I am that the splendid efforts which Derby County made did not succeed in securing for the Xᵉ a place in Division I (the English League) while I was a candidate for Derby at the last election. Derby have had football matches attended, there were victories or eye attendance — in the fourth Division and more watched ...

... but I followed the football closely during the time I succeed and I sympathise with you very much. In what rank I suppose he a disappointment to yourself. I hope you will enjoy your trip to South Africa.

Believe me,

Yours Sincerely,

Arthur Page

W. George Richards

A letter George Richards received, as Derby's captain, after the Rams had narrowly missed promotion in season 1909–10. They finished fourth, level on points with Oldham, who went up to the First Division as runners-up on goal average, and Hull City. The champions, the Manchester City team managed by former Derby manager Harry Newbould, were one point ahead.

with West Bromwich in the Cup Final at the Crystal Palace, and only two days before they defeated Albion, the past year's Second Division champions, by an extra-time goal in the replay at Bramall Lane, Sheffield. And on Thursday, April 25th, the day after that replayed final, they had to be hosts to Chelsea in the League, losing 2–0.

It was after the 1912 FA Cup Final that the rules were amended so that extra time should be played, when necessary, at the original meeting. This first happened in 1920, when Aston Villa defeated Huddersfield Town at Stamford Bridge with a 100th-minute goal by Billy Kirton. It next occurred in 1938, when Preston averted a replay against Huddersfield with a controversial penalty converted by George Mutch in the last minute of extra time. The additional half-hour was again needed in 1946, when Derby County defeated Charlton Athletic 4–1, in 1947, when Chris Duffy scored Charlton's winner against Burnley with only six minutes of the extra period left, in 1965 (Liverpool beat Leeds 2–1) and 1968 (WBA beat Everton 1–0), but it was not until 1970 that the final had to be replayed for the first time since 1912. Chelsea then defeated Leeds United 2–1 at Old Trafford following a 2–2 draw after extra time at Wembley. There have since been five more replayed finals.

On the Saturday of Barnsley's 1912 Cup Final stalemate with the Throstles in London, Derby County comfortably beat bottom-of-the-table Gainsborough Trinity in their final home League match, Leonard doing the hat-trick, and at that stage they led the way on goal average from Burnley, who, at the expense of lowly Huddersfield, also completed their home programme with a convincing win. Both had 52 points with one game left, and Chelsea, who were without a game that day because of Barnsley's prior Cup commitment, were four points behind in third place—but with three matches to play.

The Stamford Bridge club narrowed the gap by dispatching their visitors from Blackpool while Derby were clinching promotion with their win at Barnsley on the following Monday. Then came Chelsea's victory in their rearranged game at Oakwell, which put them level on points with Burnley, but left them still third on goal average. On the season's last Saturday two days later, April 27th, Chelsea snatched the second promotion place with another win, by an only goal at home to Bradford, while Burnley forfeited it by losing at Wolverhampton. This delayed the Lancashire club's return to the First Division for one more year, when made it as runners-up to Preston North End. These were the final leading positions in 1912:

	P	W	D	L	F	A	Pts
Derby County	38	23	8	7	74	28	54
Chelsea	38	24	6	8	64	34	54
Burnley	38	22	8	8	77	41	52

As those goals figures indicate, a key factor was the strength of Derby's defence, into the centre of which the dominant Frank Buckley had been brought from Birmingham as an admirable successor to Ben Hall. Of the club's record low number of 28 goals in the against column, only one was conceded in the last 11 games—a late equaliser by a former County player, Irish international Billy Halligan, when Wolves were the visitors.

Halligan, an ex-Belfast Distillery forward who reached the Rams from Leeds City, won the first of his two caps during his 16 months on the Baseball Ground staff, getting his country's goal in a 2–1 defeat by Wales in Belfast in January, 1911, but he missed the match with England, who won by the same score, in Derby a fortnight later. He made his £450 move to Wolves that summer after playing only 22 League games (eight goals) under Jimmy Methven's management, and it was while he was with the Wanderers that he did face England. On that occasion, in Dublin, the margin of Ireland's failure was increased to 6–1.

For two seasons Halligan, in better luck than he had been at Derby, was Wolves' top scorer, with 41 goals in 73 League and Cup games. For the next two—though outscored by Sammy Stevens, a successor to Tommy Browell from Steve Bloomer's part of the world—he was a regular with Hull City, for whom he totalled 35 goals in almost 80 appearances before war intervened. When peace returned, he completed his career with Preston, Oldham and Nelson.

There were scenes of tremendous excitement when the Derby County players arrived back from the hard-earned win at Barnsley that ensured the reinstatement of First Division football at the Baseball Ground. According to one eye-witness account, 'Midland Road was one dense mass of people…the multitude [estimated at about 20,000] stretched far down London Road…Derby County favours were sported on every hand…musical and unmusical instruments blared at every turn.'

Although the gates at the railway station had been locked in an attempt to keep the cheering thousands at bay, many of the crowd managed to break onto the platform. As the train steamed in, these delighted fans hauled the players out and carried them to the exit. Some were placed in cabs 'which were immediately mounted by as many people as the vehicles could accommodate at a crush', and taken through the packed streets to the official reception at the Royal Hotel. Not until the FA Cup at last came to Derby 34 years later were a Rams team returning in triumph given such a delirious welcome home, for the two further promotions back to the First Division that had to be achieved in the meantime, in 1915 and 1926, were not clinched in an away match.

When the team returned from their Wembley win in the first FA Cup Final after the Second World War, the victory parade began from outside the Blue Peter Hotel on the borough outskirts at Alvaston, where the players transferred from their motor coach to a decorated eight-ton beer truck which carried a ram's head, supplied by a local butcher, on the cabin front. So many cars infiltrated from side roads along the route to the town centre that the aldermen and councillors who were following in a double-decker Corporation bus fell so far behind that the official reception at the police buildings had already begun by the time they got there.

The players who had brought the Cup to Derby for the first time were themselves also delayed, for they needed a police escort to complete the journey on foot when the thousands jamming all approaches to the destination caused the procession to grind to a halt after it had set off down London Road headed by a troop of mounted police and Derby Borough Military Band. Before dismounting from the truck, skipper Jack Nicholas passed the Cup round to every member of the team in turn, to the accompaniment of deafening cheers, and was then led by the arm through the crowd by the Chief Constable, Col. H. Rawlings.

Many fainted as the crowd remained outside the police buildings after the players had been introduced from the balcony. Inside, the proposed celebratory dinner against which there had been an outcry in those early post-war days of acute food shortages was replaced by 'another type of function which, while doing equally sincere honour to the club, will not entail the provision of food for 250 guests'. Unique though the occasion was—and has obstinately continued to remain—there were also those who, to quote one who voiced his objection in the local paper, considered that 'to allocate ratepayers' money for a function of this kind at the present time is open to criticism'.

Such considerations did not arise when Steve Bloomer and his merry band received their tumultuous welcome back from Barnsley. The privations of a world war were then not far over the horizon, however, and, as in 1946, prosperity for Derby County on the field was not for long to be sustained after the high point they reached in 1912.

Hat-tricks for Bloomer in successive home victories against Liverpool and Sheffield United soon demonstrated that the old master was still a force to be reckoned with in Division One, but his scoring rate fell away disconcertingly just over midway through his first season of 1912–13 back in that sphere. Indeed, it was snuffed out completely after he had taken his seasonal goals tally to 14 with a couple in a 5–0 trouncing of Tottenham in mid-January (Bauchop got the three others). He played in only nine of the Rams' 16 remaining games, and did not score in any of them.

Despite the sudden defusing of their hero's striking power, Derby County went unbeaten through the final month of that campaign to end in seventh position, but any reassurance that may have gathered from such a commendable effort was swiftly dispelled the following season when they again became embroiled in a struggle against relegation from which they were unable to extricate themselves. Their number of victories was more than halved to a mere eight, and the 71 goals they conceded were exceeded in the first two divisions only by the 76 of Nottingham Forest, who finished at the foot of the Second. With a paltry 27 points, Derby also trailed in last—three points adrift of Preston, who were then even more of a yo-yo team than the Rams. It was North End's second relegation in three years, separated by a Second Division title, and they were to make an immediate return to the elite with Derby a year later.

These were the figures for the positions at the extremes of the tables for those two successive seasons of contrast:

1913–14 : Div 1 The bottom four

	P	W	D	L	F	A	Pts
Tottenham Hotspur	38	12	10	16	50	62	34
The Wednesday	38	13	8	17	53	70	34
Preston North End	38	12	6	20	52	69	30
Derby County	38	8	11	19	55	71	27

1914–15: Div 2 The top four

	P	W	D	L	F	A	Pts
Derby County	38	23	7	8	71	33	53
Preston North End	38	20	10	8	61	42	50
Barnsley	38	22	3	13	51	51	47
Wolverhampton W.	38	19	7	12	77	52	45

Steve Bloomer played in only five League matches and one Cup-tie during the 1913–14 season of Derby's second demotion that marked the conclusion of his magnificent, inspirational playing career. He scored just twice in those games—the last two of his 293 League goals for the club in their second home match, lost by 5–3 to Sheffield United—and, as his falling-off the goal standard had indicated during the second half of the previous campaign, age was at last catching up him. Having turned 40, he did

A 1913–14 Rams group.
Back row (left to right): Atkin, Barbour, Scattergood, Buckley, Walker, Waugh.
Front row: Grimes, Moore, Fordham, Barnes, Fellows.
(Albert Wilkes & Son)

not appear in the first team for the last three months of his final season, and the Rams won only two of their last 14 matches after he had made his League farewell in a scoreless draw away to Bradford City on January 24th, 1914.

A week later, Horace Barnes and Bob Waugh, a reserve full-back from Newcastle, were Derby's scorers when Bloomer bowed out in a 3–2 Cup defeat at Burnley. His total of 525 first-team games stood as the club's record for more than half a century, Kevin Hector, Ron Webster and Roy McFarland then pushing him down to fourth place.

The last of Bloomer's 38 FA Cup goals for Derby (discounting the one in the match with the Wednesday in 1893 that was officially nullified after the Sheffield club's protest) came in his 50th game in the competition for the Rams. It was not enough to avert defeat in a first-round match at the Baseball Ground on January 15th, 1913, but it was the only one Aston Villa conceded in going on to win the trophy for the fifth time.

Harold Halse, the former Manchester United inside-forward who only three months earlier had scored five goals against the Rams in a League match at Villa Park, netted twice in the 3–1 victory at Derby that put Villa ahead by four wins to three in their Cup clashes with the County.

Halse's five goals in a 5–1 First Division win against Derby on October 19th, 1912, in his ninth match for Villa and his first for them after being switched from inside-right to centre-forward in the absence of Harry Hampton through illness, equalled the club record Hampton had set in a 10–0 defeat of the Wednesday in the previous League game at Villa Park a fortnight earlier. Hampton was Villa's other scorer in the Cup defeat of the Rams the following January. Villa's opponents in the next three rounds, West Ham United, Crystal Palace and Bradford, were each beaten 5–0, after which Oldham Athletic, in their first semi-final, and Sunderland, at the Crystal Palace, both fell to an only goal.

The result of the final against Sunderland, to whose champions Villa were runners-up that season, was exactly as predicted by Clem Stephenson—even to the extent of the scorer. Stephenson, the Aston club's inside-left whose brother George was later a key member of Derby County's attack, told Charlie Buchan during the game that he had dreamt Villa would win 1–0, and that Tommy Barber, their right-half, would head the goal.

The dream threatened to become a Villa nightmare when Sunderland took control early in the second half while Sam Hardy, Villa's England goalkeeper, was off the field receiving attention to a knee he injured in a hefty collision. But that period of domination petered out after Hardy had hobbled back to take over from his stand-in Jimmy Harrop, the centre-half who had been transferred with him from Liverpool, and with a quarter of an hour to go Sunderland's unsighted goalkeeper, Joe Butler, was powerless to intervene as Barber duly headed the winner from right-winger Charlie Wallace's corner kick.

The prediction would have come unstuck, though, if Wallace had shown similar accuracy with an excellent chance to open the scoring after the first 15 minutes. Villa were then awarded a penalty after Stephenson had been brought down by full-back Charlie Gladwin's clumsy challenge, only for Wallace to become the first player to fail from the spot in an FA Cup Final by shooting hopelessly wide.

So the scene was saved for Villa skipper Joe Bache still to collect the trophy through a dream come true, but there was an unpleasant sequel. Hampton and another Charlie—Thomson, the Sunderland centre-half—were frequently at loggerheads during the game, and at a special hearing soon after it both were suspended along with Arthur Adams, the referee from Nottingham.

CHAPTER 16

Derbyshire-born Goalkeepers

Scattergood only ever-present in Derby's meanest defence – Robinson's departure upsets fans – FA inquiry into transfer to New Brighton – Switch South twice leads to Cup Final – Latham and John Goodall answer emergency calls – Maskrey follows Scattergood from Ripley – Caught out by late recall – Hardy the most gifted – Unhappy debut for Scattergood's son – Fade-out at Alfreton

T HAT SPLENDIDLY-NAMED goalkeeper Ernald Oak Scattergood was the only ever-present member of the meanest defence Derby County have fielded in the Football League. The club's lowest total of 28 in the goals-against column of their 1911–12 push to promotion has most closely been approached in their two championship campaigns of Brian Clough's six and a bit seasons as manager, though comparisons cannot be accurate because four fewer fixtures were fulfilled in Scattergood's time.

Ernald Scattergood, goalkeeping ever-present member of Derby County's meanest defence.

In the 42 games of 1968–69, only 32 goals were conceded in the runaway Second Division title success that brought top-grade soccer back to Derby after a lapse of 16 years. In 1971–72, the Rams' opponents were restricted to 33 as pride of place was at long last secured in the First Division.

Scattergood was a most worthy addition to the distinguished line of Derbyshire-born players who have guarded Derby County's goal—a line which, as far as players who completed at least a century of appearances are concerned, dated back to the introduction of Jack Robinson at the start of the 1891–92 season. Controversy crowned Robinson's Derby career, but he was freely acknowledged, at his best, as the outstanding goalkeeper of his day, a first choice for England across five years and still generally regarded as one of the finest ever to represent the Rams.

He had to contend with competition from such redoubtable rivals as another Derbyshire product, Billy Foulke, who had his hey-day with Sheffield United before he became too bulky, the Oxford University amateur G.B. Raikes, John Sutcliffe (Bolton Wanderers and Millwall Athletic), Jack Hillman (Burnley), Matt Kingsley, Newcastle's first international player, and Billy George (Aston Villa), but he missed only two of 13 successive England games from the day of his international debut, in a 6–0 defeat of Ireland at Trent Bridge, Nottingham, on February 20th, 1897, until his last appearance in a 3–0 win against the same country on March 9th, 1901, at the home of the club for which he was then playing, Southampton.

Hillman, a Devonian who stood more than 6ft and weighed 16st, was another controversial character. He was suspended for a complete season after being accused of trying to bribe Nottingham Forest players to 'throw' their last match of the 1899–1900 season, at Turf Moor, to enable Burnley to avoid relegation from the First Division. Forest won 4–0, and the Lancashire club went down with Glossop North End. Hillman won his only international cap in the 13–2 defeat of Ireland at Sunderland in 1899. After the bribery scandal he moved to Manchester City, with whom he won a Second Division championship medal in 1903 and an FA Cup winner's medal in 1904.

Hillman, whose family moved from Tavistock to Burnley when he was a child, had three spells at Turf Moor. He first left there for Everton, and was also briefly with Dundee before going back. His second departure led him from Manchester to Millwall, where an elbow injury ended his playing career after a total of more than 350 League and Cup appearances. That was when he joined Burnley for the third time—first as trainer with the Reserves, then with the first team.

In view of the years of great service Jack Robinson rendered the Rams, not missing a match as they ended his last two seasons with them second and third in the First Division table, it was most unfortunate for all concerned that he should leave the Baseball Ground staff in circumstances which aroused a considerable amount of public feeling against him throughout Derbyshire. At the end of the 1896–97 season there was not even an inkling of the 'sensational' events that were so soon to follow, but on August 28th, 1897, one local newspaper writer told his readers:

> Despite his protestations of loyalty, Robinson has resolved not to play any more for Derby County. It would be idle to suggest that this loss will not be felt in Derby, but the County have surmounted difficulties of equal magnitude before and will be able to do so again. If Robinson thinks he can enhance his reputation by joining a mushroom organisation like New Brighton whose

purse may not always be so heavy as at present he has done well to leave Derby. But this belief of his is not likely to be shared by those he is leaving behind.

That comment about the New Brighton club's prosperity not being assured came true even sooner than the man who made it could have imagined, for New Brighton Tower—so named because they played at the Tower Ground at Wallasey—resigned from the League in 1901, only three years after they had entered it. Not until 1923, when a club known just as New Brighton entered the Northern Section of the Third Division with Doncaster Rovers on its extension to 22 clubs, did that district of Merseyside again have a team in the Football League. New Brighton then maintained membership until 1951, when they failed to gain re-election after finishing at the foot of the table and went into the Lancashire Combination.

At the time of Robinson's defection from Derby, New Brighton Tower were affluent enough to tempt top talent, but their overtures towards the Rams' goalkeeper provoked a dispute between the two clubs that stirred a Football Association Commission to decide that before the Cheshire club could be affiliated to the FA they 'must furnish proof that they had purchased the interests of all the shareholders in the New Brighton Tower Company and produce the transfers'.

Pending the provision of that proof, the FA cancelled the contract Robinson signed with New Brighton and ruled that his registration with the Rams was also invalid because 'Derby County knew that Robinson had entered into a legal agreement which would prevent him from carrying out his engagement with them'. The matter was resolved when New Brighton did become affiliated. Robinson persevered with his intention to join them, but, ironically, he left after only one season even though they were then elected to the Second Division of the Football League, along with Barnsley, Glossop North End and Port Vale, when its membership was increased for 1898–99.

It said much for the high regard in which he was held as a goalkeeper that he retained his place in the England team despite being out of the Football League. He played against all three of the other home countries while on Tower's books, and made the last six of his international appearances after moving into the Southern League with Southampton.

That switch to the South took him to two FA Cup finals—or, to be precise, three, as the second of them went to a replay. In each of them his team-mates included Arthur Turner, an England winger who in the month after that replay was transferred to Derby County for a short stay from which he made his way back to the Saints by way of Newcastle and Tottenham.

The replay, like their first final, ended in defeat for Southampton, who had to wait until 1976 to carry off the Cup. In 1900 they lost 4–0 to a Bury team that included six of the players who helped to rout the Rams three years later. In 1902, after knocking out holders Spurs at the third attempt in the first round, they were beaten 2–1 at the Crystal Palace, following a 1–1 draw, by Sheffield United, who over the two matches fielded eight of the men against whom Derby had failed in the final three years earlier.

And Derby-born John Wilks Robinson so nearly faced his home-town team instead of United, for that was the season in which the Blades reached the final for the third time in four years only after putting paid to Derby County by one goal in a third semi-final meeting.

Southampton made up for their Cup disappointments by winning the Southern League title three times during Robinson's days at the Dell, to which they had just moved, but he soured his stay with his alleged attempt to poach Steve Bloomer from the Rams before he went West with Plymouth Argyle in 1903 and, two years later, Exeter City. A short spell with a Plymouth club named Green Waves followed, after which he rejoined Exeter, then returned to the Midlands with Stoke City before finally setting out for the United States in 1912 to take up an offer from the Rochester club in New York. He was 65 when he died in October, 1931.

To fill the considerable gap left by Robinson's departure, Derby County first turned to Joseph Frail, who had been signed from Glossop to follow George Dockery, formerly of Third Lanark, and Joe Green, a local lad who was later with Belper Town, in the rewardless role as the England 'keeper's club deputy. Frail, one of only ten men his home club, Burslem Port Vale, had been able to field in losing their first League game by 5–1 away to Small Heath in 1892, kept goal in the Rams' first eight matches of 1897–98, but he played in just two more towards the end of that season before going back to Glossop via Chatham, Middlesbrough, Luton, Brentford and Stockport.

The man to whom he had to give way at Derby was Jack Fryer, the 6ft 2in beanpole from Cromford whose excellence over six seasons was so sadly sullied by his ill-advised decision to defy injury in the 1903 Cup Final, his third losing appearance with the Rams at the Crystal Palace in his 199th and last game for the club.

Fryer was one of those goalkeepers who did not begin in that position. He was something of a utility player in Derbyshire minor football before, as the tallest man in his team, he was asked to take over one day when the regular 'keeper failed to turn up. It was not altogether surprising that he promptly showed himself good enough to stay there, for he was a competent wicketkeeper in the Ind Coope brewery cricket team at Burton, where he worked.

After leaving Derby County in the unpleasant aftermath of the record Cup Final defeat by Bury, Fryer made 170 appearances during his fruitful seasons with Fulham until his enforced retirement through injury, and he stayed south to run a public house near Chelsea's ground. It was in London, at Westminster, that he died in December, 1933, aged 56.

As already recalled, one of Jack Fryer's goalkeeping deputies with Derby County was the luckless Tom Harrison who was limited to just one first-team game through missing his train en route to what would have been his second appearance in the match at Blackburn for which Arthur Latham, the trainer and former full-back, had to come out of his lengthy playing retirement to deputise. Fryer was available again for the remaining two games of the 1901–02 season, and Harrison, who played for South Normanton Town, Stanton Hill Town and Ripley Athletic before joining the Rams, left the following September for Pinxton.

An earlier one-off emergency call by Derby County for a goalkeeper had been answered by John Goodall for a match at Wolverhampton during the England forward's first season with the club, in January, 1890. The Rams lost that game, in which Latham played at right-back, by 2–1. The only other instance of a player other than a recognised goalkeeper occupying that position for the club in a whole match occurred in September, 1944, when Jack Nicholas played there in a 2–0 war-time defeat at Barnsley after Frank Boulton had missed his train connection in Birmingham and his deputy, a youngster named Vanham, had answered an emergency call too late to travel with the team.

Jack Fryer's firm hold on the goalkeeping position while he was with Derby led to the Rams losing another player from within the county. This was Harry Linacre, whose restriction to just a couple of games as the big man's deputy made him only too ready to follow his uncles, the Forman brothers, to Nottingham Forest, where he found the greater scope that lifted him into the England team. Like the Formans, he was born just inside Derbyshire's southern border at Aston-on-Trent, and he played for that village, as well as Loughborough Grammar School and Draycott Mills, before his short stay at the Baseball Ground.

Recommended to Forest by Frank Forman, Linacre was an ideal successor to Dennis Allsop, that other Forest goalkeeping stalwart who slipped through Derby's grasp, and he became a firm favourite at the City Ground. It was significant that Forest lost the First Division status he helped them to gain in 1907 not long after he had played the last of his 335 League and Cup games for them.

Fortunately for Derby County, it was only a few years after they had allowed one future international goalkeeper, Linacre, to get away from them that they discovered another, also on their doorstep, who was fit to follow Fryer. He was Dronfield-born Harry Maskrey, who, like his own successor, Ernald Scattergood, arrived from Ripley Athletic.

**Harry Linacre and (right) Frank Forman, who both played for England
after leaving Derby County for Nottingham Forest.**

Maskrey cut an imposing figure—more than six feet in height and measuring as much again between the finger-tips of his outstretched arms—which made him ideally suited as a Grenadier Guardsman in the 1914–18 War. Derby County gave him his first League chance in a draw with Grimsby in their last home game of the 1902–03 season on the Wednesday after the Palace pounding by Bury, but he was not an automatic choice at the beginning of the following campaign. For its first dozen matches preference was given to Walter Whittaker, a Mancunian of many clubs newly signed from Grimsby Town, but a change was then considered necessary after a keenly-felt 6–2 home defeat by the club Derby County and their fans hate losing to most of all, Nottingham Forest.

The reinstated Maskrey had the misfortune to concede the only goal of the next game, away to the Wednesday, when, only five minutes after the kick-off, one of his clearances was blown back into the goalmouth by the strong wind and provided George Simpson, the Owls' outside-left successor to Fred Spiksley, with an easy heading opportunity. Undeterred, Maskrey proceeded to give a masterly display that guaranteed him an extended run, and from that day he was a regular member of the defence until Scattergood came into prominence early in the 1909–10 season.

For all his consistent excellence, Maskrey found the competition at international level so strong that he played only once for his country, joining his Derby team-mate Ben Warren

**Harry Maskrey, recalled by the Rams
in a goalkeeping emergency.**

in the side that defeated Ireland 3–1 in Belfast in February, 1908. He and another Derbyshire goalkeeper, the amateur Horace Bailey, were the ones who that year interrupted the England reign of Sam Hardy. Bailey, then of Leicester Fosse, took over for games in which Wales (7–1), Austria (6–1 and 11–1), Hungary (7–0) and Bohemia (4–0) were all heavily beaten.

Maskrey was still firmly established in the Derby side when he returned from a cricket coaching appointment in Scotland in August, 1909, but he had to give way to Scattergood because of an abscess which developed under an arm after the third match of the new season. He was recalled for a home game against Grimsby three weeks later, only to be injured in making one of his saves as the Rams coasted to a 6–0 victory on the strength of a Bentley hat-trick. Back came Scattergood, and, with Maskrey soon afterwards on his way from the Baseball Ground, this time in Ernald stayed—to hold down the job until George Lawrence, the last, but certainly not the least, of the club's locally-born goalkeepers of that era, stepped in on a regular basis early in a 1914–15 season which continued, not without some protests, despite the start of a world war.

I shall always remember Harry Maskrey for the fact that he was the subject of one of the readers' sporting queries that caught me out in a weekly answers column I conducted for the *Derby Evening Telegraph*. I was asked to give details of his final game for Derby County, so I looked up the records, found that he was transferred to Bradford City in October, 1909, and therefore confidently announced that he made his farewell in that big win over Grimsby, the Rams' last match before he left them. Wrong! What I had overlooked was that he was back in Derby, working for British Celanese, when the County called upon him again in a goalkeeping emergency which arose soon after the start of the 1920–21 season.

With George Lawrence, by then the first choice, and Jimmy Kidd, the reserve signed from Bolton Wanderers after starting out with Blackpool, both out of action, Maskrey was brought back for the club's first three games in September, and then for two more shortly before Christmas. Derby were beaten in all five of those matches, but that was no adverse reflection on Maskrey, who reached his 40th birthday between his two periods of recall, for that was the season in which they made such a habit of losing— a then record 22 times, including a Cup exit at Wolverhampton—that they again dropped out of the First Division.

The correct answer to the reader's query, therefore, was that Maskrey, who was said to have 'all the collier's contempt for hard knocks,' last played for Derby County on December 4th, 1920, in a 2–0 defeat at Blackburn during the Rams' depressing sequence of eight matches without scoring. His five extra appearances edged him past 200 for the club in League games, to a total of 222 with the addition of his 20 Cup-ties. And he still had some good goalkeeping left in him, with a winding-up spell at Burton All Saints. In common with so many former League footballers in those days, he took over the running of a public house, the New Inn in Derby's Russell Street, but he was in only his mid-forties when he collapsed and died there in 1927.

Riddings, a village a few miles from Alfreton, was the birthplace of Ernald Oak Scattergood, who, after following Maskrey to the Baseball Ground from Ripley Athletic, had to remain patient for a couple of seasons before also following him as Derby's regular goalkeeper. He then proved most dependable—never more so than when he kept a clean sheet in 21 of their 38 matches during the 1911–12 season in which he gained his Second Division title medal as the only ever-present member of the team.

His continued efficiency in face of the top forwards of the day during the following season, despite the lack of some height for a goalkeeper at 5ft 8in, earned him selection in March, 1913, against Wales at Bristol City's Ashton Gate ground in place of Middlesbrough's 'Tim' Williamson a month after England had lost to Ireland, in Belfast, for the first time. Williamson, whose given forenames were Reginald Garnet, played the last of his seven games for England in that 2–1 defeat by the Irish, but he went on to reach 602 League and Cup games for Boro—a club record that still stands. There was a gap of six years between his first and second caps, due to the brilliance of Sam Hardy, that most worthy addition to the impressive ranks of Derbyshire-born goalkeepers.

England defeated Wales when Ernald Scattergood made his international debut, but only just, by 4–3, and, like Harry Maskrey, he was not called upon at that level again. For the sterner test against Scotland at Chelsea a few weeks later there was a recall for Hardy, who had first been capped in 1907. Hardy stayed in for England's next six matches after the Scots had been beaten by a Harry Hampton goal, and he made the last of his 21 appearances in full internationals (he also took part in three of the fixtures in the 1919 Victory series) in the 5–4 win over Scotland at Sheffield in 1920 in which Derby's Alf Quantrill scored his one goal for England.

Born at nearby Newbold, Hardy came to the fore with Chesterfield, whose many other top-notch goalkeepers have included Gordon Banks and Ray Middleton, and after helping Liverpool to the First Division title in his first season at Anfield (1905–06) he was twice an FA Cup winner with Aston Villa (in 1913 and 1920) before injury compelled him to conclude his League career of more than 550 matches at the age of 41 in 1924, while with Nottingham Forest.

Of all the gifted Derbyshire-born goalkeepers, Hardy clearly still stands out as the most accomplished. Banks, otherwise the one player many might rate more highly, cannot be counted in that distinguished company because he hailed from Sheffield. What a pity it was from a Derby County point of view that the £500 transfer fee Chesterfield received for Hardy was handed over not by the Rams but by Liverpool, who were undeterred by the fact that he had recently conceded six goals in a Second Division match against them.

Ernald Scattergood could have wished for better than being beaten three times in his only game for England, but any disappointment he may have felt was as nothing compared with what his son Kenneth had to endure when he made his League debut for Derby County. That happened at Goodison Park on Christmas Day, 1936, when, with his team handicapped by injuries to Dai Astley, Jack Barker and Sammy Crooks, the Rams' second Scattergood had the depressing experience of having to pick the ball out of his net on seven occasions, with not even one goal scored in reply.

Three days later, Derby gained some measure of revenge with a 3–1 victory in the return game, Astley doing the hat-trick, but Ken Scattergood had to endure further fusillades that culminated in an 8–1 defeat early the following season at Stoke, from where he had been signed after short spells with Wolves and Bristol City. When the Rams released him soon afterwards he had let in 62 goals in his 25 senior matches.

Ernald Scattergood, in contrast, was Derby's first choice for five seasons and got to within eight of 200 appearances for them in League and Cup before his transfer after the first seven games of the 1914–15 season let in George Lawrence. As with Maskrey, Scattergood's move took him to Bradford, but to Park Avenue, not Valley Parade. It also restored him to the First Division, to which Bradford had been promoted for the first time in the previous season of the Rams' relegation from it.

Those were heady days for the Yorkshire city, with both its clubs in the League's top section, but leaner times were only just around the corner. Bradford Park Avenue dropped out after only three seasons, and Bradford City followed them down a year later. Both subsequently fell as far as the Fourth Division, and in 1970 Bradford went out of the League altogether as Cambridge United were voted into their place. That left City to soldier on for Bradford mainly in the lower regions until a belated revival in the 1990s briefly brought them back to centre stage in the affluent Premiership.

Scattergood's first two League seasons with Bradford PA were separated by the First World War, in which he survived being gassed, and in the second of them Derby County's immediate return to the First Division gave him the chance to make an impressive reappearance at the Baseball Ground in a scoreless draw. Bradford finished both those seasons in mid-table, but in the next one of 1920–21 they went down with a record that was inferior even to the worst in the history of the club that accompanied them—Derby County. These were the figures:

	P	W	D	L	F	A	Pts
Derby County	42	5	16	21	32	58	26
Bradford	42	8	8	26	43	76	24

Sheffield United, the club directly above that relegated pair, had 30 points.

For the first few seasons after the war, clubs met each other home and away on successive Saturdays. Derby won just one of their four First Division meetings with Bradford, Bill Paterson scoring the only goal at the Baseball Ground in March, 1921, the week after the Rams had lost 2–1 at Park Avenue on the day Harry Storer played the first of his 274 games for them. The result at that venue the year before was a 1–1 draw.

Despite Bradford's decline, Scattergood gave them excellent value over almost 300 matches, fully justifying the high opinion held of him by the manager who signed him for the Park Avenue club, the aforesaid Tom Maley who had preceded Harry Newbould at Manchester City. Scattergood not only prevented goals, he also scored them in the role of penalty-taker in which he continued after tucking away three spot kicks for Derby. He did so, that is, until, after four further successes, he had one saved by Willis Walker, the South Shields goalkeeper and Nottinghamshire cricketer, at Easter in 1922. He had such a scare in only just managing to get back to his own goal in time that he readily agreed to hand the job over to somebody else after that. He had a final tally of eight goals, scoring the other one in open play as an injured 'passenger' during Bradford's Boxing Day game against Clapton Orient in 1921.

It was no novelty for goalkeepers to take penalties in those days. One of them, Arnold Birch, converted a record five for Chesterfield in the Third Division North during the 1923–24 season. In more recent times it has become such a rarity that Alex Stepney made news by taking Manchester United's penalties while Tommy Docherty was their manager—a poor reflection on the recognised strikers.

From Bradford, Ernald Scattergood returned to Derbyshire by joining Alfreton Town, who were embarking upon a switch to the Midland League after being runners-up, and then twice champions, in their last three seasons in the Central Alliance.

They made a fairly successful start in that new sphere, but they had a poor season financially in 1926–27 and resigned membership. For an area which had produced so many outstanding players, the disbandonment of the club that had arisen in 1921, in the wake of the one for which other men associated with Derby County also played, came as a severe blow, and brought down a most unwelcome curtain on an influential phase in Derbyshire's soccer history.

The current Alfreton Town club came into existence in 1959, following the merger of Alfreton Miners' Welfare and Alfreton United. Playing on a new ground in North Street provided by the local council, they entered the Northern section of the Central Alliance's First Division, and soon progressed to the Midland Counties League, of which they were three times champions in addition to winning the Midland League Cup for three successive seasons.

Further success came in the Northern Counties (East) League after the merger of the Midland and Yorkshire leagues in 1982, and they soon also won the League Cup and championship at that level, earning a place in the newly-formed Division One of the Northern Premier League in 1987. Nine seasons later they added further to the fine traditions of the area by gaining promotion to the Premier Division.

Sam Hardy, the outstanding Derbyshire-born goalkeeper who was capped by England while with Liverpool and Aston Villa.

CHAPTER 17

Three Relegations, Two Promotions

*Ups and downs of Methven's managership – Subterfuge
to sign Lawrence – Belated title reward – Luckless
Argyle make it at ninth attempt – Three Ritchies with
the Rams – Derby winger scores in epic England win –
Quantrill in rush to last cap – Versatile Wightman
battles back to aid another promotion*

THE DOZEN FOOTBALL LEAGUE SEASONS of Jimmy Methven's managership of Derby County (excluding the four lost to the First World War) included some of the most difficult in the club's history, with three relegations from the First Division to offset two promotions as champions of the Second.

And although the Rams only twice failed to finish in the top half of the table during the nine seasons Methven was in charge before the break from League football caused by the war (six of them in the Second Division), he was unable to maintain that standard through the first three seasons after it as they ended them 18th and last in the top division, then 12th in the lower section, never in the running for another rise.

The team with which the Rams re-entered the First Division when the League got under way again on August 30th, 1919 contained seven of the men who had done most to help them to win promotion in 1914–15. They were goalkeeper George Lawrence, full-backs Jack Atkin and Tommy Barbour, wing-half Jimmy Bagshaw, and forwards Jim Moore, Harry Leonard and Bill Baker. As already recalled, of the four other regular members of the side that had given the club their second Division Two championship in four years, inside-right Tom Benfield and left-half George Brooks had been killed in action, right-winger Billy Grimes had moved to Tottenham, and centre-half Bill Eadie had retired.

George Lawrence was born just over the county border in Nottinghamshire, at Basford, but he could be counted as the last of the locally-produced goalkeepers who gave the Rams such sterling service over 26 seasons of League football from Jack Robinson's introduction in 1891, through the tenures of Fryer, Maskrey and Scattergood, and continuing until Lawrence lost his regular place at the beginning of 1922.

Jimmy Methven resorted to one of his subterfuges in negotiating the transfer of Lawrence after spotting him in action with Ilkeston United against Ripley Town towards the end of the 1909–10 season. Realising that word of his interest would spread, increasing the risk of other clubs attempting to steal a march on him, if he made an immediate offer, the Rams' manager decided to bide his time until the season was over. He also knew that he could not make a direct approach to Lawrence without the Ilkeston club's officials finding out, so, in order to make sure that he did not miss his man, he asked a friend, Harry ('Inky') Ellison, who was one of Derby County's oldest supporters, to tell the goalkeeper not to sign any forms until he (Methven) saw him after the season finished.

This Ellison duly did, and afterwards he always claimed that he was the one who got Lawrence to Derby. But it was not all plain sailing. Far from it, and Methven had to make a hasty journey to Ilkeston to clinch the deal when several other clubs did threaten to beat him to it after Lawrence had met the Derby manager's wishes by refusing to re-sign. And even then there was a late snag to be overcome. In his hurry, Methven had forgotten to take the necessary forms, but, showing an admirable presence of mind, he produced an old Amateur League form and held his hand over the printed matter while Lawrence penned his name to it.

The legal papers were completed the next day, only for Lawrence soon to be given plenty of cause to wonder if he had done the right thing as Scattergood's consistent form kept him waiting impatiently in the reserves. Quite a number of his transfer requests had to be warded off until Scattergood's departure to Bradford finally gave him his chance of a regular first-team place in October, 1914, and he not only took it avidly but also had the reward of ending that season with a Second Division championship medal.

He had turned 30 by the time League football was resumed in 1919 after its war-enforced four-season break, but he remained first choice for most of the first three peacetime seasons, and, including his wartime games, he exceeded 150 appearances before leaving for Bristol City in September, 1924 almost a year after his last League match for the Rams, a 3–3 home draw with Fulham. His exit was little more straightforward than his arrival, for he objected to the £500 transfer fee being asked and successfully applied for its reduction to £100. After one season in the West Country he moved to Lincoln City, then ended his playing days back at Ilkeston.

Bill Baker, a winger from Dartford, missed only three matches in the 1914–15 promotion season after displacing Edwin Neve, a Lancastrian who had more than 100 League games for Hull City behind him but left for short spells with Nottingham Forest and Chesterfield after his only full Derby season, in the outside-left position he had been sharing with Ivan Sharpe, unfortunately coincided with relegation. For Baker, too, a regular place in the Rams' first team was to last for only the one season, but he remained on the Baseball Ground staff for two more after returning from the war, in which he was wounded and gassed.

Baker's next stop was at Plymouth, where he was the Argyle's left-winger for the first three of the six successive seasons in which they had the shattering experience of being runners-up for the Third Division South's one promotion spot—first on goal average, and by only one point on two of the other occasions. After then finishing third and fourth, they finally made it at the ninth attempt as champions in 1930.

The replacement for Baker as Derby County's outside-left in 1919 was Alf Quantrill, a real speed merchant who was adept at centring the ball on the run. Born in India, at Rawalpindi, he was brought to England at an early age and some seven or eight

George Lawrence, an impatient reserve in waiting.

Alf Quantrill, who had a hectic journey to Cardiff after a late England call-up.
(Albert Wilkes and Son)

years later, at 15, he played in the Lincolnshire League for Grimsby Rovers. From there he joined Boston Swifts, and it was while he was with them that he was spotted by a Derby scout in a cup game. Invited to the Baseball Ground for a 14-day trial, he made such an immediate impression that he was offered terms after his first private try-out, and he was signed, aged $17^1/2$, in August, 1914, exactly a week after the outbreak of war.

He had only a few first-team chances in the promotion season, at the end of which he joined the Derbyshire Yeomanry along with Tommy Barbour and Stuart McMillan, son of the former Rams winger and destined, just more than 30 years later, to be the manager who brought the FA Cup to Derby. Stuart McMillan's only League game for the County as a player, at outside-right, was also one of those in which Quantrill turned out on the left wing—a 1–1 home draw with Glossop at the beginning of 1915.

In May, 1918, after spending two years with the Yeomanry in Salonika, Quantrill was invalided home with recurrent malaria and transferred to the 5th Dragoon Guards, with whom he served first in France and then, after the armistice, in Germany. Resuming football regularly, he scored 84 goals from inside-right in a Services season and helped his team to win the Cavalry Corps Cup. In the final, on a snow-covered ground, they won 2–0 after extra time.

Back at Derby, his progress was so remarkable that he gained the first of his four England caps within six months of ousting Bill Baker for his First Division debut in a narrow home win over Aston Villa. The only goal of that visit by Villa on a Monday in early September, 1919, was scored by Bill Ritchie, an inside-forward from Carlisle who was also making his Derby debut after war service, but was given only three other first-team opportunities before moving to Millwall. He was subsequently with Ashington and Barrow before emigrating to Canada.

The Rams had two other players named Ritchie around that period—Archie, a full-back from Glasgow Rangers who features prominently in the penultimate chapter, and Duncan, an outside-left previously with Dumbarton, Raith Rovers and Sheffield United who played only twice in the League side (in the 1913–14 relegation season).

England lost 2–1 to Wales at Highbury when Alf Quantrill was first on their left wing in March 1920, but he was retained against Scotland at Hillsborough the following month (the only forward to keep his place), and he scored one of the goals in a classic 5–4 home victory. The main individual honours, however, went to Bob Kelly and Fred Morris, two more newcomers to international football, who, in heavy rain, transformed this hectic game from a 2–4 interval deficit with three goals in seven minutes midway through the second half, the Burnley player netting twice. Jack Cock, who, like Quantrill, had played for England only once previously, was the other man on the mark in this team:

> **Hardy** (Aston Villa); **Longworth** (Liverpool), **Pennington** (West Bromwich Albion); **Ducat** (Aston Villa), **McCall** (Preston North End), **Grimsdell** (Tottenham Hotspur); **Wallace** (Aston Villa), **Kelly** (Burnley), **Cock** (Chelsea), **Morris** (West Bromwich Albion), **Quantrill** (Derby County).

Miller (2), Wilson and Donaldson scored for Scotland, whose defeat handed the home championship to Wales. The Scots' line-up was:

> **Campbell** (Liverpool); **McNair** (Glasgow Celtic), **Blair** (Wednesday); **Bowie** (Glasgow Rangers), **Low** (Newcastle United), **Gordon** (Rangers); **Donaldson** (Bolton Wanderers), **Miller** (Liverpool), **Wilson** (Dunfermline Athletic), **Paterson** (Leicester City), **Troup** (Dundee).

Later that year, Quantrill also played in a 2–0 win gained over Ireland at Sunderland with goals by Kelly and, on his international debut, Villa's Billy Walker, but the Derby winger was not originally selected for England's next match, a scoreless draw with Wales at Cardiff in March, 1921. The story behind what was to be his final cap call-up makes especially interesting reading in view of the current elaborate arrangements for squad training before such matches. This was how Alf Quantrill told it to me:

A policeman called at my lodgings about nine o'clock one Sunday evening and said that Mr Morgan Roberts, then the Derbyshire FA secretary and a Derby County director, had 'phoned to say that I was to travel to Cardiff to play against Wales the next day in place of Dimmock, of the Spurs, who had dropped out because of injury. I had to go to the other end of town to fetch Tom Page, the groundsman, to the Baseball Ground in order to get my boots. I caught an early train on the Monday morning to Cardiff, had a sandwich lunch from a station trolley en route, and arrived in Cardiff with only half-an-hour to spare. Ninian Park is some way from the station, and my only hope of getting there in time for the kick-off was to take a taxi. This I did, and just managed to get onto the field before the whistle blew to start the game. After the match, I went to collect my expenses, but when I asked for 3s 6d [17p] to cover the taxi fare the FA councillor in charge refused to pay it, saying that taxi fares were not allowed. What a change there is today!

What a change indeed! And his 'today' (he was speaking in the early 1950s) was getting on for half a century ago. How transformed the treatment of international players has become since then.

Quantrill played in 72 League games and four Cup-ties for Derby County, scoring five goals, before their return to the Second Division precipitated his departure to

The England team which Derby's Alf Quantrill had a hectic journey to join for the match with Wales at Cardiff in 1921. Back row (left to right): Wilson (Wednesday), Bamber (Liverpool), Cresswell (South Shields), E.G.H. Coleman (Dulwich Hamlet), Silcock (Manchester United), Bromilow (Liverpool). Front row: Chedgzoy (Everton), Kelly (Burnley), Buchan (Sunderland, captain), Chambers (Liverpool), Quantrill (Derby County). The game, which was briefly stopped by a thunderstorm, ended in a scoreless draw, but in the trial before it at Burnley three goals were scored in a 6–1 win for the North by Buchan, who, as recalled in Chapter 12, was unsuccessfully sought by the Rams while he was an unknown amateur in the Kent League.

Preston North End in the summer of 1921—shortly after he had married Steve Bloomer's eldest daughter. His description of his three years at Deepdale as 'not very happy ones' was hardly surprising considering that in only his second game for North End he displaced a cartilage in his right knee and, in being put out of action for the rest of the season, lost the chance to play in the 1922 FA Cup Final in which Preston lost to Huddersfield Town by a controversial penalty.

North End left behind their lucky black cat in favour of a sprig of white heather—and a film of the match showed that luck deserted them in confirming that left-winger Billy Smith was brought down just outside the area for the award of the decisive spot kick he converted in the 67th minute. Huddersfield were generally considered the better side, however, and one reporter said 'it was one of the best mistakes the referee [J.W.P. Fowler, of Sunderland] ever made in his career'.

By a remarkable coincidence, that outcome was reversed in similar circumstances when these clubs next met in the final 16 years later. At Wembley in 1938, George Mutch, Preston's inside-right, scored the only goal of the game by converting a controversial penalty that was awarded in the last minute of extra time. Referee A.J. Jewell, of London, ruled that Alf Young, Huddersfield's centre-half and captain, tripped Mutch just inside the penalty area, but a published photograph of the incident indicated that the North End forward was just outside the line of the area in the split second before the offence occurred.

Alf Quantrill's next moves after Preston were to Chorley, then Bradford, where he spent six years before joining Nottingham Forest. About two years after that, however, he developed a duodenal ulcer and therefore decided to hang up his boots at the end of the 1931–32 season. Having been one of the few footballers of his day who had believed in having a job outside the game, doing his training in the evenings, he had wisely safeguarded his future by obtaining employment in accountancy, then insurance, after abandoning his original aim to become a solicitor, and he rose to be manager of the Scottish Union Insurance Company's North-West territory, based in Manchester, until his retirement several years before his death in 1968.

Two of the players new to League football who were among Quantrill's Derby County team-mates when soccer got back to its peacetime footing in the 1919–20 season both had a Nottingham Forest connection before him, as guests during the First World War. As we have seen, one of them, Noah Burton, put in a second, and longer, spell with Forest, but although his last two seasons on their books coincided with the couple Quantrill spent at the City Ground, they did not appear together in the first team. The other, defender Harold Wightman, also rejoined Forest—but that was not until the summer of 1936, when he was the first team manager they appointed.

The dire season of 1920–21 which deposited Derby County back in the Second Division with their worst record up to that time—only five wins, 32 goals and 26 points from their 42—games was the last with the Rams not only for Burton and Quantrill, but also for 'Tiddler' Murray, an inside-forward who had won an England amateur cap before leaving Bishop Auckland to turn professional at the Baseball Ground. Seeking to escape the goal drought in which he had been caught up, Murray moved to Middlesbrough after just that one season with Derby, but he had only limited opportunities with Boro back in the First Division before going into Scottish football with Hearts and Dunfermline. The year after he left Ayresome Park Middlesbrough themselves were relegated, but they were Second Division champions the season following Derby County's own promotion, in 1926, as runners-up to the Wednesday.

Harold Wightman, who was born at Sutton-in-Ashfield, first took part in organised football at the age of 12, when he was a forward with Summit United in the Skegby and District League. From there he went to Mansfield Mechanics, a Notts and Derbyshire League club, and at 15 he signed an amateur form for Notts County, but did not play for them. For the next two seasons he assisted Sutton Town as an inside-left in the Central Alliance, and after helping them to finish runners-up to Derby County Reserves he played in the same competition for Eastwood Rangers.

Then, still as a teenager, he spent a couple of years with Chesterfield in the Midland League, mainly as a centre-forward, before his 138 wartime games as a guest for Forest, the first club to realise that centre-half was his best position. He was on the winning side in each of his three appearances for the Reds against the Rams, and there was much disappointment in Nottingham when Jimmy Methven astutely nipped in to secure his signature in May, 1919, the month after he had been with Burton in the Forest team that landed the Victory Shield at Everton's expense. As an ever-

**Harold Wightman, whose astute signing by
Jimmy Methven foiled Forest.**
(Derby Evening Telegraph)

present with Derby in the first post-war season, he earned this praise in the local paper:

> Out of necessity, he shone mostly in defensive tactics, but when the stress and strain of defending was the exception to the rule he revealed his constructive ability, which was more in evidence when he was better supported. Wightman would be an acquistion to any side, and he can be placed high in the list of leading centre-halves.

Several other members of the team were not deserving of similar praise as the Rams had a desperate struggle to avoid relegation that season, but Wightman survived both that trauma and the even worse one that followed, when the club did go down, to get within sight of a 200th appearance before going back to Chesterfield at the end of a decade with Derby.

As the trapdoor into the Second Division inexorably opened in the spring of 1921, he lost his place to Charlie Rance, a member of Tottenham's 1919–20 title-winning promotion side who was signed, along with the combative Harry Storer from Grimsby, in Methven's last attempt to beat the drop, but he soon regained it to prompt Rance's return to London with Queen's Park Rangers. When a more formidable rival was encountered as Harry Thoms rejoined Methven's successor, Cecil Potter, from Hartlepools United, Wightman again battled back to make such a successful switch to full-back that he played a significant part—as the partner for Tom Crilly, Potter's other recruit from his former club—in the regaining of First Division rank in the first season of another manager from the North-East, the formidable George Jobey.

Wightman filled the vacancy left by the transfer to Newcastle United of Bert Chandler, for four seasons an automatic choice since taking over from Jack Atkin. Chandler, who was born at Carlisle in January, 1897 and died back there in the same month of 1963, joined the Rams after leaving the Army, in which he survived a gas attack in 1918 after being commissioned in the Machine Gun Corps of the Border Regiment. He cost Newcastle more than £3,000, a sizeable sum for those days, but spent only just over one season with them before a fee of about £2,500 took him to Sheffield United, with whom he also did not stay long. Derby County clearly benefited from his best footballing years.

Harold Wightman's first-team days at Derby were finally numbered to just one in each of his last two seasons by the arrival of snowy-haired Tommy Cooper from Port Vale, and he played his last League game for the Rams while Cooper, who went on to captain both club and country, was winning his first international cap in Belfast. That was on October 22nd, 1927, in a 5–0 away defeat by Manchester United, the club against which Wightman had made his debut for Derby in a 1–1 draw at the Baseball Ground on August 30th, 1919.

For his last year with the County, Wightman was manager George Jobey's assistant. After spending another year back at Chesterfield, he was coach and assistant to manager Horace Henshall with Notts County, who had just descended into the Third Division but gained immediate promotion as the Southern Section's 1930–31 champions. That was Wightman's only season at Meadow Lane, after which he had spells as manager of the Towns of Luton and Mansfield, separated by a brief return to Derby as chief scout.

At Luton, where his signings included Joe Payne, scorer of ten goals in his first League game at centre-forward (against Bristol Rovers on Easter Monday in 1936), Wightman laid the basis of the side that won promotion from the Third South in 1936–37, but that success was achieved under the direction of Ned Liddell, a former Orient defender who had previously managed Southend, QPR and Fulham. Wightman resigned in the autumn of 1935 because of a difference of opinion with his board of directors.

The man he succeeded at Mansfield early in 1936 was Charles Bell, a Scot whose clubs as a player had included Chesterfield, and who had been a captain in Frank Buckley's Footballers' Battalion during the First World War. Like Bell, who resigned after admitting to losing control of his players, Wightman held that post for only a few months, for he soon let it be known that he wanted to leave at the end of the season. Resisting Mansfield's offer of a three-year contract with an increased salary, he eagerly took up the challenge of trying to revive Nottingham Forest's fortunes—only to find the task well beyond him.

From finishing his first season back at the City Ground 18th out of 22 in Division Two in 1937, Forest deteriorated still further to have an escape the following year 'in circumstances dramatic enough to be without parallel in football's history'.

That quote is taken from the report by the highly respected Nottingham journalist Arthur Turner of the match on the 1937–38 season's last day in which Forest saved themselves by the two-hundredth part of a goal with an equaliser five minutes from time at Barnsley. The 2–2 draw left both clubs on 36 points, five immediately above already-doomed Stockport County, so it was Barnsley who went down instead of Forest, with respective goals figures of 50–64 to 47–60. Newcastle United, beaten 4–1 at Luton in their last game, also escaped narrowly on goal average, as these final bottom-of-the-table positions show:

	W	P	D	L	W	D	L	F	A	Pts
Newcastle	42	12	4	5	2	4	15	51	58	36
Forest	42	12	3	6	2	5	14	47	60	36
Barnsley	42	7	11	3	4	3	14	50	64	36
Stockport	42	8	6	7	3	3	15	43	70	31

The scorer of the late goal that so sensationally switched the misery of relegation from one team to the other was David ('Boy') Martin, the Northern Ireland international signed by Wightman from Wolves. This was how Turner described it:

> Trim [the Forest right-back from Arsenal who guested for Derby County during the 1939–45 War] planked the ball into the arms of Barnsley's goalkeeper, Binns, and Martin, no bustler of goalkeepers in the ordinary way, let loose a full-blooded charge that had Binns rocking and turning...turning into goal with the ball in his hands. It was over the line all right, and while Forest's players danced for joy the 'keeper walked yards down the pitch, crying bitterly with his face in his hands.

Barnsley's frantic appeals were to no avail, referee P. Snape, of Swansea, sticking to his decision to award the goal after consulting a linesman. But even then Forest, who had been reduced to ten men by an injury to half-back Bob Davies, were almost undone, for their goalkeeper, Percy Ashton, was beaten by a shot from wing-half Logan that struck the woodwork.

Martin was also the scorer of Forest's first goal, giving them a 26th-minute lead with one of his fiercely-struck specials, only for Barnsley to pull level with a fluke and then get in front through a goalkeeping blunder. Ten minutes before half-time, the ball bounced off the bumpy pitch over the diving Ashton when inside-left Asquith sent in a speculative long-range shot. On the hour, a drive from Barlow, the home side's other inside-forward, should have been dealt with comfortably, but Ashton allowed the ball to squirm out of his grasp over the line.

Bert Barlow, who had wasted an excellent earlier chance, was the player who joined Wolves soon afterwards, in the 1938 close season, and then, less than a year later, made news by scoring twice against them in Portsmouth's shock victory in the last pre-war FA Cup Final a couple of months after moving from Molineux to Fratton Park.

Nottingham Forest again finished 20th in that 1938–39 season, and again survived only on goal average after an anxious final day. Even more amazingly, they were once more required to end with a visit to the other club in danger of going down. Whereas, however, they had needed a point for safety at Barnsley's expense, this time they went to Norwich knowing that they could afford to lose if they did so by fewer than four goals. What was more, they went there fresh from the benefit of a fortnight's training at Skegness, and in midweek had been without match while Norwich had been losing a hard-fought game at Plymouth—the club against which Forest had completed their home programme with a narrow win, aided by an own goal, the previous Saturday.

In the event, Norwich defeated their visitors from Nottingham by only one goal, luckily scored early in the second half when Ware, their centre-forward, was played on from an otherwise offside position as the ball was deflected to him off a defender from a free kick. So down Norwich went. They and Forest both had 31 points, three behind Swansea, the club immediately above them, and 14 ahead of the other relegated side, Tranmere Rovers. Forest had goal figures of 49–82; Norwich 50–91.

Harold Wightman was no longer Forest's manager by the time of that second successive last-ditch wriggling clear of the relegation hook. In March, 1939, he was replaced by Billy Walker, who had ended his playing days at Aston Villa with a then club record of 478 League games and a total of 214 League goals that was only one fewer than Harry Hampton's Villa best. Walker's number of League appearances has since been exceeded by full-back Charlie Aitken, who raised the club's record to 561, two of them as substitute, from 1961 to 1976, but his 30 goals in 53 FA Cup-ties took him to a Villa total of 244—two ahead of Hampton's collective tally.

Walker was unable to prevent Forest failing to survive another last-day battle against the drop in the third post-war season—despite ending on a winning note, if by just one goal—but he then led them not only out of the Third Division but back into the First. He also took them to victory in an FA Cup Final, repeating the success he had enjoyed in his first managerial post with Sheffield Wednesday before resigning there, claiming interference by the chairman in his control of team affairs, as the Hillsborough club fell on hard times. His reign at Forest lasted until 1960, when he again resigned, but he stayed with them on the committee that then ran the club until the breakdown of his health which resulted in his death towards the end of 1964.

Harold (or, as he was better known, Harry) Wightman ended his direct connection with football on leaving Forest. He died at Nottingham in April, 1945, two months short of his 51st brithday.

CHAPTER 18

Enter Gentleman Jim

*War work leads Thornewell to Rams – Only two regular
right-wingers between wars – From Derby to Cup
winner's medal with Blackburn – One match from first
Cup Final at Wembley – One goal short of promotion –
Eight games without a goal – Search for a centre-
forward – Moore scores five against Palace and has
unique distinction – One match from first Cup Final at
Wembley – Storer, stalwart as player and
manager...and county cricketer*

THERE WERE SHARPLY CONTRASTING careers at Derby for the two other new
men besides Wightman and Burton in the team that resumed League life in 1919
by drawing at home to Manchester United. Blakey Martin, a wing-half from Glossop,
was to make only five further senior appearances; George Thornewell, a nippy little
right-winger, was to be a regular selection in succession to Billy Grimes for almost 300
more. Martin, who had won the Military Medal and bar while serving with the Royal
Marines in France and Gallipoli during the war, spent only the one season with the
Rams before entering the new Third Division with Southend.

Although Thornewell, like Burton, was getting a first taste League football, he could
not, again like Burton, be termed a complete Derby newcomer. He had played in four
of the six matches with which they had resumed their activities in 1919 in the Midland
Victory League that had also involved only West Bromwich (to whom Derby had been
runners-up on goal average), Wolves and Aston Villa. Five players, Atkin, Barbour,
Lawrence, Leonard and Moore, took part in all six games, and Burton made the second
of his appearances for the Rams in that competition the month before scoring Forest's
Victory Shield winner at Everton.

George Thornewell first came to Jimmy Methven's attention while he and the Derby
County manager were working at the Rolls-Royce factory in Derby during the war
following the Rams' temporary closedown after finishing at the foot of the Midlands
league table in 1916 (they gained only 16 points from their 26 matches, suffering 17
defeats). Though born at Romiley, near Stockport in Cheshire, Thornewell, the youngest
of eight children, was only a few years old when he moved to Derby after his father's
death, and he played for St. James's Road School and Derby Boys before impressing
Methven in the Rolls-Royce works team.

He left his apprentice training at the factory to train as a pilot in the Royal Air Force,
as the Royal Flying Corps had just become known, but the war ended before he could

go into action and he returned to complete his apprenticeship. Methven, picking up the Rams reins, promptly made sure of securing his registration. It was yet another of the astute signings to which the manager was to add in his few remaining years in charge by also acquiring such prominent players as Johnny McIntyre, Ben Olney, Harry Storer and Lionel ('Spud') Murphy.

Those four, plus Thornewell, Harold Wightman and Syd Plackett, were bargains from the Methven era who were inherited by George Jobey and were regular members of the team that regained First Division status in his first season, 1925–26, as Derby's manager. Before that, in addition to Bert Chandler, they were regulars through the three seasons in which Cecil Potter was Methven's immediate successor—seasons of near-misses in both Cup and League.

In 1923, the Rams got to within one game of the first FA Cup Final to be played at Wembley. They did not concede a goal in the first four rounds, but then were two down in the first nine minutes of a semi-final at Chelsea's ground that they lost to West Ham by 5–2. In the following season, they were involved in a second-round Cup marathon with Newcastle which went to three replays, and lasted altogether for seven hours— then a record for the competition proper—before United continued along the path that took them to victory over Aston Villa in the final.

These were the details, with Derby's scorers, of those two memorable Cup runs in successive years:

1922–23

First round:	H	2–0	Blackpool	Moore, Lyons
Second round:	A	3–0	Bristol City	Moore 2, Lyons (pen)
Third round:	H	1–0	Wednesday	Moore
Fourth round:	A	1–0	Tottenham H	Galloway
Semi-final:		2–5	West Ham	Moore, Henderson (og)

(at Stamford Bridge, Chelsea)

1923-24

First round:	H	2–1	Bury	Murphy, Whitehouse
Second round:	H	2–2	Newcastle U	Storer 2
	A	2–2	Newcastle U	Galloway, Mooney (og)
		2–2	Newcastle U	Galloway, Thornewell

(at Burnden Park, Bolton)

| | A | 3–5 | Newcastle U | Galloway 2, Storer |

(Newcastle won toss of coin to decide venue)

Billy Brown and Billy Moore (two goals each) and Jimmy Ruffell scored against the Rams at Stamford Bridge for West Ham, who were beaten 2–0 by Bolton Wanderers at Wembley but had the consolation of gaining promotion to the First Division as runners-up to Notts County. Derby County, meanwhile, fell away to a disappointing 14th place after their semi-final exit, winning only one of their remaining ten League games—and that by a lone goal at home to Bury scored by Randolph Galloway, a former boy musician in the Army who had served in the Yorkshire Regiment during the 1914–18 War.

It was through his Army service that Sunderland-born Galloway met 'Spud' Murphy, the forward from Melton Mowbray who became Alf Quantrill's successor on Derby's left wing, and on whose recommendation he joined the Rams soon after Cecil Potter's arrival from Hartlepools United. Galloway was a forceful leader of the County's attack for the best part of two seasons, but then lost his place to Albert Fairclough, a free scorer from Bristol City, and shared the rest of his League career between Nottingham Forest, Luton Town, Coventry City and Tottenham Hotspur.

Newcastle's main scorer in what remains Derby County's longest Cup serial in the February of 1924 was Neil Harris, who also netted the first of the two late goals that accounted for Villa in the final a fortnight before he returned to Wembley as Scotland's centre-forward in a draw that an own goal earned with England. Harris, whose later travels took him into the Derby area as manager of Burton Town, scored three of his four goals against the Rams in their fourth, decisive meeting. His son, John, best-known as a Chelsea defender and Sheffield United manager, played at Wembley too, in two wartime finals, and also just the once for Scotland, in a heavy defeat by England in Glasgow the month before the end of the 1939–45 War, when caps were not awarded.

The 1923–24 season of Derby County's protracted Cup tussle with Newcastle was the one they agonisingly ended just one goal short of the 5–0 win they needed to rejoin the Geordies back in the First Division. At home to Leicester City in their last match, they twice struck an upright in their desperate, but availing, efforts to add to the four-goal lead they built up with almost half-an-hour to go, and therefore yielded the second promotion place, three points behind Leeds United, to Bury by 0.015 of a goal. They and the Lancashire club, who had completed their programme the week before with, ironically, a 5–0 home win against Coventry City, both won 21, drew nine and lost 12 of their 42 matches, but Bury's goals figures of 63–35 to Derby's 75–42 edged them ahead on goal average by 1.800 to 1.785.

Derby again finished third the following season, but on that occasion they were two points behind Manchester United, who went up with Leicester City. A narrow defeat at Stoke cost the Rams a place in the top two with only two games to go, and they were unable to make up the lost ground as both those matches, away to Coventry City and at home to Blackpool, were drawn.

Bitterly disappointing as their last-ditch frustrations were in both Cup and League during Potter's reign, the Rams at least could feel that they were running on the right lines, as the promotion under Jobey promptly proved, in marked contrast to the tribulations of the woeful season of 1920–21 in which they were relegated with what was then the worst record in their history.

Lack of finishing power was the main reason for that plight. Their defence did a decent job in conceding 58 goals—with only one exception the lowest number outside the top eight clubs in the table—but in managing to score a paltry 32 themselves they failed to find the net in 19 of their 42 matches, and on 16 other occasions they were unable to score more than once. In one desolate sequence they went eight games without a goal from late October to mid-December.

The search for another scoring centre-forward to follow Harry Leonard spread to Scotland after the barren pre-Christmas spell. Just over £3,000, a substantial fee for those days and one that the Rams could ill afford in their parlous financial state, was forked out to obtain Bill Paterson from Cowdenbeath, but his supply of goals also dried up after had notched seven in his first nine games. In three years with Derby he altogether scored 24 in 68 outings with the first team before going back to where he had come from. His second venture into English football from Cowdenbeath took him to Coventry, for whom he netted another two dozen in the Third Division before setting off to Springfield in the United States.

The problem Paterson was bought to attempt to solve at Derby was so acute that he was but one of nine players who were tried at centre-forward during the relegation season in which he was signed. They ranged from Jimmy Lyons, who came from Hednesford Town and in 86 appearances, chiefly at inside-forward, scored 33 goals (four of them in one game against Rotherham) before leaving for Wrexham, to George Minney, a product of Hertfordshire junior football who played in just the last two matches, for which Paterson was unavailable.

The others included two defenders, Bert Chandler and Harold Wightman, who were one-offs at the head of the attack in common with Albert Shiner, a short-term signing from the Seaview club on the Isle of Wight. For four consecutive games the position was entrusted to William Gardner, a squat but sturdy chap who arrived with excellent amateur credentials from Bishop Auckland at the same time as 'Tiddler' Murray. Gardner had played in the 1915 Amateur Cup Final, if in a side beaten by Clapton, and in the 1919–20 season he had scored 72 goals—four of them for England's amateurs against Wales. For Derby, however, he netted only once, and after quickly returning north to join Spennymoor United he was a restless traveller by way of QPR, Ashington, Grimsby, Darlington, Torquay, York, Crewe and Rochdale.

Noah Burton and Jim Moore made up the nine, but also only briefly. Both were more at home at inside-forward. As has already been noted, Burton, with his modest total of 80 goals in nearly 400 games, was never a ready scorer in any case. 'Gentleman Jim' Moore, whose 218 appearances for the Rams produced 82 goals, did have his sharp-shooting moments—the best of them when he scored the first five out of six (as an inside-left) against Crystal Palace on Christmas Day, 1922—but his exceptional dribbling ability made for a natural conversion from the centre-forward role in which he made his £1,500 move to Derby from Glossop in the autumn of 1913.

One England cap was scant reward for the consistently good form Moore showed both before the First World War—when he was top scorer with 22 goals, and an ever-present with the ill-starred Tom Benfield, in the side that won the Second Division championship—and during the first few seasons after it. The fact that he was involved in another unsuccessful struggle against relegation soon after peace returned, and therefore spent his two most profitable post-war seasons out of the First Division, clearly counted against him.

Moore's lone international call-up came on May 21st, 1923, a couple of months after he had scored his fifth goal of the FA Cup run that took Derby County to the last four in the year of Wembley's first final. His performances on the path to the semi-final, coupled with his being the club's joint leading scorer, with Lyons, in the League, earned him a place on England's close-season Continental tour. He missed the opening match, won by 4–1 against France in Paris, then formed an all-Derby right-wing pairing with George Thornewell, who was also winning his first cap, against Sweden in Stockholm.

The centre-forward on Moore's left was Derbyshire-born Harry Bedford, who was shortly to be made a County colleague in leaving Blackpool to replace Albert Fairclough, who moved to Gillingham, and becoming the first of the international attack leaders fielded by the Rams during the years up to the Second World War while George Jobey was their manager. After Bedford came Jack Bowers, Hughie Gallacher, Dai Astley and Dave McCulloch, a formidable array indeed.

Although Moore, like Thornewell, was among the scorers in a 4–2 defeat of the Swedes, he was not retained for the game with the same country at the same venue three days later. The Moore who scored twice in a 3–1 victory that day was West Ham's, the Tynesider Billy Moore. But for that Moore, too, there was to be no more. In fact, not one of the 25 players called upon for those three tour matches was chosen for England's next game, in Belfast the following October.

Jimmy Moore, who hailed from Handsworth and learned his football in the Birmingham district, was captain of the Derby team that put the club into the Cup's semi-finals for the ninth time. He also had the distinction of being the only member of the Rams' promotion side of 1914–15 to play for the club when they next rose from the Second Division 11 years later. By then, however, his first-team opportunities had been curtailed by the switching of Harry Storer from wing-half to the forward line, and although he enjoyed a three-month recall while Storer was out with a knee injury during the 1924–25 season, he himself then had the misfortune to damage a knee that had to be operated upon.

He recovered in time to play just twice during the run to promotion the following season—first as deputy for Bedford at centre-forward, finally as the stand-in at inside-right for Jackie Whitehouse, a wartime guest with the Rams and Chelsea who had been signed by Cecil Potter from Moore's own part of the country, Birmingham. Whitehouse was an invaluable schemer-scorer in exactly 200 games for the Rams, forming a formidable inside trio with Galloway and Storer, and his outstanding feat, four goals

**'Gentleman Jim' Moore gave the Rams a
five-goal Christmas present.**

in an 8–0 trouncing of the Wednesday, no doubt had a big bearing on his next transfer taking him to Hillsborough.

It was in an away match with the Wednesday that Jimmy Moore made his debut for Derby County on the first day of November in 1913, when he scored in a 3–1 win. He was also close to a scoring farewell, for he netted on his penultimate appearance in a 2–1 defeat at Southampton, but bowed out as two goals were conceded without reply at Swansea three days later, on February 13th, 1926. In the following month he was one of eight players placed on the transfer list, and Chesterfield, whom he had assisted in the war, signed him on deadline day.

It was therefore in the Third Division North that he ended his Football League career with the Saltergate club, for his last two stops were at Mansfield and Worcester. He left Mansfield Town two years before their election, in 1931, to the League's Southern Section (from which they were switched to the Northern after one season), and he also went from Southern League Worcester City before Jackie Whitehouse was appointed as that club's player-manager. Whitehouse made his way there from Sheffield via Bournemouth and Folkestone, but before the Thirties were out he was back in service with Derby County as a scout.

**George Thornewell, a Cup winner with
Blackburn within months of leaving Derby.**
(Derby Evening Telegraph)

It spoke volumes for the ability and application of Harold Wightman, George Thornewell and Harry Storer that they were still around to play prominent parts in the winning of promotion in 1925–26 after having been involved in the depressing relegation season of 1920–21. Indeed, for the first eight post-war seasons the nippy little Thornewell was unchallenged as Derby County's outside-right, winning four England caps along the way, and he got to within five of 300 appearances before his eventual exclusion in favour of Sammy Crooks, to whom he originally lost his place through injury, led to his transfer to Blackburn Rovers late in 1927.

Within a few months of that move, Thornewell was climbing Wembley's 39 steps to collect his FA Cup winner's medal after figuring prominently in the move that produced the then quickest goal at the stadium in the defeat of Huddersfield Town.

James Roscamp gave Blackburn the lead just inside the first minute (one reporter exaggerated by saying it was after 'barely 30 seconds'). The ball was bundled out of goalkeeper Willie Mercer's grasp and over the line at the end of a move in which Syd Puddefoot and George Thornewell shared. In 1955, Jackie Milburn headed the first of Newcastle's goals in their 3–1 defeat of Manchester City after 45 or 55 seconds—depending upon which account you believe—but the fastest goal of all the FA Cup finals at Wembley was scored after 43 seconds by Roberto Di Matteo in Chelsea's 2–0 win against Middlesbrough in 1997. In the 1895 final at the Crystal Palace, Aston Villa's winning goal against West Bromwich Albion was scored after 40 seconds—credited to Bob Chatt by some reports, to John Devey by others.

For Sammy Crooks, regrettably, there was to be no story similar to Thornewell's of ultimate success in the national knock-out competition. He was Derby County's only other regular right-winger of the inter-war years, and also had the distinction of becoming their most-capped player,[1] but injury cruelly denied him the chance to crown his career as a member of the side that carried off the trophy for the Rams 18 years after Thornewell had shared in Blackburn's triumph.

From Ewood Park, Thornewell followed Jim Moore to Chesterfield, where he enjoyed his second promotion success by helping to win the Third North championship in 1930–31. He had his final fling with Newark Town, then concentrated on running the White Hart public house at Duffield, just to the north of Derby, but also found time to serve on the committee of the Derby County Supporters' Association. He was nearly 88 when he died in 1986, outliving Sammy Crooks by five years.

Unlike Thornewell, who missed only five matches in the relegation season of 1920–21, and Wightman, absent from just seven until dislodged by Charlie Rance, Harry Storer came late into Derby's team as the drop loomed. His debut, in fact, coincided with the last game Wightman played, in a defeat at Bradford on March 12th, 1921, before losing his place to the centre-half from Tottenham.

---

1. Sammy Crooks played 26 times for England, from April, 1930 to December, 1936. For international appearances, he has since been overtaken among Derby County players by Alan Durban (27 appearances for Wales), Colin Todd (27 for England), Roy McFarland (28 for England) and Peter Shilton, who played 34 of his record 125 matches in England's goal while with the Rams.

Signed for £2,500 from Grimsby Town, Storer was brought in at left-half for the Rams' last dozen games of that wretched season, and that was the position in which he also made all but one of his last 80 appearances for the club before his £4,250 transfer to Burnley in February, 1929. In between, besides six appearances at both left-back and centre-forward, and another at right-half, he turned out at inside-left 130 times, only one fewer than his total of matches at left-half in his complete tally of 274, and he was the club's top scorer with 27 goals in 1923–24.

Those goals included two lots of four—the first in late September as Derby gained their record 8–0 away win against Bristol City the week after losing to that club at home, the other at Christmas in a 6–0 home victory over Nelson the day after losing to that club away. Having been switched into the attack because, on his return from injury, he found Syd Plackett playing too well at left-half to be displaced, he did so well there that it was as a forward that he earned his first England call-up against France, in Paris, a fortnight after Derby had so dramatically fallen fractionally short of promotion against Leicester. What was more, he made it a scoring debut in a 3–1 win, in a front line that also included George Thornewell.

Storer's unrelenting style made him frequently prone to injury, and it was after one of his lengthy absences that he showed his disregard for personal safety in the County's

Harry Storer, scorer of four goals in a record away win.
(Derby Evening Telegraph)

cause by going straight back onto the casualty list as he scored the winner against Chelsea. He was injured again early in that game, but he carried on with typical determination until he had to be carried off with torn rib ligaments suffered in striking the ball into the net from some 20 yards.

His return from another injury during Derby's first season back in Division One led him to revert to left-half, with Jackie Whitehouse having taken over at inside-left, and in October, 1927, he was awarded his other England cap in the middle line against Ireland in Belfast. Again he had a County colleague for company—Tommy Cooper, the fair-haired full-back from Port Vale who was Jobey's second big signing after Bedford—but there was no repeat victory. The Irish won 2–0.

Whereas relegation was unavoidable in Storer's first dozen games for Derby, he did help to ward it off in his first dozen for Burnley. Even so, it was back in the Second Division that he completed his playing career in football after being restricted by further injury to three appearances during the following 1929–30 season in which the Turf Moor club did go down. He was back to being a Burnley regular, missing only five of their matches in 1930–31, when the managerial vacancy at Coventry occurred with the dismissal of James McIntyre, a former City player, but he needed to look to his future at the age of 33 and, although there were many other applicants, he so greatly impressed Coventry's chairman, Walter Brandish, when he went for an interview at Highfield Road that he was offered the job on the spot.

That it was a wise appointment was swiftly made apparent. And Storer's success as a manager with Coventry City went hand in hand with his cricketing success as an opening batsman with Derbyshire. In three consecutive soccer seasons from 1933–34 to 1935–36, Coventry were second, third and first in the Third Division South; in the three summer seasons of 1934, 1935 and 1936 (his last first-class cricket) Derbyshire were third, second and first in the County Championship. He did not qualify for Derbyshire by birth, having been born at West Derby on Merseyside while his father was Liverpool's goalkeeper, but he moved to the county with his parents at the age of four and regarded himself as a Derbyshire man.

In the early stages of his career as a county cricketer, the combative Storer needed all of the steely resolve for which he was renowned in order to progress. As if he did not have enough on his plate in attempting to help to revive Derby County's fortunes after their demoralising season of 1920–21, he had the atrocious luck to find his entry into first-class cricket coinciding with the worst season in Derbyshire's history—the one in which the county finished last in 1920 with not a point to their name.

In his 24 innings that year, Storer accumulated only 147 runs, with a highest score of 32 and an average of 6.68. He improved the next summer, scoring his first century and increasing his aggregate to 758 for an average of 22.96, but after continuing to show promise for two more years he fell away to such an extent as Derbyshire again tumbled to last place in 1924, having a paltry highest score of 18 in his 26 innings for an average once more below seven, that he had to go into league cricket to try to rebuild his form and confidence.

It was typical of the man that he did so to such a high degree that Will Taylor came to describe him as the best batsman he had seen play for the county during his many years as the club's secretary. Storer retired in 1936 not only with more than 13,500 first-class runs to his credit, but also with having made a notable contribution as a bowler and fielder in exceeding 200 for both wickets and catches. Six times he passed 1,000 runs in a season. His 18 centuries included two in one match (equalling his uncle's achievement) and the first two double-centuries by one batsman for Derbyshire—both against Essex at Derby, 209 in the county's record opening stand of 322 in 1929, and 232 in 1933.

In view of the determination and maximum effort that Storer put into his cricket and football as a player, it was no wonder that he had the lowest of tolerance levels for faint hearts when he went into management. Nor was it any real surprise when the climb into the Second Division with Coventry became the first of three promotions as a manager that he added to the one in which he had shared as a player with Derby.

Having unexpectedly left Coventry after 14 years, he guided Birmingham City to the Second Division championship in 1947–48, two seasons after limbering up with the transitional League South title. Then, undeterred by an ill-advised return to Coventry that ended with conflicting reports that he had either resigned or been sacked, he rejoined Derby County, whom he had left as captain, and in 1956–57 he dragooned the Rams out of the Third North wilderness into which they had plunged within seven years of their long-overdue victory in an FA Cup Final.

He was unable to take his old club any further up the football ladder, but he stayed on at the Baseball Ground for five more years following his final winning of promotion before going into a well-deserved retirement which lasted until the beginning of September in 1967, when he died in Derby at the age of 69.

CHAPTER 19

From Rams Reserves to First Cap

Discarded Olney leaves with record on quick route to England place – Johnny McIntyre, £10 bargain solves problem in 10-year stay – Ritchie the war hero – Early death of Tom Lamph – Rejected by Murphy – Reserves move up to Central League – Financial crisis ends third-team venture – Methven leaves after more than 30 years

DERBY COUNTY WERE ALREADY DOOMED to their third relegation from the First Division when goalkeeper Ben Olney was signed by Jimmy Methven from Stourbridge just in time to play in their last two fixtures of the 1920–21 season. Both were against mid-table Manchester United, who were held to a 1–1 draw at the Baseball Ground by an Archie Ritchie penalty but won the return game at Old Trafford by 3–0.

George Lawrence, however, was reinstated as first choice after Jimmy Kidd had deputised in the first two matches of the following season, and Olney had to wait until the club's first League game of 1922, a 2–2 draw at Fulham, before being given another chance. That, with Lawrence unfit, was in preference to Kidd, who the previous Saturday had been beaten six times in the first-round FA Cup-tie at Villa Park in which, as recalled earlier, the veteran Jack Atkin had made his unhappy final first-team appearance.

Olney's recall lasted for only two more games, Lawrence returning after another heavy defeat, by 5–1 at Bradford, but three matches later Ben was again brought back—and this time he was back to stay, breaking the Rams' sequence of established Derbyshire-born goalkeepers.

For the rest of that season, and for the next five, Olney was the undisputed first choice. From February 25th, 1922, the date when he was third time lucky in embarking upon his long run as a regular, until September 17th, 1927, when he guarded Derby's goal for the last time, he missed only 11 matches out of 247—all through injury or illness, and seven of them in succession. In three seasons he was absent only once, including the promotion-winning one of 1925–26; in another he was an ever-present.

By the time he left for Aston Villa in December, 1927 (soon after losing his place to Harry Wilkes, who had been rejected by Villa for supposedly being too small) he had made more first-team appearances for Derby County than any other goalkeeper. Not until 1968 was his total of 240 overtaken by Reg Matthews, whose 246 lasted as the record until Colin Boulton, the only ever-present member of the Rams' two First Division title teams in the 1970s, came along to push it up to 344. For League games alone, Olney totalled 223, Matthews 225, Boulton 272.

Olney fittingly spent his last full season with Derby in the First Division, but he was languishing in the reserve side when Villa snapped him up only a few days after the County had completed their first League double over them by winning 1–0 at Villa Park the day after inflicting a 5–0 Boxing Day beating at the Baseball Ground.

Less than five months later, Olney gained the first of his two England caps in a 5–1 defeat of France in Paris. Two of the goals were scored by George Stephenson, who for a few weeks had been a Derby County colleague after making a move opposite to his own in joining the Rams from Aston Villa.

That match was played on May 17th, 1928, and two days later Olney and Stephenson helped towards a 3–1 victory over Belgium in Antwerp. This was the England line-up in both games:

Olney (Aston Villa); **Goodall** (Huddersfield Town), **Blenkinsop** (Sheffield Wednesday); **Edwards** (Leeds United), **Matthews** (Sheffield United), **Green** (Sheffield United); **Bruton** (Burnley), **Jack** (Bolton Wanderers), **Dean** (Everton), **Stephenson** (Derby County), **Barry** (Leicester City).

'Dixie' Dean (2) and David Jack were the other scorers against France. Dean netted twice more in Antwerp, where Vincent Matthews was also on the mark.

Ben Olney, who was born in London, at Holborn, but raised in Birmingham, did not take up football seriously until he was in the Army during the First Word War. After being demobilised, he assisted a Birmingham works side, Fairleys Athletic, and Aston Park Rangers before joining Stourbridge. While with that club, he played against Scotland in a junior international match at Villa Park, and it was his outstanding display on that occasion which caught Derby County's attention, persuading them to snap him up from under Villa's noses for a bargain £800.

**Ben Olney, undisputed first choice in goal for
the best part of six seasons.**

When Villa did eventually sign him, he became as big a favourite of their fans as he had been of Derby's—especially during the 1928–29 season in which they were third in the First Division, only one win away from Wednesday's champions, and reached the FA Cup semi-finals before just one goal by Portsmouth at Highbury brought him the disappointment of missing Wembley that he had first experienced with the Rams against West Ham. He was also unfortunate not to be capped again by England, though he was chosen twice more against South Africa.

With Villa, he took over from Tommy Jackson, who had been Sam Hardy's successor, and he got to within three of another century of appearances before leaving the League for Bilston United in the summer of 1930. A year later he was appointed that club's player-manager, but in the following August he answered an emergency by re-entering the League with Third Division Walsall. After a season there, he moved to Shrewsbury Town, then, in 1933, became a publican in Birmingham and joined the Moor Green team in which he made one nostalgic reappearance at the Baseball Ground.

His playing days finally over, he returned to live in Derby, and after a spell as licensee of the Normanton Hotel he took a job at the Rolls-Royce factory. He was working there at the time of an illness that resulted in his death in September, 1943, at the early age of 44.

The international recognition that came to Olney, if belatedly, was also deserved, but denied, in the case of Glaswegian Johnny McIntyre, who was desperately unlucky never to be capped. It was his misfortune to be well worthy of consideration at a time when, as in Jimmy Methven's playing days, Anglo-Scots were not exactly looked upon with favour by his country's selectors. Transferred from Stenhousemuir in June, 1921, the month after Derby's headlong plunge out of the First Division and shortly after the arrival of Storer and Olney at the Baseball Ground, McIntyre became, for just the £10 signing-on fee, one of the biggest of the bargains acquired while Methven was manager. He was a key member of the side during Cecil Potter's three seasons at the helm, and for the first six seasons during which George Jobey was the next man in charge.

Converted from an adequate inside-forward into a resolute right-half of considerable skill and constructive ability, McIntyre formed with pivot Harry Thoms and Syd Plackett a half-back line that was an integral part of the team in all but six of Derby's 42 matches on the path to promotion in 1925–26. Had it not been for injuries they would have turned out together throughout that memorable season. While Plackett, on the left flank, was the team's only ever-present, Thoms who, with full-back Tom Crilly, followed Potter from Hartlepools United missed just two games, and McIntyre was kept out of four of the last five.

Johnny Mac, as he was known, made a scoring debut for the Rams from inside-right in a 4–2 defeat at Blackpool on the opening day of the 1921–22 season. After only three more games there, he was also tried at inside-left and on the left wing before settling down in the right-half position that had been filled by no fewer than nine other players since the long-serving Jimmy Bagshaw's departure to Notts County early in 1920.

That list ranged from Tommy Barbour, who, as we have seen, is best remembered as Jack Atkin's full-back partner, to Bernard McLaverty, who had to contend with strong competition for a first-team place in almost eight years at Derby but still managed to take his number of appearances into three figures. McLaverty made only four of them as the County clinched their return to the First Division, in the late absence of the injured McIntyre, but he played a more prominent part in their first season back there

Johnny McIntyre, unlucky not to be capped by Scotland.

Bernard McLaverty, a versatile player who had to contend with strong competition for a place.

as Plackett faded from the scene. During that period, in the autumn of 1926, he scored his only League goal for the Rams, in a 4–1 home win against Tottenham Hotspur.

In addition to occupying both wing-half positions, McLaverty occasionally turned out at centre-half, where he had started out in junior football and also played for Leadgate Park in his native North-East (he was born at Chester Moor, a village near Chester-le-Street). He switched to wing-half with his next club, Durham City, and came to Derby County's attention while captaining them to fifth place in the North-Eastern League during the 1919–20 season in which they were also winners of the Newcastle Infirmary Cup and runners-up for the Durham Senior Cup.

From Derby, he moved to Norwich City, then returned to Derbyshire with Heanor Town towards the end of 1932. After hanging up his boots, he remained in the county as a licensee at Duffield, where he died on Christmas Eve in 1952, aged 54.

The seven other players who preceded Johnny McIntyre at right-half in Derby's team in the early months of the 1920s were Harry Walker, Harry Boxley, Tom Lamph, Frank Waterhouse, Archie Ritchie, Noah Burton and Bill Morton. Of these, the most experienced was Ritchie, but although he also played at centre-half and left-half, he was primarily a full-back. Like McIntyre, he started out in the Scottish Central League with Stenhousemuir, his home town, and he represented that league against the Scottish League before moving to Dumbarton shortly after his 18th birthday.

On the outbreak of war in 1914, Ritchie enlisted in the Royal Engineers. He served overseas for the four years it lasted, and in 1917 he was awarded the Distinguished Conduct Medal for volunteering to replace casualties and helping to repair a bridge 'at all costs' at Nieuwpoort, in Belgium. After the armistice, he was with the Army of Occupation in Germany, where he made up for some of the time lost to football by helping the Royal Engineers to win the Brigade Cup. He was also chosen to play for the British Army against the Belgian Army, but had to turn down the invitation because the Engineers needed him on the same day for an Army Cup-tie.

Ritchie returned to Dumbarton when he was demobilised in 1919, but he was soon snapped up by Glasgow Rangers, and in what was to be his only season at Ibrox he gained a Scottish League championship medal. Rangers lost only two of their 42 matches, conceded a mere 25 goals while scoring just over 100, and had three points to spare over their great rivals Celtic, who had narrowly beaten them to the title the year before.

Tempted south by Derby County in the summer of 1920, Ritchie proved the perfect full-back partner for first Jack Atkin and then Bert Chandler, but on the last Saturday before Christmas in 1921 he had to be assisted from the field at West Ham with a serious knee injury that virtually put paid to his days as an automatic choice. The Hammers were also reduced to ten men, losing right-back Jack Hebden with a broken ankle, but they overcame their handicap to win 3–1.

Hebden did not play in League football again that season, and he made only rare appearances in each of the next three before re-establishing himself so successfully that he captained the side prior to leaving for Fulham with another West Ham full-back, George Horler. Ritchie reappeared for the Rams after an absence of nearly three months, only to break down once more while preparing for the 1922–23 season. After that, with newcomer Crilly firmly established alongside Chandler in his absence, he had only three first-team opportunities in as many seasons before injuries to first Wightman and then Crilly, following Chandler's departure to Newcastle, enabled him to make a partial comeback of 14 games during the push to promotion under George Jobey.

Ritchie altogether totalled 87 League matches and six Cup-ties for Derby before leaving to take over as Guildford City's player-manager. His farewell appearance, as deputy for Crilly at home to Blackburn in November, 1926, was certainly eventful, though not with a happy outcome for the Rams. They seemed set to remain unbeaten at the Baseball Ground that season when they were 3–1 ahead in only 15 minutes, but the Rovers rallied to triumph 5–4. Derby again scored four without winning, but salvaged a point, in the return game at Ewood Park a week before also drawing 4–4 with their Easter visitors from Huddersfield…after being three down inside the opening half-hour, twice hitting the goal's framework and missing a penalty.

Ritchie played just one game for Derby at right-half, as did Noah Burton. Of Johnny McIntyre's other immediate predecessors in that position, the highest number of senior appearances for the club, 88, were made by Harry Walker and he played mainly, if often infrequently, in the forward line until the 1914–15 promotion season in which he was the mostly-used right-half. One of the recruits from within Derbyshire, this Wirksworth-born signing from Clay Cross was with the Rams for ten years from the summer of 1910, but in the next four he had six more clubs: Notts County, Fulham, Reading, Aberdare Athletic, Bournemouth and Chesterfield.

Walker left Derby shortly after Tom Lamph and Frank Waterhouse moved in, both signed by Jimmy Methven in March, 1920, to help stave off the relegation that so emphatically became unavoidable a year later. The Gateshead-born Lamph, who arrived from Manchester City within six months of being among the players put up for auction after Leeds City's expulsion from the Football League, represented the North-Eastern League against the Southern and Central leagues while an amateur with Spennymoor, but he played fewer than a dozen first-team games for each of his two Cities, very few more for Derby, and even fewer after returning to Leeds to join the new United.

His time with Derby County petered out soon after he had briefly been involved in their bleak sequence of eight games without a goal, and not long before their relegation fate was sealed in that woeful season of 1920–21. Back at Leeds, his health failed, and, forced into premature retirement in 1922, he died at the early age of 32 on February 24th, 1926—almost exactly five years to the day since leaving Derby.

Frank Waterhouse reached the Rams as a player of considerable experience with West Bromwich Albion. His 172 League games for the Throstles included all 38, at centre-half, in their Second Division title-winning team of 1910–11, his first full season after joining them from Wednesbury Old Athletic. With Derby, however, he managed only 26, dropping out midway through their unsuccessful struggle to keep afloat in the First Division as Jimmy Methven's term as manager also neared its end.

William Henry Morton totalled two fewer appearances than Waterhouse in the Rams' League side. Signed from Ilkeston United after service during the war, having played for another of his home town's clubs, Ilkeston St. John's, as well as West Hallam, before it, he had the misfortune to find his first five games, all at left-half, coinciding with the first five of the scoreless sequence of eight that turned the team towards the inescapable descent into Division Two. He was brought back, chiefly at right-half, to take part in all but one of Derby's last 18 matches as relegation became inevitable, but lost his place to McLaverty after defeats in the opening two fixtures of the following 1921–22 season. There was no first-team room for him at his next club, Newcastle, and he soon moved again, to Lincoln City, then Wigan Borough.

Archie Ritchie, who was awarded the DCM for bravery in the 1914–18 War.

Harry Boxley was another player Derby recruited from outside the Football League after the 1914–18 War, his previous experience having been gained with Stourbridge (where he was born), Shrewsbury Town and Wellington Town. He first turned out for the Rams in a 4–0 home victory, to which Noah Burton contributed a hat-trick, against Wolverhampton Wanderers in the Midland Victory League of 1919, but he played only seven times in the first post-war First Division season before becoming one of the first signings former Derby defender Ben Hall made as manager of Bristol Rovers. On August 28th in 1920, Boxley was the Rovers' right-half for their first match in the new Third Division. They started with a 2–0 defeat at Millwall, but ended in mid-table, winning more matches than they lost—just.

Those, then, were the men among whom Derby County rang the right-half changes during the first two seasons after the First World War before Johnny McIntyre made the position his own from around Christmas-time in 1921 until September, 1931. But for his injuries, he would have played even more than his near-370 League and Cup games for the Rams. After making the short move to Chesterfield along with Tom Ruddy, a forward who had joined Derby from Darlington and was later with Linfield in the Irish League, he went out of direct contact with the game before rendering further excellent service at the Baseball Ground as coach and scout until his retirement some 14 years before his death in 1974.

From running a pub and hotel in Derby and working as a fitter at the Rolls-Royce factory, he originally returned to the Rams as a member of the ground staff, then became one of the four group supervisors in the revised training programme while Jack Barker, the club's former captain, was briefly manager in the 1950s.

Lionel ('Spud' Murphy, a force on
the left of Derby's attack.

McIntyre was but one of a good number of former Derby County players who had no connection with Derby before they joined the Rams, but who returned to live in the town or surrounding area after their footballing days were over. 'Spud' Murphy, who, with a dozen goals, was second only to Harry Bedford's 27 among the club's scorers in the promotion-winning season of 1925–26 (in common with McIntyre he missed just four matches) was another. After 235 games and 49 goals for the County, Murphy became the fourth player to leave within 16 days (after Olney, Thornewell and McLaverty) when, in January, 1928, he moved to Bolton Wanderers in part exchange for Albert Picken, but he made his home in Derby again after also playing for Mansfield Town, Norwich City and Luton Town. Picken, a fellow left-winger, failed to progress from the reserves with the Rams—as had also been his misfortune with Wolves after drawing himself to their attention at Wellington Town.

I would have welcomed the chance to have added Murphy to the former Derby players I interviewed throughout one season in the 1950s for a *What They're Doing Now* series of articles in the *Derby Evening Telegraph*, yet I failed to get beyond the front door of his house. The message that he was not interested was relayed to me through the female member of the household who answered my knock, but a disagreeable-sounding voice from the nether regions had already made it abundantly clear that he wanted nothing to do with me if there was no money in it for him. Word had obviously got around about the evening newspaper's tight purse strings.

Unthinkable as it would be nowadays, no payment was made to those former Rams players for the interviews they gave me, though for some of them it was a free advert for their business or the pub they ran. As far as I know, a fee was not even considered at the outset by those in authority. I certainly was given no encouragement when I subsequently suggested it, such was the parsimonious outlook then prevailing in that particular branch of provincial journalism.

Of all the players from whom I sought an interview, the only other one to refuse was Jack Barker. He was just as firm as Murphy in sending me packing, but more pleasant about it. With his build of a heavyweight boxer (he put me in mind of Bruce Woodcock), he was a daunting figure as he looked down on me from his front doorway, but he did have the grace to invite me in and allow me to start the interview. Then, however, this bluff, no-nonsense Yorkshireman suddenly asked me how much he would be getting for the article I was preparing. When he received the inevitable answer he promptly told me to put my notebook away and politely wished me good evening. Not long afterwards, I was able to meet him again after he had been appointed manager of Derby County, but I never had the opportunity to find out for myself that, as I had been told, Murphy was 'quite a lively lad'.

Murphy, who died in Derby in 1968, just over 73 years after his birth at the North Yorkshire village of Hovingham, was acclaimed as 'without doubt the discovery of the year' by one anonymous local journalist soon after ending Derby County's search for a successor to Alf Quantrill. Another dubbed him 'a genius'. Though that might be considered going overboard a bit, he was a first choice of three managers from February 11th, 1922, when he made his League debut in a 3–0 home victory over Clapton Orient—only a few days after turning professional—until October 29th, 1927, the date of his final appearance for Derby in a 1–1 home draw with Tottenham Hotspur.

For most of that time he applied his progressive style to marked effect in the outside-left position which had caused such a problem since Quantrill's departure that seven players had been tried there in little more than five months, but he also gave a good account of himself in a number of matches at inside-left alongside Georgie Mee, the cheerful little chap from Blackpool who was Derby's next established left-winger. This was especially so as five consecutive wins clinched promotion in April, 1926.

Johnny McIntyre was among those seven predecessors on the attack's left flank—for just one game, lost at Bury, before he found his true niche at right-half. Only one appearance on the left wing was also made by George Webb, normally a wing-half, who joined the Rams after being loaned out to Nuneaton Borough while Aston Villa had held his registration and was soon on the move again, to Bristol Rovers. That, too, was the destination from Derby for John Pattison, a North-Easterner who was given the most chances, all 15 of them, in the gap left by Quantrill during that difficult period. Pattison had two spells with his home club, Durham City, either side of a short stay at Newcastle, before going to the Baseball Ground, and he went back for a third one from Bristol. He was subsequently signed by South Shields, then went West again with Torquay United and Bath City.

The four others who filled the outside-left position for Derby in the 1921–22 season before Murphy's arrival were George Thornewell, in rare switches from the opposite wing, and the inexperienced Jim Barnes, George Birdsall and Bob Taylor. Barnes and Taylor were from the Blyth area of Northumbria, Birdsall from the village of Saxton, near Tadcaster in North Yorkshire. That trio played only seven League games on the left wing between them, though Birdsall, formerly of Brompton, in the Northallerton League, and Harpenden Town, had half-a-dozen other opportunities at left-back during his short stay.

So few of Derby's reserve players made sufficient progress to warrant an extended run in the senior side in those early years after the First World War that the second team was withdrawn from the Central Alliance and entered in the Central League to provide the players with stronger competition by opposing the reserves of clubs belonging to the First and Second divisions of the Football League. At the same time, Steve Bloomer was appointed coach, and a third, or 'A', side was formed with the intention of eliminating what 'County Onlooker' described in the *Derby Football Express* as 'the very unsatisfactory procedure of chopping and changing the reserve side about in order to give try-outs to new men'.

The third team, however, had to be abandoned after only one season because of the pressing need to reduce running costs and the size of the playing staff as the club's financial situation became the worst in their history up to that time. In such unenviable circumstances, it was scarcely surprising that Jimmy Methven was powerless to revive the Rams' fortunes during the closing months of his managership. Even so, their descent into the Second Division was not the sole reason why his long association with Derby County, dating back to 1891, was brought to an end in the summer of 1922, shortly after they had finished their first season after relegation just below the halfway mark in the table. He had to go into hospital for treatment of the eye trouble which, after an unsuccessful operation, was to cost him his sight towards the end of his life.

On finally leaving Derby County, he did some scouting for Stoke City, then worked for Derby Corporation before his failing sight compelled him to retire in the 1930s. Following the death of his wife, he spent his last years quietly with his daughter Constance and son James at their home in the Littleover district of Derby. He was in his 85th year when he died in Derby's Manor Hospital on March 25th, 1953.

Of Methven's six sons (he and his wife also had three daughters), Harold, a centre-forward with Sheffield United and Portsmouth, was the only one to play football professionally. James Junior was briefly an amateur with Derby County, and he played once in their first team at inside-right in a defeat at Bolton in March, 1914, while they were on their way back to the Second Division.

For Cecil Bertram Potter, the path from Derby three years after Jimmy Methven's exit led him in the opposite direction to what he had intended. Instead of carrying out his plan to take over a dairy business in Sussex, his home county, he was persuaded to stay in soccer at Huddersfield, where he undertook the daunting task of filling the void left by the legendary Herbert Chapman's departure to Arsenal. Potter saw the Yorkshire club through to the title hat-trick to which Chapman also pointed the Gunners before his untimely death, but the strain took such a toll of his health that he resigned after just the one season at Leeds Road.

Against his better judgement, Potter was tempted back into the game to manage Norwich City, for whom he had played between leaving Ipswich Town and guesting for Hull and Tottenham during the First World War, but that venture ended in the disillusionment of dismissal after a string of poor results culminating in a heavy Cup defeat by the Corinthians' amateurs. There was to be no further comeback. Potter went into a long retirement that lasted until the autumn of 1975, when he died at the age of 86.

CHAPTER 20

The Final Tributes

*Steve Bloomer interned in Germany – Back to Derby
as coach – A double-take penalty ploy – Farewell
game at Belper – His finest team – Health causes
concern – Cruise to Australasia only delays the
inevitable – In soccer's Hall of Fame – Site of
Bloomer monument arouses some criticism –
Honoured at his birthplace*

STEVE BLOOMER, the sharpshooting forward who for so long was the ace marksman in English football, once played at full-back for Tottenham Hotspur.

Yes, that is taking some liberties with the exact truth, but it did actually happen in one sense, and it was all down to the First World War. When that terrible conflict broke out in August, 1914, Bloomer was stranded in Germany, where he had gone only the previous month as the Berlin Britannia club's coach after ending his first-team playing days with Derby County. As a result, he was interned at a camp at Ruhleben, a racecourse just outside the German capital.

Others who shared that fate included three fellow former international footballers. They were Sam Wolstenholme, a wing-half who had won his three caps in the same England teams as Bloomer (the first in 1904 while with Everton, the two others in 1905 after his transfer to Blackburn), Fred Pentland, who, as a Middlesbrough right-winger, had played the first of his five games for England in 1909, a couple of years after Steve had last turned out for his country, and 'Jock' Cameron, a full-back whose two appearances for Scotland had been made five years apart—the first in Dublin before his move from St. Mirren, the other against England (and Pentland) in 1909, by which time he was with Chelsea.

To help pass the time, they organised a knock-out competition for which the internees formed teams that adopted the names of English professional clubs, and that was how Steve Bloomer came to play at full-back, of all places, for 'Tottenham Hotspur'. He helped them to beat 'Oldham Athletic' (described as 'a scratch team of public schoolboys') by 9–2 in the final, watched by a crowd of some 2,000.

On his return home after the armistice, Bloomer rejoined Derby County to assist in the coaching of youngsters, and a few weeks before the Christmas of 1918 he captained the Pick of the Derby Wartime League against the Royal Engineers at Newark. He took part in other charity matches in addition to playing occasionally for the reserves, and in April, 1923 he was in an Old Internationals side against the Rams in a game played at the Baseball Ground in aid of Derby's War Memorial Fund that became specially remembered for a penalty kick taken by Billy Meredith. Putting one of his own ideas into operation, the Welsh winger tapped the ball forward from the spot, just far enough to comply with the laws, and George Wall, who had been in the forward lines of England with Bloomer and Manchester United with Meredith, rushed forward to hit it past goalkeeper Ben Olney.

Bloomer scored two of the other goals in the Old Internationals' 5–3 victory—one of them a gift from Bert Chandler, the County's right-back, who passed the ball to him instead of clearing his lines. The term 'Old Internationals' was used loosely. Two of the four uncapped players in the side, Harry Leonard and Spurs centre-forward Jimmy Cantrell, were their other scorers in a 5–3 win. Jim Moore (2) and Bill Hurst, a signing from the North-East who soon left for QPR, replied. These were the teams:

Derby County: Olney; Chandler, Crilly; McIntyre, Thoms, Plackett; Thornewell, Hurst, Galloway, Moore, Murphy. **Old Internationals:** Maskrey; Crompton, Morris; Barbour, Leake, Lloyd; Meredith, Bloomer, Cantrell, Leonard, Wall.

The double-take penalty ruse was to be repeated at the Baseball Ground more than 30 years later, when former Rams players Peter Doherty and Jimmy Hagan worked it successfully during the match arranged in aid of the dependants of 'Chick' Musson, the strong-tackling wing-half in the club's 1946 Cup-winning team who died in only his mid-thirties. Doherty also operated it with his old Derby partner Raich Carter in floodlit exhibition games.

September 31st, 1931 was the date of Steve Bloomer's last game in Derby area football. Then 57, he captained the Belper British Legion Club in a charity match with the Herbert Strutt School at the school's ground in Belper. Partnered on the right wing by Herbert Varney,[1] who had played for Belper Town both before and after making two League appearances for Derby County (the first of them also as Bloomer's partner in a 2–2 home draw with the Wednesday in 1902), he scored from a penalty—in the orthodox manner—after one of his shots had been handled, but on that occasion he was on the losing side. A young man named Dick More did the hat-trick in the school's 4–3 victory.

Supper was given in Bloomer's honour after the match, and it is interesting to recall that in his speech of thanks he gave what he considered to be his finest team.

It was: **Jack Robinson** (Derby County); **Howard Spencer** (Aston Villa), **Billy Williams** (West Bromwich Albion); **Ben Warren** (Derby County), **Alec Raisbeck** (Liverpool), **Ernest Needham** (Sheffield United); **Billy Meredith** (Manchester City), **Bobby Walker** (Hearts), **G.O. Smith** (Corinthians), **Joe Bache** (Aston Villa), **Fred Spiksley** (Wednesday). The clubs listed are those with which Bloomer remembered the players at their best. It is indeed surprising that he could find no place for John Goodall, his Rams mentor.

---

1. Varney ended his second spell with Belper Town by joining West Bromwich Albion, for whom he played in five League games before going back to Belper after the 1906–07 season. The charity match in which he again teamed up with Steve Bloomer, 15 years since he had last played, was watched by about 500 to 600 people and raised £10 5s.

By the time of that charity game at Belper, Bloomer had returned to Derby County as a general assistant at the Baseball Ground, following further spells of coaching abroad, in Canada and Spain,[2] and he could occasionally be seen, clad in overalls, chatting to the club's players during breaks in training. One of those players, the gentlemanly Tim Ward, who went on to captain the Rams and play for England but made a contrastingly unrewarding return to the club as manager, had an amusing story

Steve Bloomer, then on the ground staff at the Baseball Ground, makes a point to a group of Derby players during the 1930s. They are, left to right, Sammy Crooks, 'Dally' Duncan, Jack Nicholas, Jack Barker and Jack Bowers.

---

2.   In Spain, Bloomer was with Real Irun, an amateur club in the Basque country. They won the King's Cup in his first season with them, beating Seville, Barcelona and, in the final, Real Madrid.

Steve Bloomer in middle age.
(W.W. Winter, Derby)

Steve Bloomer (left) aboard ship during his cruise to Australasia shortly before his death.

to tell of one day not long after he had been signed by George Jobey from Cheltenham Town in the late Thirties. During a pause in a training stint at the Baseball Ground, one of his new clubmates told him to kick the ball towards an old man who was standing in a group of other Derby players. Ward did so, and the ball looked like hitting the old man, who had his back to it, until someone shouted a 'Look out!' warning. Instead of ducking out of the way, the veteran, then in his sixties, turned quickly and volleyed the ball into the far-away net. 'There,' said Ward's mischievous colleague, 'now you can tell your grandchildren that you played football with Steve Bloomer'.

Another Derby player of those times in the 1930s, left-winger Dave Halford, has told me of how Bloomer used to sit in the main stand during a training session at the Baseball Ground and co-operate with George Jobey by calling out to exchange views on tactics and performances while the manager was supervising from his closer vantage point down on the running track alongside the pitch.

Sadly, however, Bloomer's health had by then been causing concern for some while, and there was a marked deterioration in his condition after the death of his wife Sarah, daughter of a Derby bootmaker, in 1935. Increasingly troubled by asthma and bronchitis, he was sent on a cruise to Australia and New Zealand in the hope of bringing about a recovery, but it only delayed the inevitable. He was taken ill again on the day after his arrival home, and on April 16th, 1938, less than a month since his return, he died at the Great Northern Inn in Junction Street, Derby, the home of his daughter and son-in-law, Mr and Mrs Cyril Richards. He was 64. Thousands of mourners lined the streets for his funeral. The service was held at Derby Cathedral, with burial at Nottingham Road cemetery.

The trip to Australasia was made possible by a fund organised by a committee of four—George Jobey, Ben Robshaw (a future chairman of the Rams), Dick Mooney and T. Stephenson—with the support of the FA, Derby County and many of the other League clubs. It raised more than £500.

Many had considered it a slight when the FA had surprisingly omitted to send Steve Bloomer an invitation to their jubilee banquet in 1913, but getting on for 60 years later, in January, 1971, he was posthumously given the national accolade he deserved by being among the first dozen leading personalities selected for soccer's Hall of Fame. In alphabetical order, he was in the excellent company of:

> **Herbert Chapman**, the manager who put Arsenal on the path to emulating the hat-trick of First Division titles on which he had set his previous club, Huddersfield Town; **William Ralph ('Dixie') Dean**, whose 379 League goals included the record number for one season, 60 for Everton in 1927–28; **Duncan Edwards**, the outstanding Manchester United and England wing-half who was only 21 when he was fatally injured in the Munich airport disaster in 1958; **Tom Finney**, the gifted and versatile Preston forward who played 76 times for England, scoring 30 goals, and was later knighted; **Alex James**, one of the 'Wembley Wizards' who defeated England 5–1 in 1928, and a star performer with Preston and Arsenal; **Sir Stanley Matthews**, the 'Wizard of Dribble' who excelled on the wing for Stoke City, Blackpool and England during a playing career that did not end until he was in his 51st year; **William McGregor**, founder of the Football League; **Billy Meredith**, the skilful, scoring winger who played for both Manchester

clubs, and whose international career with Wales spanned 25 years; **Sir Stanley Rous**, a leading referee, secretary of the FA, and president of FIFA; **Frank Swift**, of Manchester City, one of the game's greatest goalkeepers, the first player in that position to captain England, and, as a journalist with the *News of the World*, another to lose his life through injuries suffered in the crash at Munich while accompanying the Manchester United party back from the European Cup-tie in Belgrade; and **Billy Wright**, captain of England, for whom he was the first to make 100 appearances, and Wolverhampton Wanderers.

Derby County paid their own tribute, following Bloomer's death, by displaying a bronze commemorative plaque at the Baseball Ground. It is now in the Baseball Bar at Pride Park and bears this inscription:

IN MEMORY
OF
STEVE BLOOMER
1874 –1938
THIS TABLET WAS ERECTED
BY MANY OF HIS FRIENDS AND
ADMIRERS AS AN APPRECIATION
OF HIS SERVICES TO
DERBY COUNTY FOOTBALL CLUB
AND HIS COUNTRY
ALSO AS A TRIBUTE TO ONE OF
THE GREATEST PLAYERS THE
GAME HAS PRODUCED

The plaque that has been moved from
the Baseball Ground to Pride Park.

In October, 1996 a memorial plinth was unveiled in Derby's Lock-up Yard, home of the city's fish market, from the proceeds of an auction of his England caps and contributions from his descendants. Some of the caps were bought by Belper-born Michael Knighton, who had been a schoolboy apprentice with Derby County and had played as an amateur for Ilkeston Town and Heanor Town after a short spell as a professional with Coventry City had been ended by a ruptured thigh muscle.

Knighton, a businessman better known for his attempted take-over of Manchester United and his later chairmanship of Carlisle United, was among those who attended the unveiling of the Bloomer memorial outside Derby's Market Hall. The others included the Mayor of Derby and former international footballers Tom Finney, Nat Lofthouse, Wilf Mannion and ex-Rams forward Johnny Morris, plus Arthur Rowley, the current successor to Bloomer as the highest scorer in Football League history.

The location of the plinth, however, did not meet with general approval, and just over a year later Bert Mozley, the former Rams and England full-back, declared himself 'horrified' when he saw where it was during the return visit he made from his Canadian home in the autumn of 1997 to celebrate his 74th birthday. Mozley, who called for it to be moved to the club's new home at Pride Park, stated:

> I couldn't even find it at first. What a place to put a memorial to a player who was one of the best in the world in his day. Can you imagine the outcry in Staffordshire if the powers-that-be had erected the statues of Stanley Matthews and Billy Wright in their local fish markets? I was very impressed by the new stadium, and I think it would be a more suitable location for such a great player.

But those with a contrary view had the influential backing of Bloomer's grandson Steve Richards, who pointed out:

> If it was at Pride Park, people would get to see it only on match days. The Lock-up Yard is central, with lots of people walking past. If the club was still at the Baseball Ground, where my grandfather played, it might have been different, but I think he would have preferred its present location himself.

The wording on the memorial reads:

> STEVE BLOOMER, FIRST KING OF ENGLISH
> FOOTBALL GOALSCORERS, ENTERED THE 20th CENTURY
> WITH HIS FAME AS DERBY COUNTY'S OUTSTANDING
> MARKSMAN ALREADY ESTABLISHED.
> AS THE NEXT CENTURY BECKONED WHEN THIS
> MONUMENT WAS ERECTED IN 1996 HIS RAMS' ALL-GAMES
> RECORD OF 332 GOALS WAS STILL UNSURPASSED.
> HIS 353 FOOTBALL LEAGUE GOALS FOR DERBY COUNTY
> AND MIDDLESBROUGH WAS A RECORD UNTIL NEAR
> HIS DEATH IN 1938 AT 64.
> BLOOMER'S 28 GOALS IN 23 ENGLAND GAMES GAVE
> HIM A THEN UNIQUE AVERAGE OF 1.21 PER CAP.
> THE SON OF A MIDLANDS' BLACKSMITH, BLOOMER WAS A
> PUPIL AT ST. JAMES' SCHOOL IN DERBY. HE WAS DESCRIBED
> AS A 'WORKING CLASS HERO' BY NOTTINGHAM TRENT
> UNIVERSITY STUDENT JONATHAN BELSHAW IN HIS 1990s
> STUDY OF VICTORIAN SOCIAL CHANGES.
> THE MONUMENT, ERECTED THROUGH THE AUCTION
> OF BLOOMER'S ENGLAND CAPS, PLUS FAMILY
> CONTRIBUTIONS, HAS BEEN PRESENTED
> TO DERBY CITY COUNCIL
> BY HIS DESCENDANTS.

The official unveiling of the Bloomer memorial in Derby's Lock-up Yard. The Mayor of Derby is pictured with (left to right) Johnny Morris, the former Rams player who cost the then record transfer fee when signed from Manchester United in 1949, Arthur Rowley, current holder of the League scoring record once held by Steve Bloomer, Michael Knighton, a Derbyshire-born businessman who bought some of Bloomer's international caps, Nat Lofthouse (partially hidden), the former Bolton and England centre-forward, Tom Finney, the former Preston and England forward, and the late Wilf Mannion, formerly of Middlesbrough and England. Steve Richards, Bloomer's grandson, is on the extreme left of this picture.

(Raymonds Press Agency)

In 1998, another posthumous honour was bestowed upon Bloomer, at national level, when he was among the 100 League Legends named by the Football League to mark their 100th season. That list includes seven other former Derby County players, as shown in the appendix.

A memento mug was also produced, co-sponsored by the Professional Footballers' Association and the *Derby Evening Telegraph*, and manufactured by Keramikos, ceramic decorators of Matlock. It bore the inscription 'STEVE BLOOMER THE GREATEST goalscorer in Derby County Football Club history', and listed his scoring achievements. And a Rams 'anthem', entitled 'Steve Bloomer's Watching', became a familiar part of the match-day proceedings as it was played over the loudspeakers at Pride Park.

Then, on September 14th, 2000, Bloomer was honoured at his home town of Cradley, where a memorial plaque opposite the house in Bridge Street where he was born was unveiled at a ceremony in which the Mayor of Dudley was joined by Jimmy Dunn, the former Wolves and Derby player who lives at neighbouring Cradley Heath, and Bloomer's grandson Steve Richards.

At a reception at the New Collier public house in Bridge Street that followed, Steve Richards, who was a sports writer for *The Sun* and the *Daily Herald* in the 1960s when they were broadsheets,[3] and later did public relations work in the United States, said that Steve Bloomer had 'scored one of his most memorable goals simply by being honoured in this way in his home town of Cradley, the very street where he was born'.

He considered that his grandfather had played a major role in influencing his future. 'His silence when he saw me play football several times told me I wasn't going to be the next Steve Bloomer!'

Jimmy Dunn, son of the former Everton and Scotland forward of the same name, recalled that when he joined Derby County in the 1950s everybody at the club was still talking about the legend. From all he had heard 'he must have been one hell of a player'. He added: 'I am often asked how would the players of yesteryear fare today, and I say players like Steve Bloomer and Stanley Matthews would be just as good as they were in their day because they would have adapted to what was going on'.

The memorial plaque at Cradley, Bloomer's birthplace.

---

3. His son Mark has followed him into the newspaper business as a freelance photographer contracted to the *Daily Mail.*

The Official Unveiling
of the
Steve Bloomer
Memorial Plaque

in Bridge Street, Cradley on
Thursday 14th September 2000 at
11.30am by The Mayor of Dudley,
Mr. Steve Richards, and
Mr. Jimmy Dunn

**The front page of the souvenir brochure produced for the
official unveiling of the plaque at Cradley.**

Bev Pegg, whose firm Cradley Castings part-sponsored the Memorial unveiling ceremony, recalled that he had also lived in Bridge Street as a child and, having been told about the player by his parents, was therefore able to tell the Council exactly where the house in which Bloomer was born had been situated.

Steve Bloomer's 332 goals in his 525 games for Derby County (38 of them in his 50 Cup-ties) set a record for one club which has since been overtaken by Bill Dean, with 377 in 431 appearances for Everton, and George Camsell, with 345 in 453 matches for Middlesbrough. With the addition of his goals for Boro—59 in 125 League games and three in five FA Cup-ties—Bloomer had an aggregate of 394 in 655 matches, plus his 28 in 23 internationals.

As far as League games only are concerned, Bloomer's 294 goals for Derby (including one in the 1895 'test' against Notts County) have been surpassed as a club record by Dean (349 for Everton), Camsell (326 for Middlesbrough), John Atyeo (314 for Bristol City) and Vic Watson (298 for West Ham United). After Bloomer come Arthur Chandler (259 for Leicester City), Nat Lofthouse (255 for Bolton Wanderers) and the overall record League scorer, Arthur Rowley (251 for Leicester City).

The Bloomer family's gravestone at the Nottingham Road cemetery in Derby.
(Raymonds Press Agency)

Only one other player from the 19th century shares with Bloomer the distinction of still being his club's highest scorer. Grenville Morris,[4] first capped by Wales in 1896 at the age of 18, while with Aberystwyth, fell just one goal short of 200 in his 15 years with Nottingham Forest, for whom he was a bargain signing at £200 from Swindon Town in 1898. At about £1 a goal that was very good business, but bettered by the return Derby County obtained on their outlay for Steve Bloomer.

The seat dedicated to Steve Bloomer in the Nottingham Road cemetery at Derby. The wording on it reads: In Memory of the Legendary STEVE BLOOMER...of Derby County and England.
(Raymonds Press Agency)

---

4. Morris altogether played 21 times for Wales. He scored the first of his seven goals for his country on his debut, in a 6–1 victory against Ireland at Wrexham on February 29th, 1896. His last international appearance was in a 2–0 defeat by England, also at Wrexham, on March 11th, 1912. In addition to his 199 goals in 423 League games for Forest, he scored 18 in 37 FA Cup-ties.

Appendix One

DERBY COUNTY'S FA CUP FINALS

April 16th, 1898	*Derby County 1, Nottingham Forest 3* *At Crystal Palace*
Derby County:	Fryer; Methven, Leiper; Cox, Goodall A., Turner; Goodall J., Bloomer, Boag, Stevenson, McQueen.
Nottingham Forest:	Allsop; Ritchie, Scott; Forman (Frank), McPherson, Wragg; McInnes, Richards, Benbow, Capes, Spouncer.
Referee:	J. Lewis (Blackburn).
Scorers:	*Derby County*: Bloomer (31 minutes); *Nottingham Forest*: Capes (19 and 42 mins), McPherson (86).
Attendance:	62,017
Receipts:	£2,312

Derby's team was the same as that fielded in the First Division match between the clubs at the Baseball Ground on April 11th, when the Rams won 5–0 with goals from Bloomer (3), Boag and Turner. Forest's line-up in that game was: Allsop; Ritchie, Iremonger; Shaw, Frank Forman, McCracken; Bradshaw, Richards, Benbow, Fred Forman, McInnes.

April 15th, 1899	*Derby County 1, Sheffield United 4* *At Crystal Palace*
Derby County:	Fryer; Methven, Staley; Cox, Paterson, May; Arkesden, Bloomer, Boag, McDonald, Allen.
Sheffield United:	Foulke; Thickett, Boyle; Johnson, Morren, Needham; Bennett, Beer, Hedley, Almond, Priest.
Referee:	A. Scragg (Crewe).
Scorers:	*Derby County*: Boag (12 mins); *Sheffield United*: Bennett (59), Beer (65), Almond (70), Priest (87).
Attendance:	73,833
Receipts:	£2,747

April 18th, 1903	**Bury 6, Derby County 0** *At Crystal Palace*
Bury:	Monteith; Lindsay, McEwen; Johnston, Thorpe, Ross; Richards W., Wood, Sagar, Leeming, Plant.
Derby County:	Fryer; Methven, Morris; Warren, Goodall A., May; Warrington, York, Boag, Richards G., Davis G.
Referee:	J. Adams (Birmingham).
Scorers:	Ross (20 mins), Sagar (48), Leeming (56 and 75), Wood (57), Plant (59).
Attendance:	63,102
Receipts:	£2,470

The record FA Cup Final victory. The previous widest winning margin was 6–1, by Blackburn Rovers against the Wednesday in 1890.

April 27th, 1946	**Charlton Athletic 1, Derby County 4** *after extra time (score 1–1 after 90 minutes)* *At Wembley*
Charlton Athletic:	Bartram; Phipps, Shreeve; Turner Bert, Oakes John, Johnson; Fell, Brown, A.A. Turner, Welsh, Duffy.
Derby County:	Woodley; Nicholas, Howe; Bullions, Leuty, Musson; Harrison, Carter, Stamps, Doherty, Duncan.
Referee:	E.D. Smith (Whitehaven).
Scorers:	*Charlton*: Bert Turner (86 mins); *Derby County*: Bert Turner, own goal (85), Doherty (91), Stamps (97 and 106).
Attendance:	98,215
Receipts:	£45,000

OTHER OUTSTANDING FA CUP-TIES

(Up to the beginning of George Jobey's time as manager)

November 14th, 1885 *Second round: Derby County 2, Aston Villa 0*

Derby County: Luntley; Morley, Williamson; Cooper G.F., Flowers, Warmby; Bakewell, Spilsbury, Evans, Smith, Cooper L.

Aston Villa: Hobson; Jones, Riddell; Burton J., Price, Whateley; Albert Brown, Hunter, Arthur Brown, Vaughton, Davis.

Scorers: Smith, Evans.

Attendance: 5,000

The victory that put Derby County on the soccer map as a force to be reckoned with.

January 18th, 1890 *First round: Everton 11, Derby County 2*

Everton: Smalley; Hannah, Doyle; Kirkwood, Holt, Parry; Latta, Brady, Geary, Chadwick, Milward.

Derby County: Bromage; Latham, Ferguson; Williamson, Goodall A., Roulstone; Bakewell, Higgins, Goodall J., Cooper, Milarvie.

Scorers: *Everton*: Brady 3, Geary 3, Milward 3, Doyle, Kirkwood; *Derby*: Goodall J. 2.

Attendance: 25,000

Derby's heaviest defeat after leading 2–1.

January 21st, 1893 *First round: The Wednesday 3, Derby County 2*

Wednesday: Allan; Brandon T., Mumford; Brandon H., Betts, Chalmers; Davis, Brown, Rowan, Brady, Spiksley.

Derby County: Robinson; Methven, Leiper; Hickinbottom, Goodall A., Roulstone; Mills, Bloomer, Goodall J., McMillan, Little.

Scorers: *Derby*: Goodall J., Bloomer; *Wednesday*: Spiksley 3.

Attendance: 20,000

January 30th, 1893   (*replay after protest*) **Derby County 1, The Wednesday 0**

Derby County: Unchanged.

Wednesday: Allan; Brandon T., Darroch; Brandon H., Betts, Chalmers; Davis, Brown, Rowan, Woolhouse, Spiksley.

Scorer: Goodall J.

Attendance: 15,000

February 2nd, 1893   (*replay after protest*) **The Wednesday 4, Derby County 2**

Wednesday: Unchanged.

Derby County: Robinson; Methven, Leiper; Hickinbottom, Goodall A., Roulstone; Mills, Storer W., Goodall J., McMillan, Little.

Scorers: *Wednesday*: Betts, Spiksley, Woolhouse, Chalmers; *Derby County*: Goodall J., Little.

Attendance: 10,000

Tommy Little's goal was the first of only two he scored for the Rams in just 17 first-team appearances. The other one came in a 5–1 home win over Newton Heath in a League game on February 11th. He moved to Manchester City in June, 1895. In the following October he went to Baltimore in the United States, but returned to City a month later and subsequently played for Ashton North End, Wellingborough, Swindon , Barnsley and Dumfries.

February 1st, 1896   **First round: Derby County 4, Aston Villa (holders) 2**

Derby County: Robinson; Methven, Leiper; Cox, Goodall A., Kinsey; Goodall J., Bloomer, Miller, Stevenson, McQueen.

Aston Villa: Wilkes; Spencer, Crabtree; Burton, Jas. Cowan, Chatt; Athersmith, Devey, Campbell, Hodgetts, Cowan J.

Scorers: *Derby County*: Bloomer 2, Miller 2; *Aston Villa*: Burton, Hodgetts.

Attendance: 20,000

January 29th, 1898　　*First round: Derby County 1, Aston Villa (holders) 0*

Derby County:　　Fryer; Methven, Leiper; Cox, Goodall A., Turner J.; Paul,
　　　　　　　　　　Goodall J., Maconnachie, Stevenson, McQueen.

Aston Villa:　　Whitehouse; Bowman, Evans; Sharp B., Cowan Jas.,
　　　　　　　　　Crabtree; Athersmith, Cowan J., Sharp J., Wheldon, Smith.

Scorer:　　McQueen.

Attendance:　　12,000

John Paul played on both wings for Derby, and also at inside-forward, scoring nine goals in 30 League appearances (including the 'test' against Notts County), but this was his only Cup-tie. He was with Hibernian before joining the Rams, and afterwards went to Bristol Rovers. Alex Maconnachie spent just this one season with Derby, scoring nine times in 26 games, but lost his place for the third-round replay with Liverpool to John Boag, who did the hat-trick in a 5–1 win and stayed in the side for the semi-final against Everton and the County's first final, in which they lost to Nottingham Forest. Maconnachie moved to Notts County in March, 1898, and to Third Lanark in 1901.

March 19th 1898　　*Semi-final: Derby County 3, Everton 1*
　　　　　　　　　　At Wolverhampton

Derby County:　　Fryer; Methven, Leiper; Cox, Goodall A., Turner J.;
　　　　　　　　　　Goodall J., Bloomer, Boag, Stevenson, McQueen.

Everton:　　Muir; Balmer W., Storrier; Stewart, Holt, Robertson; Taylor,
　　　　　　　Divers, Bell L., Chadwick, Bell J.

Scorers:　　*Derby:* Bloomer (2), Goodall J.;
　　　　　　　Everton: Chadwick.

Attendance:　　30,000

This victory, in their third successive semi-final, avenged Derby's defeat by Everton at Stoke the previous year. Jimmy Methven regarded it as the most memorable of his 511 games for the Rams.

February 27th, 1902   **Third round replay: Derby County 6, Portsmouth 3**

Derby County: Fryer; Methven, Morris; Raisbeck, Goodall A., Leckie; Wombwell, Bloomer, Boag, Warren, Davis G.

Portsmouth: Reilly; Wilkie, Turner; Stringfellow, Chadwick, Blythe; Marshall, Cunliffe, MacAuley, W. Smith, Corrin.

Scorers: *Derby:* Bloomer 3, Warren 2, Boag; *Portsmouth:* W. Smith, Chadwick (pen.), Cunliffe.

Attendance: 17,836

Following a scoreless draw in the original tie at Portsmouth, four goals, three of them to the Rams, came in 18 minutes during the first half of the replay, and four more in slightly more than five minutes in the second half. After the interval, Bloomer increased the home lead to 5–1 by scoring twice, then Chadwick converted a penalty after Methven had brought down Smith, and Cunliffe further reduced the visitors' deficit almost immediately. Bloomer completed his hat-trick with a header three minutes from time. Portsmouth's changes from the first game brought in Wilkie and MacAuley in the absence of Burgess and Steve Smith through injury, with Corrin switching from centre-forward to the left wing.

March 27th, 1902   **Semi-final, second replay: Derby County 0, Sheffield United 1**
At City Ground, Nottingham

Derby County: Fryer; Methven, Morris; Warren, Goodall A., Leckie; Wombwell, Bloomer, Boag, Warrington, Davis G.

Sheffield United: Foulke; Thickett, Boyle; Johnson, Wilkinson, Parker; Bennett, Common, Hedley, Priest, Lipsham.

Scorer: Priest.

Attendance: 15,000

This followed 1–1 draws at West Bromwich and Wolverhampton. Sheffield United, who had been taken to two games by Newcastle United in their quarter-final, needed another replay to defeat Southampton, 2–1, in the final.

March 19th, 1904	*Semi-final: Bolton Wanderers 1, Derby County 0* *At Molineux, Wolverhampton.*
Bolton Wanderers:	Davies D.; Brown, Struthers; Freebairn, Greenhalgh, Boyd; Stokes, Marsh, Yenson, White, Taylor.
Derby County:	Maskrey; Methven, Morris; Warren, Hall, May; Mercer, Bloomer, Warrington, Richards, Davis G.
Scorer:	Taylor.
Attendance:	20,180

March 31st, 1909	*Semi-final replay: Bristol City 2, Derby County 1* *At St. Andrew's, Birmingham.*
Bristol City:	Clay; Annan, Cottle; Marr, Wedlock, Spear; Staniforth, Gilligan, Rippon, Burton, Hardy.
Derby County:	Maskrey; Nicholas, Morris; Barbour, Hall, Richards; Thompson, Garry, Bentley, Barnes, Davis J.
Scorers:	Bristol City: Rippon (pen.), Hardy; Derby: Davis J.
Attendance:	27,600

As in the first meeting, at Stamford Bridge, full-back Nicholas conceded a penalty.

March 24th, 1923	*Semi-final: West Ham United 5, Derby County 2* *At Stamford Bridge*
West Ham:	Hufton; Henderson, Young; Bishop, Kay, Tresadern; Richards, Brown, Watson, Moore W., Ruffell.
Derby County:	Olney; Chandler, Crilly; McIntyre, Thoms, Plackett; Thornewell, Lyons, Galloway, Moore J., Murphy.
Scorers:	*West Ham:* Brown 2, Moore 2, Ruffell; *Derby:* Moore, Henderson (o.g.).
Attendance:	50,795

February 2nd, 1924   *Second round: Derby County 2, Newcastle United 2*

Derby County: Olney; Chandler, Crilly; McIntyre, Thoms, Plackett; Thornewell, Whitehouse, Galloway, Storer, Murphy.

Newcastle Utd: Mutch; Russell, Hunter; Curry, Mooney, Gibson; Low, Cowan, Harris, McDonald, Seymour.

Scorers: *Derby*: Storer 2; *Newcastle*: McDonald 2.

Attendance: 27,873

February 6th, 1924   *Replay: Newcastle United 2, Derby County 2*

Both teams unchanged.

Scorers: *Newcastle*: Harris, Cowan; *Derby*: Galloway, Mooney (o.g.).

Attendance: 50,393

February 11th, 1924   *Second replay: Derby County 2, Newcastle United 2*
    At Burnden Park, Bolton

Derby County: Unchanged.

Newcastle Utd: Mutch; Hampson, Hudspeth; Curry, Spencer, Gibson; Low, Aitken, Harris, Cowan, Seymour.

Scorers: *Derby*: Galloway, Thornewell; *Newcastle*: Seymour, Hudspeth (pen.).

Attendance: 17,300

February 13th, 1924   *Third replay: Newcastle United 5, Derby County 3*
    At St. James's Park, Newcastle

Newcastle Utd: Mutch; Hampson, Hudspeth; Mooney, Spencer, Gibson; Low, Cowan, Harris, McDonald, Seymour.

Derby County: Unchanged.

Scorers: *Newcastle*: Seymour, Harris 3, Cowan; *Derby*: Galloway 2, Storer.

Attendance: 32,496

Appendix Two

⚽

OUTSTANDING LEAGUE MATCHES PLAYED BY DERBY COUNTY

(Up to the beginning of George Jobey's time as manager)

September 8th, 1888   *Bolton Wanderers 3, Derby County 6*

Bolton Wanderers: Harrison; Robinson, Mitchell; Roberts, Weir, Bullough; Davenport, Milne, Coupar, Barbour, Brogan.

Derby County: Marshall; Latham, Ferguson; Williamson, Monks, Roulstone; Bakewell, Cooper, Higgins, Plackett H., Plackett L.

Scorers: *Bolton*: Davenport 2, Brogan; *Derby*: Bakewell 2, Cooper 2, Plackett L. 2.

Attendance: 3,000

The Rams' first match in the Football League. They recovered from conceding two goals in the first five minutes and going 3–0 down shortly afterwards.

September 6th, 1890   *Derby County 8, Blackburn Rovers 5*

Derby County:	Haddow; Hopkins, Latham; Chalmers, Goodall A., Roulstone; Bakewell, McLachlan, Goodall J., Holmes, Nelson.
Blackburn Rovers:	Lowe; Brandon, Forbes; Barton, Dewar, Forrest; Lofthouse, Campbell, Southworth, Walton, Whitehead.
Scorers:	*Derby*: Goodall J. 3, Nelson 2, Goodall A., Chalmers, McLachlan; *Blackburn*: Southworth 3, Walton, Whitehead.
Attendance:	4,500

- The highest aggregate of goals in a Derby County match in the Football League, most closely approached by the 9–3 defeat of West Bromwich Albion at the Baseball Ground on December 8th, 1935. There were also 13 goals when Everton defeated Derby 11–2 in an FA Cup-tie in 1890, and 12, all scored by the Rams, in a UEFA Cup-tie with Finn Harps in 1976.
- Jimmy McLachlan, signed from Vale of Leven in 1890, was a regular choice at inside-right for two seasons after the departure of 'Sandy' Higgins before moving to Notts County in September, 1893. He played mostly on the right wing after rejoining the Rams a year later, then signed for Ilkeston Town in May, 1895.
- Sam Holmes, a local signing from Crich midway through the second League season, scored eight times in 22 games. His left-wing partner, Jim Nelson, made only three other first-team appearances despite his two-goal debut.

January 3rd, 1891   *Blackburn Rovers 8, Derby County 0*

Blackburn Rovers:	Gow; Brandon, Forbes; Barton, Dewar, Almond; Lofthouse, Campbell, Southworth, Hall, Townley.
Derby County:	Haddow; Baker, Goodall A.; Walker, Chalmers, Roulstone; Bakewell, McLachlan, Daft T., Cooper, McMillan.
Scorers:	Hall 4, Southworth 3, Townley.
Attendance:	3,000

This was the last of three League appearances made for Derby by Daft, one of the players recruited from Derby Midland. It was also the last League game for the Rams for goalkeeper David Haddow, who conceded 69 goals in his 16 League matches but went on to play for Scotland and gain winner's medals with Glasgow Rangers (Scottish Cup), Burnley (Division Two title) and Tottenham Hotspur (Southern League title).

January 10th, 1891   *Derby County 9, Wolverhampton Wanderers 0*

Derby County: Bunyan; Roberts, Goodall A. ; Walker, Chalmers, Roulstone; Bakewell, McLachlan, Goodall J., Holmes, McMillan.

Wolverhampton W: Rose; Baugh, Brodie; Fletcher, Allen, Lowder; Wykes, Booth, Thomson, Wood, Bowdler.

Scorers: McMillan 5, Holmes 2, Roulstone, Goodall J..

Attendance: 3,000

Derby set club record for the margin of a League victory, with a team that showed four changes from their crushing defeat at Blackburn the week before.

October 19th, 1892   *Derby County 4, Notts County 5*

Derby County: Robinson; Methven, Staley; Cox, Goodall A., Roulstone; Mills, Goodall J., Storer W., Bloomer, McMillan.

Notts County: Toone; Whitelaw, Hendry; Bramley, Calderhead, Shelton McGregor, Oswald, Bruce, Walkerdine, Daft H.

Scorers: *Derby*: Storer 2, McMillan, Goodall J.;
Notts County: Bruce 2, Daft 2, McGregor.

Attendance: 5,000

Notts County were relegated for the first time at the end of this season, losing to Darwen in the 'test' series from which Derby escaped by finishing 13th out of 16, three points ahead of 14th-placed Notts. As a result of the 'tests', Birmingham, the first champions of Division Two, did not gain promotion, and Manchester United, the First Division's bottom club, were not relegated. Darwen, who had finished third in the Second Division, went up with runners-up Sheffield United; Notts went down with Accrington, who resigned before the next season started.

September 9th, 1893 *Derby County 7, Everton 3*

Derby County: Robinson; Methven, Leiper; Cox, Goodall A., Docherty; Keay, Bloomer, Goodall J., Allan, McMillan.

Everton: Williams; Kelso, Howarth; Boyle, Holt, Stewart; Latta, Bell, Southworth, Chadwick, Milward.

Scorers: *Derby*: Bloomer 2, McMillan 2, Goodall A., Allan, Keay; *Everton*: Chadwick, Milward, Southworth.

Attendance: 8,000

Derby ended this season third in the First Division, two points behind runners-up Sunderland and eight adrift of champions Aston Villa. Everton, who were sixth, recovered from this heavy defeat to beat Sunderland 7–1 on the last day of September, and in October they had another big home win, by 8–1 against Darwen. On successive Saturdays in December, they scored eight more against the Wednesday, and seven against West Bromwich Albion. In their return game with the Rams they lost 2–1.

April 27th, 1895 *Derby County 2, Notts County 1* (*Test match to avoid relegation*) *At Walnut Street, Leicester*

Derby County: Robinson; Methven, Leiper; Cox, Goodall A., Staley; Francis, Bloomer, Goodall J., McMillan, Paul.

Notts County: Toone; Stothert, Hendry; Bramley, Calderhead, Shelton; Chadburn, Allsopp, Allan, Sissons, Fletcher.

Scorers: *Derby*: Bloomer, McMillan; *Notts County*: Fletcher.

Attendance: 8,000

Fred Fletcher and John Allan had both started that season with Derby County. Allan, signed from Glasgow Thistle, was an ever-present in his only full season with the Rams, 1893–94, mostly as a right-winger. Fletcher, a local player, made only three League appearances for Derby before joining Notts in November 1894, the month before Allan made the same move.

September 19th, 1896 **Derby County 4, Wolverhampton Wanderers 3**

Derby County: Robinson; Methven, Leiper; Cox, Goodall A., Kinsey; Goodall J., Bloomer, Miller, Stevenson, McQueen.

Wolverhampton W: Tennant; Eccles, Dunn; Griffiths, Malpass, Owen; Tonks, Pheasant, Beats, Wood, Miller.

Scorers: *Derby*: Bloomer 4; *Wolves*: Beats 2, Wood.

Attendance: 5,000

A week later, Bloomer scored three times in a 7–2 home win against Bury. He also did the hat-trick that season in an 8–1 home victory over West Bromwich Albion, and in FA Cup-ties against Barnsley St. Peters's, who were beaten 8–1 in the first round, and Bolton Wanderers, who lost 4–1 in the fourth. Bloomer's goals total for the season was 31 (24 in the League, seven in the Cup), breaking the club record he had set with 27 the previous season. In both 1898-99 and 1900–01 he scored 24 goals, all in the League.

October 15th, 1898 **Derby County 5, Everton 5**

Derby County: Ford; Methven, Kifford; Cox, Goodall A., May; Handley, Goodall J., Bloomer, Arkesden, McQueen.

Everton: Muir; Balmer, Molyneux; Boyle, Owen, Taylor; Clarke, Bell, Oldham, Kirwan, Schofield.

Scorers: *Derby*: McQueen, Arkesden 2, Bloomer 2 (1 pen.); *Everton*: Owen 2 (1 pen.), Ford (o.g.), Kirwan, Bell.

Attendance: 7,000

Derby were 2–1 down within 15 minutes, with Fryer's deputy David Ford at fault and another reserve, Jack Kifford, off form. It was reported that 'the crowd, in their disappointment, were extremely derisive, and there was a brief cessation owing to certain ill-mannered persons throwing at the linesman on the railway side. An official of the club went across urging them to desist.' The score was 3–3 at half-time, but Ford then made two more costly mistakes and 'was subjected to ironic applause for stopping an easy shot shortly afterwards.' Bloomer forced the draw with two late goals, the second of them only a few minutes from time.

January 21st, 1899	*Derby County 9, The Wednesday 0*

Derby County: Fryer; Methven, Staley; Cox, Goodall A., May; Oakden, Bloomer, Boag, MacDonald, Allen.

The Wednesday: Massey; Earp, Langley; Ferrier, Crawshaw, Ruddlesdin; Dryburgh, Hemmingfield, Kaye, Wright, Spiksley.

Scorers: Bloomer 6, MacDonald, Oakden, Earp (o.g.).

Attendance: 5,000

This equalled the record victory Derby gained against Wolves in 1891. Bloomer's six goals set the club's individual record.

February 3rd, 1900	*Aston Villa 3, Derby County 2*

Aston Villa: George; Spencer, Evans; Bowman, Cowan, Crabtree; Athersmith, Devey, Garraty, Wheldon, Smith.

Derby County: Fryer; Methven, Kifford; Leckie, Goodall A., May; Wombwell, Bloomer, Boag, Shanks, McQueen.

Scorers: *Villa*: Garraty 2, Wheldon; *Derby*: Bloomer, Boag.

Attendance: 6,000

This match was notable because Derby, who led 2–0, had five 'goals' disallowed. The Football League record for the number of nullified goals in one match was then six in a First Division game in which Blackburn beat Liverpool 1–0 in September 1896. This was equalled in a Division Three South fixture between Swindon and Southend, who drew 2–2, in November 1949.

April 20th, 1907   **Derby County 1, Bristol City 3**

Derby County: Smith J.W.; Nicholas, Moore W.; Warren, Hall, Bagshaw; Armstrong, Long, Bentley, Wheatcroft, Davis G.

Bristol City: Demmery; Gale, Annan; Marr, Wedlock, Hanlin; Staniforth, Maxwell, Gilligan, Connelly, Hilton.

Scorers: *Derby*: Armstrong; *Bristol City*: Gilligan, Maxwell, Hanlin.

Attendance: 6,000

This defeat sealed Derby's first relegation to the Second Division. Arthur Armstrong, who had toured with Sanger's Circus as an acrobat before joining the Rams, scored within four minutes on his debut, but City quickly equalised and went ahead before Warren shot tamely into Demmery's hands from the penalty spot. Jack Smith, a goalkeeper from Long Eaton who was deputising for Harry Maskrey, then let a speculative long shot from Hanlin slip through his hands for the goal that clinched the visitors' victory.

October 19th, 1907   **Derby County 6, Leeds City 1**

Derby County: Maskrey; Atkin, Morris; Warren, Hall, Richards; Springthorpe, Garry, Long, Bentley, Dilly.

Leeds City: Bromage; Kay, Murray; Tompkins, Hynds, Thorpe; Parnell, Watson, McLeod, Cubberley, Croot.

Scorers: *Derby*: Bentley 4 (1 pen.), Dilly, Garry; *Leeds*: Atkin (o.g.).

Attendance: 6,000

Arbroath-born Tommy Dilly, a man of many clubs, joined the Rams from West Bromwich Albion just before this Second Division match, in which he deputised for Davis. He moved to Bradford during the following close season.

October 1st, 1910   *Derby County 5, Lincoln City 0*

Derby County: Scattergood E.; Barbour, Atkin; Garry, Hall, Bagshaw; Grimes, Bloomer, Bauchop, Barnes, Donald.

Lincoln City: Fern; Jackson, Wilson; Fraser, Gardner, Miller; Clarke, Reid, Hunter, Yule, Platts.

Scorers: Bloomer 2 (1 pen.), Barnes, Bauchop 2.

Attendance: 12,000

Steve Bloomer's first match after his return to Derby from Middlesbrough. This was how his first goal, after 20 minutes, was described in the Derby newspaper: 'Fern had just previously entangled himself with Donald and Barnes, whom he challenged at close quarters, and, with the ball just out of the goalkeeper's reach, Bloomer pounced on it with his old-time vigour and scored cleverly'. Shortly before half-time, Fern strained his side in tipping a Barnes shot over the bar and had to leave the field. He returned to take over from his deputy, Wilson, the Lincoln captain, at the beginning of the second half, but 15 minutes from the end 'he again overtaxed himself and retired from the game for good'. By then the Rams were three up, a successful header by Barnes from Donald's corner in the 55th minute having been followed 10 minutes later by Bloomer's penalty, awarded against Miller for handling the ball. Bauchop made it 4–0 with a header from Barnes's pass while Fern was being assisted off for the second time, and the same player scored again with only half a minute to go.

April 22nd, 1912   *Barnsley 0, Derby County 2*

Barnsley: Clegg; Downes, Taylor; Glendinning, Bratley, Utley; Bartrop, Travers, Lillycrop, Tufnell, Moore.

Derby County: Scattergood E.; Atkin, Barbour; Garry, Buckley, Richards; Grimes, Bloomer, Leonard H., Bauchop, Barnes.

Scorers: Buckley, Bauchop.

Attendance: 4,000

The win, on the last day of the season, that clinched Derby's return to the First Division.

October 19th, 1912   *Aston Villa 5, Derby County 1*

Aston Villa: Anstey; Lyons, Weston; Whittaker, Morris, Harrop; Wallace,
                       Hall, Halse, Stephenson, Bache.

Derby County: Scattergood E.; Atkin, Barbour; Matthews, Buckley,
                       Bagshaw; Grimes, Bloomer, Leonard, Bauchop, Neve.

Scorers: *Villa*: Halse 5; *Derby*: Bauchop.

Attendance: 30,000

Owing to the illness of 'Happy' Harry Hampton, who a fortnight earlier had scored
five goals in a 10–0 home win over the Wednesday, Harold Halse was switched from
inside-right to lead Villa's attack and, in only his ninth match for the club, emulated
that record Villa feat by following two goals inside the first 12 minutes with a
second-half hat-trick in 16 minutes. In the previous September Halse had scored six
goals for Manchester United in an 8–4 defeat of Swindon Town in an FA Charity
Shield game at Stamford Bridge.

January 18th, 1913   *Derby County 5, Tottenham Hotspur 0*

Derby County: Scattergood E.; Atkin, Betts; Garry, Bagshaw, Richards;
                       Sharpe, Bloomer, Leonard, Bauchop, Neve.

Tottenham Hotspur: Joyce; Collins, Webster; Weir, Rance, Grimsdell; Tattersall,
                       Minter, Cantrell, Steel, Middlemiss.

Scorers: Bauchop 3, Bloomer 2.

Attendance: 10,000.

Charlie Rance, a former Clapton amateur, was a member of Spurs' Second Division
championship-winning team in 1919–20, but he lost his place to Charlie Walters
shortly before they began their run to victory in the 1921 FA Cup Final and moved to
Derby in March that year. He was unable to help the Rams to avoid relegation from
the First Division at the end of that season and in September 1922 he returned to
London with Queen's Park Rangers.

September 29th, 1923   *Bristol City 0, Derby County 8*

Bristol City: Goddard; Hughes, Banfield; Neesam, Hawley, Torrance;
                          Worlock, Paul, Fairclough, Sutherland, Compton.

Derby County: Olney; Chandler, Crilly; McIntyre, Thoms, Plackett;
                          Thornewell, Whitehouse, Galloway, Storer, Murphy.

Scorers: Storer 4, Galloway 2, Thornewell, Plackett.

Attendance: 20,000

Derby's record away victory. Storer again scored four goals in a 6–0 Boxing Day
home win against Nelson, and in the following month he did the hat-trick in a 6–1
victory over South Shields at the Baseball Ground. He ended the season as the
Rams' top scorer with 27 goals, three of them in the Cup.

May 3rd, 1924   *Derby County 4, Leicester City 0*

Derby County: Olney; Chandler, Crilly; McIntyre, Thoms, Wightman;
                          Thornewell, Moore, Galloway, Storer, Murphy.

Leicester City: Goodridge; Barrett, Osborne; Newton, Bamber, Watson;
                          Adcock, Middleton, Chandler, Carr, Trotter

Scorers: Moore 2, Storer, Galloway.

Attendance: 20,000

The Rams fell one goal short of the victory they needed for a return to the First
Division, yielding the second promotion place behind Leeds United to Bury by 0.015
of a goal.

Appendix Three

STEVE BLOOMER'S FIRST GAME IN THE FOOTBALL LEAGUE

September 3rd, 1892   *Stoke City 1, Derby County 3*

Stoke City: Rowley; Clare, Underwood; Christie, Proctor, Brodie; Evans, Naughton, Dickson, Schofield, Robertson.

Derby County: Robinson; Methven, Staley; Cox, Garden, Roulstone; Ekins, Bloomer, Goodall J., Rose, McMillan.

Attendance: 5,000

Scorers: *Stoke*: Schofield; *Derby*: McMillan 2, Goodall J.

HIS LAST LEAGUE MATCH

January 24th, 1914   *Bradford City 0, Derby County 0*

Bradford City: Ewart; Campbell, Boocock; Hargreaves, Torrance, Brennan; Bond, Wild, Storer C., Chesser, Logan.

Derby County: Lawrence; Atkin, Waugh; Barbour, Buckley, Bagshaw; Grimes, Moore, Bloomer, Barnes, Neve.

Attendance: 15,000

Bloomer scored his last League goals at home to Sheffield United on September 6th, 1913, netting twice in a 5–3 defeat.

STEVE BLOOMER'S LAST FA CUP-TIE

January 31st, 1914	*Second round: Burnley 3, Derby County 2*
Burnley:	Dawson; Bamford, Taylor; Halley, Boyle, Watson; Nesbitt, Lindley, Freeman, Hodgson, Mosscrop.
Derby County:	Lawrence; Atkin, Waugh; Barbour, Buckley, Bagshaw; Grimes, Moore, Bloomer, Barnes, Walker.
Scorers:	*Burnley:* Hodgson 3; *Derby:* Barnes, Waugh.
Attendance:	30,000

- This was the only goal scored for Derby by Robert Waugh, a full-back signed from Newcastle United as cover for Charlie Betts, another former Newcastle defender. Waugh was later deputy for Tommy Barbour when that player reclaimed the left-back position, and he also stood in at right-back for Jack Atkin in making 29 senior appearances before moving to Jarrow in 1919.
- Burnley went on to win the Cup, beating Liverpool in the final with a goal by Freeman.

HIS FIRST INTERNATIONAL MATCH

March 9th, 1895	*England 9, Ireland 0 (at County Ground, Derby)*
England:	**Sutcliffe** (Bolton Wanderers); **Crabtree** (Burnley), **Holmes** (Preston North End); **Howell** (Sheffield United), **Crawshaw** (Wednesday), **Turner** (Stoke City); **Bassett** (West Bromwich Albion), **Bloomer** (Derby County), **Goodall J.** (Derby County), **Becton** (Preston NE), **Schofield** (Stoke City).
Ireland:	**Gordon T.** (Linfield); **Gordon H.** (Linfield), **Torrans** (Linfield); **McKie** (Cliftonville), **Milne** (Linfield), **Burnett** (Glentoran); **Morrison** (Glentoran), **Gaffikin** (Linfield), **Stanfield** (Distillery), **Sherrard** (Cliftonville), **Jordan** (Linfield).
Scorers:	Bloomer, Goodall, Becton 2 each, Schofield, Bassett, Howell.

Jimmy Turner, who had made his England debut in a 6–0 defeat of Wales at Stoke in 1893 while with Bolton Wanderers, was winning his second England cap. He gained his third and final one in a 3–2 win over Ireland in Belfast in 1898 after a dispute with Stoke City had led to his transfer to Derby County. He played for the Rams in their 3–1 defeat by Nottingham Forest in the 1898 FA Cup Final, but settled his differences with Stoke and rejoined them in August that year.

...AND HIS LAST

April 6th, 1907	*England 1, Scotland 1 (at Newcastle)*
England:	**Hardy** (Liverpool); **Crompton** (Blackburn Rovers), **Pennington** (West Bromwich Albion); **Warren** (Derby County), **Wedlock** (Bristol City), **Veitch** (Newcastle United); **Rutherford** (Newcastle United), **Bloomer** (Middlesbrough), **V. Woodward** (Tottenham Hotspur), **Stewart J.** (Wednesday), **Hardman** (Everton).
Scotland:	**McBride** (Preston North End); **J. Sharp** (Arsenal), **Thomson** (Hearts); **Aitken** (Middlesbrough), **Raisbeck** (Liverpool), **McWilliam** (Newcastle United); **Stewart G.** (Manchester City), **Walker R.** (Hearts), **Wilson A.** (Wednesday), (Bolton Wanderers), **Wilson G.W.** (Everton).
Scorers:	*England*: Bloomer; *Scotland*: Crompton (o.g.).

In addition to the 1895 match, England met Ireland in Derby, at the Baseball Ground, on February 11th, 1911, winning 2–1 with this team:

> **Williamson** (Middlesbrough); **Crompton** (Blackburn Rovers), **Pennington** (West Bromwich Albion); **Warren** (Chelsea; ex-Derby County), **Wedlock** (Bristol City), **Sturgess** (Sheffield United); **Simpson** (Blackburn Rovers), **Fleming** (Swindon Town), **Shepherd** (Newcastle United), **Woodger** (Oldham Athletic), **Evans** (Sheffield United).

Ireland's team was:	**Scott W.** (Everton); **Burnison** (Bradford), **McCann** (Glentoran); **Harris** (Everton), **Connor** (Belfast Celtic), **Hampton** (Bradford City); **Lacey** (Everton), **Hannon** (Bohemians), **McDonnell** (Bohemians), **McAuley** (Huddersfield Town), **Thompson** (Bradford City).
Scorers:	*England*: Shepherd, Evans; *Ireland*: McAuley.

An amateur international match was played in Derby on November 18th, 1919, when England defeated Ireland by 5–0 at the Baseball Ground. The England team was:

> **J.F. Mitchell** (Northern Nomads); **L. Golightly** (Darlington), **A.E. Knight** (Portsmouth); **R.F. Popham** (Casuals), **K.R. G. Hunt** (Corinthians), **C.W. Harbidge** (Reading); **W.H. Harvey** (Wednesday), **M. Howell** (Oxford University), **H.M. Prince** (Army), **R.W. Sloley** (Corinthians), **R.W. Gandar-Dower** (Casuals).

Scorers:	Prince 3, Harvey 2.

Appendix Four

DERBY COUNTY FOOTBALLERS AND DERBYSHIRE CRICKETERS

(first-team players only)

	With Rams	*With Derbyshire*
ALDERMAN, Albert	1927–34	1928–48
BUXTON, Ian	1959–67	1959–73
CARTER, Raich	1945–48	1946
CHATTERTON, William	1884–88	1882–1902
CROPPER, William	1886	1882–88
DAVIS, Jack	1905–10	1920
EXHAM, P.G.	1884	1883
FLETCHER, Thomas	1904–06	1906
GOODALL, John	1889–99	1895–96
HALL, Ian	1958–62	1959–72
McMILLAN, Stuart	1914–19	1922–24
MORLEY, Haydn	1884–89	1891
STEPHENSON, Bob	1962–64	1967–68
STORER, Harry	1921–29	1920–36
STORER, William	1891–93	1887–1905
SUGG, Frank	1884	1884–86
SWALLOW, Ray	1958–64	1959–63
WARREN, Arnold	1901–02	1897–1920
WRIGHT, L.G.	1888	1883–1909

- Haydn Morley, whose father William and brother, William Junior, were prominent figures in the formation of Derby County, was the first player to be signed by the Rams.
- Percy George Exham, a master at Repton School, played in Derby's first FA Cup-tie. Cork-born, he played cricket for Ireland in addition to making one appearance for Derbyshire, in a drawn game with Yorkshire at Derby in July, 1883.
- William Cropper, a promising all-rounder at cricket, died the day after being injured while playing soccer for Staveley against Grimsby Town on January 12th, 1889. His bowel was ruptured when the home left-back, Dan Doyle, accidentally struck him in the stomach with his knee as they challenged for a high ball.
- Chatterton, William Storer, Sugg and Warren played for England in Test cricket. Arnold Warren played in only one Test, despite taking 5–57 in Australia's first innings at Leeds in 1905. In 1910, he and Jack Chapman shared a world record ninth-wicket partnership of 283 for Derbyshire against Warwickshire at Blackwell. Chapman scored 165, Warren 123.
- Ilkeston-born Frank Sugg, who played for Yorkshire before joining Derbyshire, and for Lancashire afterwards, was the scorer of the first hat-trick for Derby County, in a 3–0 away win against Stafford Road on November 15th, 1884.
- Harry Storer (209) partnered Joe Bowden (120) in Derbyshire's record opening stand of 322 against Essex, at Derby, in 1929.

The four Derbyshire and England cricketers who played for Derby County— Above: William Chatterton and (right) William Storer. Below: Arnold Warren and (right) Frank Sugg.

Appendix Five

DERBY COUNTY PLAYERS AMONG THE 100 LEAGUE LEGENDS

named by the Football League on August 4th, 1998 to mark their 100th season

JOHN GOODALL (Preston NE, Derby, New Brighton Tower, Glossop, 1888–1904)

STEVE BLOOMER (Derby, Middlesbrough, 1892–1914)

HUGHIE GALLACHER (Newcastle, Chelsea, Derby, Notts County, Grimsby, Gateshead, 1925–1939)

RAICH CARTER (Sunderland, Derby, Hull City, 1932–1953)

PETER DOHERTY (Blackpool, Manchester City, Derby, Huddersfield Town, Doncaster Rovers, 1933–1954)

DAVE MACKAY (Tottenham Hotspur, Derby, Swindon Town, 1958–1972)

PETER SHILTON (Leicester City, Stoke City, Nottingham Forest, Southampton, Derby, Plymouth Argyle, Bolton Wanderers, Leyton Orient, 1965–1997)

PAUL McGRATH (Manchester United, Aston Villa, Derby, Sheffield United, 1981–1998)

Appendix Six

LEADING SCORERS FOR DERBY COUNTY

	League	FA Cup	Others	Total
STEVE BLOOMER	293	38	1	332
KEVIN HECTOR	155	12	34	201
JACK BOWERS	167	16		183
HARRY BEDFORD	142	10		152
JACK STAMPS	100	26		126
ALF BENTLEY	99	13		112
ALAN DURBAN	93	10	9	112
SAMMY CROOKS	101	10		111
JACK PARRY	105	5		110
BOBBY DAVISON	91	7	8	106

PLAYERS WHO HAVE MADE MOST APPEARANCES FOR DERBY COUNTY

	League	FA Cup	Others	Total
KEVIN HECTOR	486	34	69	589
RON WEBSTER	455	30	50	535
ROY McFARLAND	442	33	55	530
STEVE BLOOMER	474	50	1	525
JACK PARRY	483	20	14	517
JIMMY METHVEN	458	52	1	511
GEOFF BARROWCLIFFE	475	22	6	503
SAMMY CROOKS	408	37		445
ARCHIE GOODALL	380	42	1	423
STEVE POWELL	352	32	36	420

	League	FA Cup	Others	Total
TOMMY POWELL	380	24	2	406
ARCHIE GEMMILL	324	35	45	404
ALAN DURBAN	346	19	38	403
MICHAEL FORSYTH	325	16	43	384
JACK NICHOLAS	347	36		383
COLIN TODD	293	30	48	371
JOHNNY McINTYRE	349	20		369
STEVE BUCKLEY	323	19	24	366
JACK BARKER	326	27		353
COLIN BOULTON	272	29	43	344
GEORGE COLLIN	309	25		334
JACK ATKIN	308	17		325
BERT MOZLEY	297	24		321
GERAINT WILLIAMS	277	17	27	321
ALAN HINTON	253	20	43	316
CHARLIE MORRIS	276	35		311
GEORGE RICHARDS	284	25		309
JOHN O'HARE	248	17	43	308
GEORGE THORNEWELL	275	20		295
TOMMY BARBOUR	273	21		294
'DALLY' DUNCAN	261	28		289
REG HARRISON	254	27		281
ALBERT MAYS	272	9		281
'CHICK' MUSSON	246	34		280
GARY MICKLEWHITE	240	11	28	279
HARRY STORER	257	17		274
FRANK UPTON	259	8	5	272
BEN HALL	245	24		269
BEN WARREN	242	27		269
RAY YOUNG	254	6	9	269
TOMMY COOPER	248	18		266
JACK STAMPS	233	29		262
TIM WARD	238	22		260
PETER RAMAGE	233	22		255

- The number of appearances as a substitute in these totals were: Hector 8; McFarland 5; Parry 1; Steve Powell 11; Durban 15; Forsyth 3; Williams 2; Hinton 21; O'Hare 3; Micklewhite 24; Young 1.
- Appearances under the heading 'Others' include a 'test' played before the introduction of promotion and relegation, Football League Cup, Texaco Cup, European Cup, UEFA Cup, Anglo-Italian Cup and FA Charity Shield.

GOALKEEPERS WITH 100 OR MORE APPEARANCES FOR DERBY

	League	*FA Cup*	*Others*	*Total*
COLIN BOULTON	272	29	43	344
REG MATTHEWS	225	7	14	246
BEN OLNEY	223	17		240
HARRY MASKREY	202	20		222
HARRY WILKES	208	12		220
PETER SHILTON	175	10	18	203
JACK FRYER	173	26		199
ERNALD SCATTERGOOD	182	10		192
JACK KIRBY	173	18		191
JACK ROBINSON	163	16	1	180
TERRY WEBSTER	172	6		178
KEN OXFORD	151	6	5	162
GEORGE LAWRENCE	137	8		145
LES GREEN	107	5	17	129
RAY MIDDLETON	116	4		120
MARTIN TAYLOR	97	5	7	109

- Mart Poom, a member of the current playing staff, has also exceeded 100 appearances.

Colin Boulton, who made more appearances for Derby County than any other goalkeeper and was the only ever-present member of the club's League title-winning teams of 1971–72 and 1974–75.

Appendix Seven

DERBY COUNTY'S FIRST RELEGATION SEASON
Division One, 1906–07

Played 38, Won 9, Drew 9, Lost 20, Goals for 41, agst 59, Pts 27, Pos 19th

Date		Res	Opponents	Derby scorers	Att
Sept 1	A	0–2	Sheffield United		8,000
3	H	2–2	Manchester Utd	Morris, Warren (pen.)	5,000
8	H	2–1	Bury	Davis G., Long	5,000
15	A	0–1	Bolton Wanderers		16,000
22	H	2–2	Manchester City	Davis G., Richards	6,000
29	A	1–1	Manchester Utd	Long	25,000
Oct 6	H	1–0	Middlesbrough	Ransford	10,000
13	A	1–2	Stoke City	Wood J.	5,000
20	H	3–0	Preston NE	Wood J., Warren (pen.), Ransford	7,000
27	A	1–5	Blackburn Rovers	Ransford	15,000
Nov 3	H	0–0	Newcastle United		9,000
10	A	2–0	Sunderland	Davis J., Wood J.	10,000
17	H	0–1	Aston Villa		7,000
24	A	1–2	Birmingham	Davis J.	10,000
Dec 1	H	0–1	Liverpool		8,000
8	A	0–2	Everton		10,000
15	A	0–3	Bristol City		10,000
22	H	0–0	Woolwich Arsenal		7,000
24	H	3–0	Notts County	Warren (pen.), Long, Davis G.	8,000
25	A	1–1	Wednesday	Wood J.	22,000
29	H	3–0	Sheffield United	Bentley 2, Wood J.	7,000
Jan 1	A	0–2	Newcastle United		30,000
5	A	0–1	Bury		11,000
19	H	0–1	Bolton Wanderers		5,000
26	A	2–2	Manchester City	Davis J., Long	15,000

Date		Res	Opponents	Derby scorers	Att
Feb	9	A	1–4	Middlesbrough	Davis G.	10,000
	16	H	2–1	Stoke City	Davis G. 2	7,000
Mar	2	H	2–3	Blackburn Rovers	Davis G., Long	10,000
	9	A	0–1	Preston NE		8,000
	16	H	1–1	Sunderland	Hall	6,000
	23	A	0–2	Aston Villa		16,000
	29	A	0–4	Notts County		20,000
	30	H	1–1	Birmingham	Wheatcroft	5,000
Apr	1	H	1–0	Wednesday	Wheatcroft	10,000
	6	A	0–2	Liverpool		7,000
	13	H	5–2	Everton	Bentley 2, Long 2, Davis J.	4,000
	20	H	1–3	Bristol City	Armstrong	6,000
	27	A	2–3	Woolwich Arsenal	Davis G., Long	2,000

Appearances
37: Maskrey; *36:* Davis J., Nicholas; *34:* Warren; *32:* Davis G., Hall, Long; *29:* Morris; *26:* Wood A., Wood J.; *20:* Bagshaw; *15:* Ransford; *14:* Wheatcroft; *11:* Bentley, Richards; *7:* Moore; *6:* Lamb; *3:* Methven, Vann; *2:* Armstrong, Cleaver; *1:* Fletcher T., Smith H., Smith J., Haywood.

Scorers
8: Davis G., Long; *5:* Wood J.; *4:* Bentley, Davis J.; *3:* Ransford, Warren; *2:* Wheatcroft; *1:* Armstrong, Hall, Morris, Richards.

- Fred Haywood, a centre-forward from Mexborough Town, made his only appearance for the club in their final match of this season.
- Herbert Smith, who was born at Witney in 1879 and died at Oxford in 1951, played his one game in Derby's League side at left-back against the Wednesday on April 1st. An amateur international, he was an Amateur Cup finalist with Oxford City in 1903 and won a gold medal in the 1908 Olympic Games football competition in London. He also gained four successive caps in the full England side, in 1905 and 1906, while with Reading. He was later president of the Oxfordshire FA.
- John Smith was a reserve goalkeeper from Long Eaton St. Helen's. He played for Derby in nine League games and one FA Cup-tie before moving to Newark Town.
- Bill Moore, known as 'Doggy', altogether played 11 first-team games in three seasons after being signed from the local club Graham Street Prims that also supplied Jimmy Bagshaw to the Rams. Moore moved to Stockport County in August, 1909.
- Jimmy Long played for Clyde and Grimsby Town before joining Derby County from Reading shortly after Steve Bloomer's transfer to Middlesbrough. He scored 19 goals in 65 senior appearances for the Rams.

- These were the only three games that centre-forward Bernard Vann played in the first team in his three months with Derby County. He was previously with Northampton Town and Burton United; afterwards he played for Leicester Fosse.
- Jimmy Ransford, also a centre-forward, hailed from Blackwell. He played for Alfreton Town both before and after his short stay with the Rams, having started out with Ripley Athletic.

PROMOTED Division Two, 1911–12

Played 38, Won 23, Drew 8, Lost 7, Goals for 74, agst 28, Pts 54, Pos 1st

Date		Res	Opponents	Derby scorers	Att
Sept 2	A	0–3	Clapton Orient		16,000
9	H	3–0	Bristol City	Barnes 2, Donald	8,000
11	A	0–1	Chelsea		20,000
16	A	4–0	Birmingham	Barnes 2, Bauchop, Bloomer (pen.)	8,000
23	H	4–2	Huddersfield Town	Bloomer 2 (pens.), Grimes, Walker	10,000
30	A	0–1	Blackpool		4,000
Oct 7	H	5–0	Glossop NE	Bauchop 3, Bloomer, Barnes	10,000
14	A	0–0	Hull City		14,000
21	H	0–0	Barnsley		9,000
28	A	1–0	Bradford	Bauchop	20,000
Nov 4	H	6–1	Fulham	Leonard 4, Bauchop, Bloomer	12,000
25	H	5–2	Leeds City	Sharpe 2, Bauchop, Bloomer, Grimes	12,000
Dec 2	A	1–0	Wolves	Leonard	20,000
6	H	2–0	Burnley	Bloomer, Leonard	12,000
9	H	5–0	Leicester Fosse	Bloomer 2, Leonard 2, Wright	12,000
16	A	1–1	Gainsborough	Sharpe	1,000
23	A	3–0	Grimsby Town	Bloomer 2, Bauchop	7,000
25	H	2–1	Grimsby Town	Bloomer, Bauchop	15,000
26	A	3–1	Nottm Forest	Bloomer, Bauchop, Leonard	33,500
30	H	5–1	Clapton Orient	Bauchop 3, Bloomer, Leonard	15,000
Jan 1	A	0–4	Stockport County		10,000
6	A	1–1	Bristol City	Leonard	4,000
27	A	0–0	Huddersfield Town		8,000
Feb 10	A	1–3	Glossop NE	Bloomer (pen.)	3,000
17	H	2–3	Hull City	Bloomer 2	8,000
21	H	0–1	Birmingham		5,000

Date		Res	Opponents	Derby scorers	Att
Feb 24	H	5–1	Blackpool	Barnes 3, Sharpe 2	5,000
Mar 2	H	1–0	Bradford	Bauchop	7,000
16	A	0–0	Burnley		30,000
23	H	2–0	Stockport County	Barnes, Grimes	5,000
30	A	1–0	Leeds City	Sharpe	4,500
Apr 6	H	1–1	Wolves	Grimes	12,000
8	H	2–0	Chelsea	Leonard 2	18,000
9	H	1–0	Nottm Forest	Leonard	14,000
13	A	1–0	Leicester Fosse	Bloomer	15,000
15	A	0–0	Fulham		10,000
20	H	4–0	Gainsborough	Leonard 3, Bauchop	12,000
22	A	2–0	Barnsley	Buckley, Bauchop	4,000

Appearances
38: E. Scattergood; *36:* Bloomer; *35:* Atkin, Grimes; *33:* Bagshaw; *31:* Bauchop; *29:* Sharpe; *28:* Buckley; *27:* Betts, Leonard; *22:* Barbour, Garry, Richards; *19:* Barnes; *7:* Donald; *3:* Walker, Wright; *1:* Abbott.

Scorers
18: Bloomer; *17:* Leonard; *16:* Bauchop; *9:* Barnes; *6:* Sharpe; *4:* Grimes; *1:* Buckley, Donald, Walker, Wright.

- Right-winger Horace Wright was signed from Bulwell White Star, and scored two goals in 16 first-team games before going into the Southern League with Portsmouth in August, 1912 at a fee of £35. He was later with Coventry City and Exeter City.
- Harry Walker, a Wirksworth-born wing-half, was with the Rams from May, 1910, when he was signed from Clay Cross, until June, 1920, when he moved to Notts County after making 88 appearances. He subsequently assisted Fulham, Reading, Aberdare Athletic, Bournemouth and Chesterfield.
- Shirley Abbott was one of Alfreton Town's products. The game in which he played at wing-half in a scoreless draw at Huddersfield was his only one in Derby's League side. He was transferred to Portsmouth in August, 1913, and after helping them to win the Southern League title in 1919–20 he was a member of the first team they fielded in the Football League the following season in a 3–0 home win against Swansea Town in the new Third Division on August 28th, 1920. He moved to Queen's Park Rangers in May, 1923, then to Chesterfield in September, 1924. He became Chesterfield's trainer after ending his playing career four years later.

RELEGATED AGAIN Division One, 1913–14

Played 38, Won 8, Drew 11, Lost 19, Goals for 55, agst 71, Pts 27, Pos 20th

Date		Res	Opponents	Derby scorers	Att
Sept	1	H	1–1	Liverpool	Barnes	7,000
	6	H	3–5	Sheffield Utd	Bloomer 2, Barnes	12,000
	10	H	2–2	Middlesbrough	Barnes, Grimes	6,000
	13	A	1–1	Tottenham Hotspur	Barnes	40,000
	20	A	2–1	Manchester City	Barnes, Leonard	30,000
	27	H	3–1	Bradford City	Barnes 2, Scattergood (pen.)	12,000
Oct	4	A	1–3	Blackburn Rov	Leonard	30,000
	11	H	1–1	Sunderland	Buckley	12,000
	18	A	0–5	Everton		30,000
	25	H	1–2	West Brom Albion	Walker	12,000
Nov	1	A	3–1	Wednesday	Leonard, Barnes, Moore	20,000
	8	H	3–3	Bolton Wanderers	Barnes 2, Moore	12,000
	15	A	1–2	Chelsea	Walker	35,000
	22	H	1–2	Oldham Athletic	Barnes	12,000
	29	A	3–3	Manchester United	Moore 2, Leonard	20,000
Dec	6	H	3–1	Burnley	Leonard 2, Barnes	12,000
	13	A	0–2	Preston NE		12,000
	20	H	2–0	Newcastle United	Moore, Leonard	12,000
	25	H	0–2	Aston Villa		9,500
	27	A	2–2	Sheffield United	Leonard, Barnes	12,000
Jan	1	A	2–3	Middlesbrough	Barnes 2	18,000
	3	H	4–0	Tottenham Hotspur	Barbour, Barnes, Moore, Cartwright (o.g.)	11,000
	17	H	2–4	Manchester City	Barnes, Moore	10,000
	24	A	0–0	Bradford City		15,000
Feb	7	H	2–3	Blackburn Rovers	Moore, Barnes	10,000
	14	A	0–1	Sunderland		15,000
	21	H	1–0	Everton	Fordham	10,000
	28	A	1–2	West Brom Albion	Fellows	15,000
Mar	11	H	1–1	Wednesday	Moore	10,000
	14	A	1–3	Bolton Wanderers	Moore	18,000
	21	H	0–1	Chelsea		10,000
	28	A	0–0	Oldham Athletic		6,000
Apr	4	H	4–2	Manchester United	Barnes 2, Leonard, Scattergood (pen.)	5,000
	10	A	0–1	Liverpool		40,000
	11	A	1–5	Burnley	Barnes	18,000
	13	A	2–3	Aston Villa	Barnes 2	20,000
	18	H	0–1	Preston NE		4,000
	25	A	1–1	Newcastle United	Barnes	15,000

Appearances
37: Barbour, Barnes; *35:* Buckley; *34:* Grimes; *33:* Atkin; *29:* Neve, E. Scattergood; *27:* Moore; *26:* Bagshaw; *24:* Leonard; *22:* Walker; *14:* Waugh; *13:* Hardman, Richards; *11:* Betts; *9:* Lawrence; *6:* Fordham; *5:* Bloomer, Callender; *4:* Reader; *2:* Fellows, Ritchie; *1:* Methven (James Junior).

Scorers
24: Barnes; *10:* Moore; *9:* Leonard; *2:* Bloomer, Scattergood (2 pens.), Walker; *1:* Barbour, Buckley, Fellows, Fordham, Grimes.

- Dick Reader, signed from Ripley Athletic, made his four appearances as deputy for Billy Grimes at outside-right. During the following close season he left for Bristol City, from where he moved to Luton Town in the summer of 1922.
- Percy Fellows, a left-winger from Dudley, deputised for Edwin Neve, the former Hull City player who was later with Nottingham Forest and Chesterfield, against Everton and West Bromwich Albion in February, but had no further opportunities.
- Reginald Callender, a Cambridge Blue and England amateur international, played his five League games as another stand-in for Neve during the last two months of the season. He had previously turned out for Stockton School, St. John's College, Cambridge, and in one match for Glossop. He was killed during the First World War.

PROMOTED AGAIN Division Two, 1914–15

Played 38, Won 23, Drew 7, Lost 8, Goals for 71, agst 33, Pts 53, Pos 1st

Date		Res	Opponents	Derby scorers	Att
Sept	2	H 7–0	Barnsley	Fordham 3, Moore 2, Baker, Bethune (o.g.)	2,000
	5	A 1–1	Glossop NE	Benfield	500
	12	H 3–1	Wolves	Benfield 2, Fordham	5,000
	19	A 0–2	Fulham		14,000
	26	H 1–0	Stockport County	Benfield	5,000
Oct	3	A 0–1	Hull City		6,000
	10	H 1–2	Leeds City	Baker	6,000
	17	A 1–0	Clapton Orient	Moore	10,000
	24	H 4–0	Woolwich Arsenal	Benfield 2, Moore, Leonard	8,000
	31	H 5–0	Blackpool	Leonard 2, Moore 2, Devonshire	4,000
Nov	7	A 0–0	Lincoln City		5,000
	14	H 1–0	Birmingham	Leonard	5,000
	21	A 2–1	Grimsby Town	Leonard, Benfield	8,000
	28	H 1–0	Huddersfield Town	Leonard (pen.)	7,000

Date		Res	Opponents	Derby scorers	Att
Dec 5	A	3–2	Bristol City	Leonard, Moore, Benfield	6,000
12	H	2–1	Bury	Benfield, Moore	6,000
19	A	3–1	Preston NE	Leonard, Grimes, Benfield	8,000
25	A	2–2	Nottm Forest	Leonard (pen.), Moore	15,000
26	H	1–0	Nottm Forest	Leonard	14,000
28	A	6–0	Leicester F	Leonard 2, Moore 2, Benfield 2	5,000
Jan 2	H	1–1	Glossop NE	Leonard (pen.)	7,000
16	A	1–0	Wolves	Baker	7,000
23	H	1–1	Fulham	Benfield	6,000
30	A	2–3	Stockport Coounty	Leonard, Moore	8,000
Feb 6	H	4–1	Hull City	Moore 3, Leonard	5,000
13	A	5–3	Leeds City	Leonard 2, Moore 2, Baker	5,000
20	A	0–3	Clapton Orient		6,000
27	A	2–1	Woolwich Arsenal	Benfield, Moore	18,000
Mar 6	A	1–2	Blackpool	Grimes	5,000
13	H	3–0	Lincoln City	Moore 2, Baker	7,000
20	A	2–0	Birmingham	Moore, Leonard	18,000
27	H	1–1	Grimsby Town	Benfield	6,000
Apr 2	A	0–1	Barnsley		10,000
3	A	0–0	Huddersfield Town		6,500
5	H	1–0	Leicester F	Baker	10,000
10	H	1–0	Bristol City	Moore	7,000
17	A	0–2	Bury		6,000
24	H	2–0	Preston NE	Grimes, Leonard	12,000

Appearances
38: Benfield, Moore; *37:* Barbour; *35:* Baker; *33:* Brooks; *32:* Leonard; *31:* Eadie, Lawrence; *30:* Atkin; *28:* Grimes; *26:* Walker; *17:* Bagshaw; *10:* Waugh; *7:* Devonshire, Fordham, E. Scattergood; *6:* J. Smith; *3:* Quantrill; *1:* Hardman, S. McMillan.

Scorers
22: Moore; *19:* Leonard; *15:* Benfield; *6:* Baker; *4:* Fordham; *3:* Grimes; *1:* Devonshire.

- William Devonshire, signed as an amateur in October, 1914, played his seven games at outside-right in the absence of Billy Grimes—the last of them in December, the month in which he turned professional.

RELEGATED AGAIN Division One, 1920–21

Played 42, Won 5, Drew 16, Lost 21, Goals for 32, agst 58, Pts 26, Pos 21st

Date		Res		Opponents	Derby scorers	Att
Aug 28	H	0–0		Chelsea		21,851
30	H	2–2		Tottenham Hotspur	Burton, Lyons	18,628
Sept 4	A	1–1		Chelsea	Burton	42,000
6	A	0–2		Tottenham Hotspur		26,142
11	H	2–4		Everton	Quantrill, Gardner	17,000
18	A	1–3		Everton	Murray	35,000
25	H	1–1		West Brom Albion	Quantrill	16,969
Oct 2	A	0–3		West Brom Albion		26,893
9	H	3–0		Manchester City	Burton, Murray, Abdallah	18,000
16	A	0–0		Manchester City		35,000
23	H	1–1		Arsenal	Thornewell	19,000
30	A	0–2		Arsenal		45,000
Nov 6	H	0–0		Bolton Wanderers		15,433
13	A	0–1		Bolton Wanderers		25,000
20	A	0–1		Middlesbrough		28,000
27	H	0–1		Middlesbrough		12,500
Dec 4	A	0–2		Blackburn Rovers		25,000
11	H	0–1		Blackburn Rovers		14,000
18	A	0–2		Huddersfield Town		13,500
25	A	2–2		Bradford City	Thornewell, Burton	28,000
27	H	1–1		Bradford City	Atkin (pen.)	23,820
Jan 1	H	2–1		Huddersfield Town	Atkin (pen.), Thornewell	12,000
15	A	1–2		Preston NE	Quantrill	17,000
22	H	1–1		Preston NE	Paterson	16,000
Feb 5	H	3–3		Oldham Athletic	Paterson 2, Moore	15,000
12	A	1–2		Burnley	Paterson	30,000
14	A	1–2		Oldham Athletic	Morton	21,196
23	H	0–0		Burnley		16,000
26	A	1–0		Sheffield United	Paterson	35,000
Mar 5	H	1–1		Sheffield United	Paterson	16,000
12	A	1–2		Bradford	Murray	16,000
19	H	1–0		Bradford	Paterson	6,000
25	A	0–3		Sunderland		20,000
26	H	0–1		Newcastle United		20,000
28	H	0–1		Sunderland		16,000

Apr	2	A	1–0	Newcastle United	Lyons	35,000
	9	H	0–0	Liverpool		10,000
	16	A	1–1	Liverpool	Storer	28,000
	23	H	2–3	Aston Villa	Moore, Paterson	14,000
	30	A	0–1	Aston Villa		20,000
May	2	H	1–1	Manchester United	Ritchie (pen.)	8,000
	7	A	0–3	Manchester United		10,000

Appearances

39: A. Ritchie; *37:* Thornewell; *33:* Quantrill; *32:* Atkin; *31:* Murray; *28:* Lawrence, Wightman; *26:* Moore; *22:* Morton; *21:* Burton; *19:* McLaverty; *17:* Paterson, Waterhouse; *16:* Barbour; *13:* Lyons; *12:* Abdallah, Storer; *10:* Chandler, Rance; *7:* Kidd; *6:* Lamph; *5:* Gardner, Maskrey; *4:* Thompson; *3:* Baker; *2:* Minney, Olney; *1:* Bayliss, Hannay, Lievesley, Shepherd, Shiner.

Scorers

8: Paterson; *4:* Burton; *3:* Murray, Quantrill, Thornewell; *2:* Atkin (pens.), Lyons, Moore; *1:* Abdallah, Gardner, Morton, Ritchie (pen.), Storer.

- Bob Bayliss made his only senior appearance on Derby's left wing in the away win against Sheffield United in late February. When he was signed that month from Gresley Rovers the deal included an agreement that he could return to Gresley, where he was a big favourite, if he did not find League football to his liking, and he did so shortly afterwards.
- John Hannay, a right-winger from the Newcastle area, Wilfred Lievesley, an inside-forward formerly of Staveley Old Boys, and Albert Shiner, a centre-forward from the Isle of Wight club Seaview, also played only one game in the Rams' first team; George Shepherd, from Rochester in Staffordshire, made his second and final appearance at outside-left in the defeat at Blackburn, having played at inside-left at Burnley (who also won 2–0) the previous season. Lievesley was later with Manchester United, Exeter City, Wigan Borough and Cardiff City.
- **Promotion was next achieved in 1925–26, George Jobey's first season as manager, with the following record:**

Played 42, Won 25, Drew 7, Lost 10, Goals for 77, agst 42, Pts 57, Pos 2nd